A CUP OF COMFORT

Devotional for Mothers

Daily Inspiration for
Christian Moms

Edited by James S. Bell
& Jeanette Gardner Littleton

adamsmedia
Avon, Massachusetts

A Cup of Comfort® is a registered trademark of F+W Publications, Inc.

Published by
Adams Media, an F+W Publications Company
57 Littlefield Street, Avon, MA 02322. U.S.A.
www.adamsmedia.com

ISBN 10: 1-59869-690-4
ISBN 13: 978-1-59869-690-5
Printed in the United States of America.
J I H G F E D C B A

**Library of Congress Cataloging-in-Publication Data
available from the publisher**

This publication is designed to provide accurate and authoritative information
with regard to the subject matter covered. It is sold with the understanding that
the publisher is not engaged in rendering legal, accounting, or other professional
advice. If legal advice or other expert assistance is required, the services of a
competent professional person should be sought.
—From a *Declaration of Principles* jointly adopted by a Committee of the
American Bar Association and a Committee of Publishers and Associations

Many of the designations used by manufacturers and sellers to distinguish their
products are claimed as trademarks. Where those designations appear in this
book and Adams Media was aware of a trademark claim, the designations have
been printed with initial capital letters.

*This book is available at quantity discounts for bulk purchases.
For information, please call 1-800-289-0963.*

Contents

To my wife, Margaret, whose loving care and nurture of our four children is bearing much fruit for the next generation.

—James Stuart Bell

To the memory of my mom, Ila Elnora Gardner, and to Vidy Metsker, Rhonda Stock, and the other women who've given me mom-sense. Also to Nicole and Alisha, who welcomed me as their stepmother, and Gardner, and Elizabeth, who still give me plenty of practice!

—Jeanette Gardner Littleton

ACKNOWLEDGMENTS

I wish to acknowledge Paula Munier and the editorial team who provided the expertise in making these stories into strong testimonies of how mothers make a huge difference in our world. I thank my coauthor Jeanette Littleton for her dedication, great attitude, and empathetic understanding of the heart of motherhood.

—James Stuart Bell

Every book has a team behind it—people who champion it and guide it but seldom get their names in print. I appreciate the feedback and guidance of editor Paula Munier and her assistant, Brendan O'Neill, and the skills of others at Adams Media. Ally Littleton also provided great editorial assistance. And we received so many more submissions than we could use in this book! Our thanks go to all the moms who were so willing to share their insights and inspiration—and who blessed and encouraged me, personally, as I read their stories.

—Jeanette Gardner Littleton

INTRODUCTION

*M*others are dear to God's heart. The Bible gives us multiple stories of God answering mothers' prayers, honoring their love for their children, and providing for them. Perhaps a mother's heart—in its very nature—is a reflection of God's giving, nurturing, sacrificial heart.

In the pages of this book, you'll also find multiple stories—real-life stories—that affirm how much God still loves mothers in our world. You'll discover how God has worked in the lives and families of other moms like you. You'll find encouragement, inspiration, and blessing through these moms as they open their own hearts to you.

No matter what time of year you pick up this book, you'll find special words. Each day starts with a scripture that the mom writing for the day found illuminating in her life. She illustrates why that scripture is important to her as a mom, and even gives you a nugget of insight that you can take with you and remember through your day.

Whether you make this book part of your daily devotion time, keep a copy at work to read during coffee break, or use it to help you reflect on your day before you go to bed, we think you'll find it invaluable to your life. We think you'll find this book to be as soothing, invigorating, and refreshing as a cozy cup of tea, a bracing cup of coffee . . . a cup of reassuring comfort.

So come join us for a special few moments each day with God . . . and with other mothers who know the joys and challenges you face. Come share the sweetness of being a mother.

JANUARY

PEACE—ONLY A PRAYER AWAY

"Don't worry about anything; instead, pray about everything. Tell God what you need, and thank him for all he has done. If you do this you will experience God's peace, which is far more wonderful than the human mind can understand. His peace will guard your hearts and minds as you live in Christ Jesus."

PHILIPPIANS 4:6–7

The day was off to a bad start. I awoke to see everything covered in snow and the white flurries continued to fall at a rapid clip. Later that morning, my husband's car stalled, and despite our repeated efforts, we couldn't coax it to start back up. We managed to push it into a nearby parking lot and call a tow truck. Our mechanic told us to tow it to his shop, but he was sorry, it would be ten days before he could fix it.

Then later that day, while I wasn't looking, my son put on a little jumping routine on the sofa, which ended with a loud thud and a nice cut to the head. As I held a washcloth over my son's bleeding head, called my husband on the phone, and searched for my car keys so I could take him to the emergency room, the tension increased. I felt my anxiety level rising dangerously close to the O.O.C. (out of control) line.

As I hung up the phone and dug further in my purse for my keys, I was startled by my son's soft voice.

"Mommy, can we say a prayer?" he asked gently.

I was stopped in my tracks. "Uh, of c-course . . . of course we can," I stuttered.

With everything going on, I hadn't even stopped to do what I should have done first—turned the situation over to the Lord.

Was I ever humbled! I prayed aloud, asking God to help my son's cut stop bleeding and to relieve his pain. Then I added a silent prayer for God to ease my anxiety and give me peace.

I'd been a twisted ball of nerves when my son asked that simple request: to stop and pray. Leave it to the innocence of my child to help put everything in perspective, to remind me of my core values and priorities.

Immediately, a feeling of calm came across me after that prayer. We were in God's capable hands.

I felt as if God gave me an extra helping of patience to get through the next few hours of stress in the emergency room. Instead of being frazzled and overwhelmed, I felt completely at ease. The cut was nothing major and easily taken care of with a few staples. My son handled it bravely, with hardly a tear. To this day I am amazed at how that simple moment of prayer had provided us with a monumental amount of peace.

That stressful situation pointed out that even though I may pray eventually, it's not my typical first reaction to frustrations. Instead, I struggle with the stress in my own way, trying to manage the pressure instead of going straight to God. If I just deposited my worries with God, I would have an immediate measure of divine peace.

As I walk into a New Year, it's good to know that when the obstacles are mounting and the pressures seem insurmountable, God's peace is only a prayer away.

—KARIN LINDSTROM

A New Start Every Day

"Great is his faithfulness;
his mercies begin afresh each day."
LAMENTATIONS 3:23

My son never went through the "terrible twos." But now that he's eight, we butt heads way more than I like. At the least sign of not getting his way sometimes, he's all up in arms, freely displaying his displeasure and anger. That just doesn't work when you have a disciplinarian mom.

But what always amazes me is that no matter how stormy the day before was, each day starts fresh and new, without anger or grudges. He never remembers our challenges of the day before—even if they were intense—but expresses love and trust.

Aren't you glad that every day in parenting is a new day, a new beginning, and a new chance to have a terrific time with your kids? And each day is a new day with God, too. No matter what's happened the day before, we have a new day to enjoy Him and a deeper relationship with Him.

Every day is a chance to start anew!

—JGL

Delightfully Different

"Thank you for making me so wonderfully complex! Your
workmanship is marvelous—and how well I know it."
PSALM 139:14

"Stop playing now. You need to study!"

"But I already know it," my second-grade son replied.

"You haven't studied. How could you possibly know the
material?"

"Mama, I remember everything Mrs. Putnam told us in
class." My son then recounted volumes of information for an
upcoming history test. He did know the material, without
studying!

In that moment, the Holy Spirit whispered, He's not like
you. Remembering my own study habits, I felt he needed to
devote hours to reviewing, but my son learned differently than
I did. He learns by hearing.

We're all individually fashioned by a loving Father. I don't
need to cram my children into a mold. I've been reminded of
this as I've watched them learn, use their talents, interact with
others, grow in faith, and develop their own unique personalities. They don't have to do things my way, just God's best way
for them.

God made each of us delightfully different.

—CANDY ARRINGTON

Simple Pleasures

"She carefully watches all that
goes on in her household. . . ."
PROVERBS 31:27

The day flew by, as I went from room to room doing household chores. I was exhausted when the kids arrived home from school. The kitchen table was instantly hidden by schoolbooks and homework papers. My plans for a relaxing evening vanished. I realized I would be helping with mountains of homework instead.

My son rifled through his papers and held out his hand. "Mom, here is something for you."

I looked down at four tiny toothpicks fastened together, with my name glued on them in alphabet noodles. The flip side held a small safety pin. I held the precious name tag in my hand and my eyes filled with tears. *He even spelled my name right,* I thought.

I reflected on the many facets of motherhood. I realized I wouldn't trade the simplicity of peanut butter sandwiches and handmade projects for anything. I smiled as I started dinner.

The simple pleasures of motherhood keep us going!

—ANNETTEE BUDZBAN

Fake Parent

"You should behave instead like God's
very own children, adopted into his family."
ROMANS 8:15

As we left church my son blurted, "Mom, are you a fake parent?"

I was stunned. Had I made a promise I had not kept? What had made him think I was not genuine?

"Kyle said I don't look anything like you," Steve explained. Inwardly I smiled. Kyle, Steve's six-year-old buddy, was right. My husband and I are Caucasian and have no physical resemblance to our adopted, biracial son. The rest of the trip home, we retold the story of his adoption and answered questions about it.

We received custody of Steve when he was three weeks old. Though he doesn't look like us, he has picked up our habits and lifestyle. Still, being called a phony was unsettling. I looked through the Bible, reading the verses that mention adoption. I wondered, *Am I a spitting image of Jesus?*

> *May God always help us demonstrate
> what it looks like to be His child.*

—SALLY SMITH

An Ocean of Guilt

"Once again you will have compassion on us.
You will trample our sins under your feet
and throw them into the depths of the ocean!"
MICAH 7:19

One evening I explained to my six-year-old daughter that when we ask God to forgive us for the things we've done wrong, He throws the memory of these things into the deepest ocean! "They're gone!" I exclaimed.

She thought for a moment and said, "But what if they float back up?"

Isn't that like us? We have a hard time believing that God will really forgive us. We let those memories float up over and over. Often we can't forgive ourselves and assume God won't forgive us either, so we hide from Him or slowly drift away.

But what God wants most is for us to spend time with Him. Not believing that He has really "thrown our sins into the deepest sea" can keep us far away from him who loves us most.

*We don't have to drown in guilt. We can float
through life buoyed by God's love and forgiveness.*

—TAMARA VERMEER

Don't Sweat the Details!

"But the Lord said to her, 'My dear Martha, you are so upset over all these details! There is really only one thing worth being concerned about. Mary has discovered it—and I won't take it away from her.'"
LUKE 10:41–42

I enjoy talking to my young neighbor. Though I'm about twenty years older than she is, we have toddlers the same age. But there's a big difference between us. Carolyn worries that she's not doing everything just right for her child. Then she worries that she's worrying too much. And the things Carolyn worries about are the little things, like if Susie stays up too late, or if Carolyn skips giving Susie a bath for a day or two when life is too hectic.

I'm much more laid back than that—maybe because I'm older, maybe because my toddler is my youngest child and Susie is Carolyn's first, or maybe because I've just given up on trying to control the little things.

"Just relax," I encourage her. "If it doesn't affect the grand scheme of Susie's life, just do your best, follow your instincts, and don't go on guilt trips. Don't worry about things that don't really matter."

We all need the reminder: life, and motherhood, is too short to spend time sweating the small stuff.

—JGL

A Place of Refuge

"But let all who take refuge in you rejoice;
let them sing joyful praises forever. Protect them,
so all who love your name may be filled with joy."

PSALM 5:11

Maria definitely didn't approve of everything her daughter did. Seventeen-year-old Lucy was living with an abusive boyfriend. "I'd like to beat him up myself, but that wouldn't help any," Maria commented crisply.

Instead, Maria encouraged Lucy to come to the house frequently. And she made sure she didn't scold Lucy about her lifestyle. "The rest of the world beats her up emotionally," Maria said. "I want home to be the place of refuge, where she can always feel love and acceptance."

As a result, Lucy spent a lot of time at home. And one day, when the boyfriend abused her, she thought, "I'm treated way better than this at home," and returned home.

While we still have kids at home, sure, we need to give them instruction and guidance. But we can also make our homes centers of love and acceptance—a refuge in the middle of a crazy world.

We can be a refuge for our children, just as God is for us.

—JGL

Closer to God Than Daddy

"God is so great—higher than the heavens,
higher than the farthest stars."
JOB 22:12

My son came into the house riding on his daddy's shoulders. "You know what, Mom?" he said. "I'm closer to God than Daddy."

Although I knew he meant he was closer physically to heaven by being taller than his daddy, it made me think. Was my son closer to God than I was?

Sometimes it's difficult to feel God's closeness when you've had an exhausting day with a fussy baby, a youngster who doesn't obey, or a rebellious teenager. That's when God pulls us from the waves of frustration, wraps His loving arms around us, and lets us dwell in His closeness.

Many times my son's words have played an important part in my mind: Just how close to God am I? Am I close to God in my thoughts? In my daily tasks? In my work, church, and community? Where is God's closeness in my life?

*How close are you to God in
your thoughts and actions today?*

—JANE LANDRETH

One Principle and 40,000 Applications

"All of you should be of one mind, full of
sympathy toward each other, loving one another
with tender hearts and humble minds."
1 PETER 3:8

When I retired early from corporate life to care for my elderly mother and disabled brother, not everyone gave me a round of applause. They wondered why I would give up my career instead of choosing other viable options, such as household help, paid caregivers, or assisted living. My decision took serious consideration, yet it was not difficult to make.

When we face special needs in the family, we often clearly see what God would have us do. For some women, this means refocusing or leaving a career to provide care for children or parents. For others, it means working two jobs to ensure adequate housing, food, and medical attention for the family. For all, it means matching what we do with the principle God has given us: love one another.

"Once possessed of the principle," said poet Ralph Waldo Emerson, "it is equally easy to make forty or forty thousand applications of it."

*In Jesus, we not only possess the principle,
but the faith, heart, and mind to apply it.*

—PAT MITCHELL

Timely Help

"Those who refresh others will themselves be refreshed."
PROVERBS 11:25

When my husband and I brought our baby home from the hospital, we were filled with awe. That day, my mother came to help. She sensed my uneasiness about the needs of a newborn.

Instead of taking over, Mother identified with my feelings. "You take care of that sweet baby, and I'll do what's needed in your house," she said. Each day she boosted my confidence as I breast-fed, changed diapers, and cared for Baby Karen.

"Don't worry about doing things perfectly," she told me. "Every mother is a novice."

Mother launched into hard work. She prepared delicious meals. She scrubbed, but took time to cuddle her granddaughter. She urged me to nap.

"You're spoiling me!" I said.

"Honey, this is refreshing for me—I love being with you," she said. I also savored our closeness. I will always remember how God's love flowed through my mother's timely giving of herself.

When you identify with others, your
giving can be refreshing to all.

—CHARLOTTE ADELSPERGER

Stronger Than Nerves of Steel

> ". . . May grace and peace be yours from
> God our Father and the Lord Jesus Christ."
> ROMANS 1:7

When I looked at our screaming toddler, Elizabeth, I felt waves of nausea. Her tiny body was coated with blood and even more was gurgling from beneath her blood matted blond hair. She had fallen and hit her head on the fireplace. I'd never seen so much blood.

As we raced to the emergency room, I prayed for my daughter. And fighting more nausea, I prayed for strength.

Elizabeth was pronounced okay at the ER, and the words, "You have to have nerves of steel to be a parent," wafted through my mind.

I'd read the phrase in a story by veterinarian James Herriot. Herriot told about dropping a canine patient in his haste to see that his son was okay after a two-story fall. The dog's owner had comforted him with those words. Words spoken half a century ago, but still so true—whether it's ER visits or daily challenges.

> *Thank goodness the grace God gives us as we*
> *mother our kids is even stronger than steel nerves!*

—JGL

God, Our Interpreter!

"Come, let's go down and give them different languages.
Then they won't be able to understand each other."
GENESIS 11:7

I laughed when I read this verse. It made me think of communication with my kids. At times, it's like we speak totally different languages!

You know exactly what I mean. You tell your child to be in earlier than usual, and he comes in just two minutes before the normal curfew—which he's usually pushing. Our ideas of curfews are different, our ideas of what's clean are different, and our ideas of so much just aren't alike at all! Even when we try to communicate verbally, what I say isn't always what my kids hear. And sometimes I understand their words no better than I would if they were speaking Russian.

I'm thankful that God not only understands the language I speak, but he understands the languages my children speak, too! I'm learning to turn to him and say, "Help me understand." And without fail, he does!

We may not always understand each other,
but God makes a great translator.

—JGL

No Time to Serve Jesus!

"Once more he asked him, 'Simon son of John, do you love me?' Peter was grieved that Jesus asked the question a third time. He said, 'Lord, you know everything. You know I love you.' Jesus said, 'Then feed my sheep.'"

JOHN 21:17

Melinda's fever was gone and all three of my kids were napping. Opening my Bible, I finally had time with Jesus, after two days.

Exhausted, I prayed, "Father, I want to serve you. Show me how to find time."

Oh dear, I thought, *today's scripture is talking about the Kingdom's work again.*

"Mom-mee!" Melinda's scream pierced the silence. "Eddy's throwing up!"

My Bible slid to the floor unnoticed as I ran to the bedroom.

"It's okay, sweetie. Mommy's here. I'll fix it. Melinda, take Betsy to the playroom—maybe she won't get sick."

But she did. Around midnight I dropped into bed and mumbled, "Jesus, I love you. Help me know how to serve you."

The next morning Melinda's kisses woke me. "Mommy, Eddy's sleeping. You take such good care of us. Angela's mom gripes when she gets sick."

My heart whispered, "Thank you, Jesus. This is work I can do."

Sometimes, the least of the sheep
need the most and require our best.

—LIZ HOYT EBERLE

"Mommy! Mommy!"

"Morning, noon, and night I plead aloud
in my distress, and the Lord hears my voice."
PSALM 55:17

With five children piling in from school at the same time, I felt like the last piece of birthday cake being pulled apart by a hungry mob. I rewarded each child with a hug and a smile between doing dishes and folding clothes, but seven-year-old Clay needed more.

"Mommy! Mommy!" He tugged at my skirt.

"What is it, son?" I asked, but he kept tugging and calling. "Mommy! Mommy!"

Goodness! The child was so incessant in his tugging at my skirt and calling my name that he didn't even know I was trying to answer him. Finally, after several minutes of Clay following me around the house, I sat him down on the couch and looked straight into his eyes. "What is it, son?"

For the next ten minutes he told me about his day. Then he hopped up and went to play with the other children.

*Listening is more than hearing words;
it's a matter of heart connection.*

—SANDY CATHCART

The Strong-Willed Child

"Guard what God has entrusted to you...
May God's grace be with you.
1 TIMOTHY 6:20–21

I stood with my three-year-old at a Christian bookstore counter, to ask about a book by James Dobson. Cupping my hands over her little ears, I desperately whispered, "Do you have *The Strong-Willed Child?*"

The sympathetic clerk looked at me, then at my daughter, and with a twinkle in his eye, replied, "Yes ma'am. Do you?"

I often speak to mothers' groups and ask, "Who has a strong-willed child?" Many hands rise. I ask the rest to pray daily for these precious moms.

I assure them that God created these children for His grand purposes, and that He will use them for His work. This daughter of mine grew to hold strong convictions, boldly share her faith, and influence college roommates and some atheistic professors.

Raising a strong-willed child is not for sissies. But the rewards are terrific. Keep on, dear moms, and know your labor will not be in vain.

*The task ahead of us is never as
great as the power behind us.*

—SANDI BANKS

The Power of Praying Moms

"Rescue the poor and the helpless;
deliver them from the grasp of evil people."
PSALM 82:4

"We have a crisis. Drugs are being sold in our school. Unless we catch the sellers red-handed, we can't prosecute and remove them," the junior-high principal at our children's school explained to the room full of mothers. "I've asked you moms here today to help me find a solution."

Two weeks later we met together again. After much prayer, I suggested we divide the school roster by the number of moms willing to pray.

Some of the moms were skeptical and turned down the opportunity to participate. Eventually, ten women agreed to take one hundred names each, and read each name in prayer at least once a week.

Soon, teachers began to intercept notes about drug buys; one girl threw up the pills she had just taken—vomiting them in front of a teacher. Within a month, the student selling the drugs was apprehended and removed from school.

God's ears are always open to a mother's prayers.

—SALLY JADLOW

Following Instructions

"But Samuel replied, 'What is more pleasing to the Lord:
your burnt offerings and sacrifices or your obedience to
his voice? Obedience is far better than sacrifice. Listening
to him is much better than offering the fat of rams.'"
1 SAMUEL 15:22

"Load the dishwasher please," I directed Alisha as part of her day's chores. Unfortunately, to load the dishwasher, she needed to clean some gross, dirty dishes.

Two hours later I walked back into the kitchen. It was spotless—except for the pile of dishes in the sink. I hadn't told Alisha to clean the kitchen. She'd figured if she worked hard on something she wasn't asked to do, I'd let her off the hook on the chore she didn't want to do. She was disappointed.

This isn't a new trick. Way back in Bible days, King Saul made extravagant sacrifices rather than simply doing what God told him to do. And how many times do we pull the same stunt? God tells us to do something that we don't want to do. Instead, we sacrifice time, money, or whatever, hoping we won't have to do what we don't want to do.

*It's easier to trust God's directives
and just obey him from the start.*

—JGL

The Power of a Look

"A cheerful look brings joy to the heart..."
PROVERBS 15:30

"Do you know why I liked my kindergarten teacher so much?" my son asked.

"No, why?" I responded.

"Because she smiled all the time, even when we were bad," he explained.

I was struck to the core because I suddenly realized how much I scowled at my kids.

"Cassidy's leg is touching mine!"

A scowl from the rearview mirror.

"I don't want this for lunch."

A scowl and an eye roll.

It really doesn't take much to hurt our kids. A simple look can communicate so much. So many times, across the table or room, I give my children looks that cut and wound!

I know how good it feels when my husband or a friend smiles at me from across the room. I feel a little brighter, a little better about myself. I want my children to feel the same!

Give your children a dose of heart medication today: smile!

—TAMARA VERMEER

What a Wonder-Full World

"... Stop and consider the wonderful miracles of God!"
JOB 37:14

I spent part of my day sitting on the floor in front of the dryer even though it wasn't broken. Instead, clothes tumbled behind a glass pane in the door. The reason I set everything aside to watch a routine experience was my son, sitting in my lap.

What was normal to me was fascinating to him. "Check out the colors! Why are they moving? Who decides which clothes get to be next to the glass? Is there an order?" These are the questions we pondered. He was so fascinated by a common appliance that I got hooked, too.

When did I quit looking? When did water filling a bathtub no longer interest me? When did I begin walking right past earthworms behaving like accordions on the driveway?

My son has given me another chance to see, to be enthralled, to inhale the world around me. I get to live in wonder again.

If you stop living in wonder,
the world is no longer wonderful.

—SUSAN STANLEY

A Parent's Opinion

"People judge by outward appearance, but the
Lord looks at a person's thoughts and intentions."
1 SAMUEL 16:7

Kids can be cruel. Since I was overweight when growing up, I saw and felt that meanness. One day recently when I vividly remembered the ugly things my classmates said, I wondered why I'm not more scarred and in therapy today.

Then I realized it was probably because of my mom. Whenever the subject of my weight came up, she'd just sympathetically say, "Well, you come by it honestly, honey. Look at your dad and me."

Mom wasn't excusing my weight, but she was certainly being realistic about it. Mom let me know that people are different—some tend toward heaviness. And she let me know that was okay—that my weight wasn't the sum of who I was or what I had to offer the world. And when my body automatically shed the baby fat later, Mom didn't act like I was any better or different.

*No matter how other people view our kids,
we can help our kids know how God sees them.*

—JGL

You Get Two Stickers

"If the work survives the fire,
that builder will receive a reward."
1 CORINTHIANS 3:14

By five p.m., I was exhausted. My four-year-old had a will that tested every ounce of me, and I saw little reward for the sacrifices I was making to be a full-time mom.

Every mother makes sacrifices, giving up energy, time, and dealing with emotions. Labor goes beyond giving birth, and we give and give. All I had left to give at that point was just making sure my children ate and trying to make Jesus real to them somehow.

This particular evening, my daughter walked up to me with a pack of stickers.

"Here, Mommy. I'm giving you a sticker," she said.

"Why?" I asked.

"Because you do everything."

"What's everything?"

"You give us dinner and read us Bible verses every day. Here, you get two stickers."

Stickers were a sweet reward. Even sweeter was my daughter's acknowledging my two daily goals of giving her both physical and spiritual food.

*God knows what kind of crown we need—and when we
need the coronation ceremony!*

—LESLIE J. SHERROD

When Not to Intervene

"Protect me from the plots of the wicked, from the scheming of those who do evil. Sharp tongues are the swords they wield; bitter words are the arrows they aim."
PSALM 64:2–3

When I heard the back door slam, I walked into the kitchen to greet my eleven-year-old daughter.

"What's wrong?" I asked as soon as I saw her face.

"One of the kids at school made up a lie about me. Now everyone believes it!" she cried.

Over hot chocolate, we discussed the wounds lies can inflict and how a lie can march halfway through the school before truth even has its boots on. I suggested that Beth confront the girl who started the lie, then forgive her for starting it in the first place.

Doing this was difficult for Beth, but in a few days the ruckus died down and life returned to normal.

If I had intervened, my daughter would have missed a valuable lesson in forgiveness. She would not have learned to endure a trial or confront the one who started it.

Many lessons are lost when we lack the wisdom to know when not to intervene on our child's behalf.

—ELISA YAGER

Never Abandoned

". . . For I will be with you as I was with Moses.
I will not fail you or abandon you."
JOSHUA 1:5

"Waaaah! Waah!"

I looked up in alarm as our three-year-old threw herself on the bed and started fake crying like a baby. Then she wanted me to hold her and bottle-feed her like I did when she was tiny.

Later in the day my eight-year-old wanted me to heat his snack. "But you know how to put it in the microwave," I said. Normally he loved fixing his own food. Then, he wanted me to do something else for him that he was fully capable of doing.

"What is it with these kids today?" I muttered.

Finally I realized it. I had been out the whole day before and had been terribly involved in my work all week. My kids were acting helpless because they wanted me to take care of them, wanted my attention—and probably they wanted the reassurance that I would be there when they had needs to be met.

*We can't overemphasize to our kids
that we'll always be there for them.*

—JGL

Like a Shepherd

"He will feed his flock like a shepherd. He will carry the
lambs in his arms, holding them close to his heart.
He will gently lead the mother sheep with their young."
ISAIAH 40:11

Crash!

I had just settled into my easy chair to relax while my three
boys played in the bathtub upstairs. Their screams shrouded my
rush up the steps, and the sound of shattering glass shredded
my soul.

Three pairs of terrified eyes met mine as I threw open the
bathroom door.

"Mommy, we didn't do anything!"

The cabinet had fallen where two-year-old Joel had been
only moments before while I undressed him for his bath. Fears
of what could have been flowed through my soul after the
incident. I shook for weeks afterward. Years later I realized our
Father's faithfulness. Baby Joel is now a daddy who relies on the
Father to lead him as He led us through the years.

*One of the Lord's names is Shepherd. He fills our lives with
His presence and promises to lead and protect us always.*

—DEE EAST

Supermoms R (Not) Us!

"Be sure to do what you should, for then you will enjoy
the personal satisfaction of having done your work well,
and you won't need to compare yourself to anyone else."

GALATIANS 6:4

My sister-in-law, Vangie, is a Supermom. She pours her whole
life into her kids. She spends hours with them. They're smart
girls who have received lots of fun life experiences as their mom
has planned their days.

Sometimes I look at Vangie's structures, her time with her
kids, her natural Supermom demeanor . . . and then I look at
our home. We have less structure, enjoy fewer experiences, and
with my husband and me both self-employed and working crazy
hours, our kids often have to share us with deadlines or adjust
to a more spontaneous lifestyle. I'm far less than a Supermom.

At times I'm tempted to look at Vangie and the other
Supermoms I know and think, "Wow, I'm not like them, so I
must be a failure."

Then God gently reminds me that He didn't create all families alike—that the most important thing is to just do the best
I can in our circumstances.

Not every mom can be a Supermom, but we
can all do our best with who we are.

—JGL

The Perfect Fit

"Just as our bodies have many parts and each part has
a special function, so it is with Christ's body. We are
all parts of his one body, and each of us has different
work to do. And since we are all one body in Christ, we
belong to each other, and each of us needs all the others."
ROMANS 12:4–5

"Will you please give this room your magic touch?" I asked my
stepdaughter Nicole. We were getting ready for company and I
sensed that the room could look much better, but I had no idea
how to fix it. Nicole instinctively knew how to arrange things.
Sure enough, a half hour later, with objects just placed a bit differently, the room looked much more attractive.

I've heard the maxim that if two people in a marriage
are just alike, one of them isn't necessary. Perhaps the same
is true for families. And maybe that's one reason God put us
in families—so our strengths can compensate for each other's
weaknesses and create a complete, effectual unit. Each of my
kids has strengths in some area where I'm weak. As we work
together and serve God together, we're much more effective
than if we try to go it alone.

God has created each family to have a perfect fit.

—JGL

Faint-Free

"But those who wait on the Lord will find new strength.
They will fly high on wings like eagles. They will run
and not grow weary. They will walk and not faint."
ISAIAH 40:31

"It'll be okay, Mom. Don't worry," my fourteen-year-old daughter said with a confident smile.

"I won't worry," I assured, planting a kiss on her head.

I kept that promise for five minutes, and then stepped outside of her hospital room. Brittany had a brain tumor the size of a lemon. Fret flooded my mind until I couldn't think...pray ...breathe. When you forget to breathe, you faint. I awoke to bright lights and concerned people surrounding me.

My weak display reminded me that flat on my back and staring at the light is the type of reliance God desires. As a mommy, I'm used to fixing boo-boos and broken toys. But I couldn't fix this. I could only trust God to do it.

A year later Brittany has recovered and is running track at school—without growing weary. And I'm still learning to be faint-free.

Trust God with the big and little things in life.

—ELIZABETH DUEWEL

Because I'm the Mother and I Say So

"Pride ends in humiliation, while humility brings honor."
PROVERBS 29:23

My young son could hardly wait for a special television show. When it was time for the program, our daughter was watching another program. Our son entered the room and switched channels. Our indignant daughter protested. Both kids were wrong—our son should not have taken over the television, and our daughter should not have reacted in anger.

That's when I got into the act. I turned off the television and said neither child could watch anything.

A T-shirt slogan says, "Because I'm the mother and I say so." That was the rule that day. I spoke, and the kids had to obey.

More than thirty years have passed since that happened—thirty years to wish that I had handled it differently and helped my kids reach a compromise. The children were unhappy, but they bounced back. Fortunately for me, they haven't held a thirty-year grudge!

"Because I'm the mother and I say so"—sometimes we can find a better way.

—LeAnn Campbell

The God Who Hears

"I love the Lord because he hears and answers my prayers."
PSALM 116:1

Ordinarily, I would have never met Michele. She served meals at a conference I directed. She walked into the room to clear tables as I was giving door prizes.

"Anyone having problems with their teens?" I asked, holding up a book for parents of "prodigal" children. She set down the dirty dishes and hesitantly raised her hand. The group cheered as I gave her the book.

Later she apologized for interrupting our meeting.

"No, Michele," I responded. "I felt I should give the book away at this meal, and you happened to walk in the room just as I offered it. I think God had this book in mind for you."

"I asked Him for help on the way to work this morning," she said, starting to sob.

"Well, I think he heard you," I said as I hugged her, and let her tell me about her daughter.

A mother's prayers for help always touch the Father's heart.

—JGL

Sing Me to Sleep

"Then you will sing psalms and hymns and
spiritual songs among yourselves, making
music to the Lord in your hearts."
EPHESIANS 5:19

My daughters were born seven years apart, but with each baby, I bought a big, blue, comfy rocking chair and rocked each girl to sleep every night for the first three years of her life.

Soon, singing became part of that bedtime routine. As I rocked my little ones, I fell so in love with them and I was so thankful for them that I invited God's presence by singing. I sang all kinds of songs: folk songs, silly songs, old hymns, new praise songs, and rhythmic spirituals. Each girl had her favorites, but we always ended with a song that became our bedtime prayer.

Even though my girls are too big to rock now, they both love to sing praises to God. Music has brought them each joy and comfort. Knowing they have songs in their hearts gives me great hope for their futures.

Let God minister to you and your children through music.

—EVANGELINE BEALS GARDNER

Good Job, Mom!

"The master said, 'Well done, my good and
faithful servant. . . . Let's celebrate together!'"
MATTHEW 25:23

"He said he's only known one child worse than ours," Renee
said as she told us about her encounter with a behavior specialist who was supposed to be tops in the field. Renee hadn't
been surprised when four-year-old Daniel was diagnosed with
ADHD—when he didn't get his way, he was combative and
even violent, hitting and biting his teachers, babysitters, and
parents.

"I feel I'm a lousy parent," Renee revealed in a low voice.

But I'd known her for years. She was doing all she could
to raise her children to love God. She loved them, disciplined
them when they needed it and in appropriate ways, and had
spent lots of time with her kids. I had learned a lot about parenting by watching Renee.

"You're a great mom," I reassured her. "God has special
plans for Daniel."

Parenting is the toughest job in the world. Renee, like all
moms, needed a reminder that she's doing a great job.

*God doesn't just tell us "well done" when our parenting days
are over, but he's pleased with us all through the process.*

—JGL

February

A Chubby-Legged Cross

"Now show him that you still love him."
2 Corinthians 2:8

I did it again, Lord. Father, why? Why do I yell at Greg and the kids? I am so tired. I feel like I can't keep up with the house and their needs, and as for me, well, somehow I feel as if I have lost myself trying to be wife, mommy, and perfect housewife. LORD, help, I feel so numb. Where is the love that is supposed to accompany a husband, two kids, a minivan, and the dream home? Show me love, Lord! Show me I know how to love as I should!

I opened my eyes to see Greg kneeling beside the bed while Mikayla and Grant stared at me, wide-eyed, with their round little cheeks smattered with tearstains.

"Honey, are you okay?" Greg asked.

"No! Yes! I dunno. I'm tired, that's all," I murmured.

Mikayla clambered up on the bed and stretched out beside me, with her head resting on my chest. Grant trying to follow his big sister's climb, tried unceremoniously to follow in her footsteps, but his eighteen-month-old chubby legs could not make it. Daddy gingerly pushed his bottom from behind so Grant could climb up on Mount Bedrest with us.

"I think Mommy needs a tickle fest!" Daddy said.

Mikayla jumped up instantly, delight shining in her eyes, and began to spider-crawl her fingers across my tummy. Greg pinned my arms down, and with gusto, the two of them tackled me as if I were a treasure that must be unlocked with tickles. Grant watched and giggled with delight at Mommy's squeals as I squirmed all over the bed.

My laughter bubbled over and out and I began to shout, "No, stop! I can't take it anymore! Stop!"

Greg and Mikayla laughed at my predicament and tickled more. So I shouted louder.

Suddenly, Grant jumped on top of me and placed his chubby little body across mine. He covered as much of my legs with his as he could. He stretched out his arms across mine, and his torso covered me. He cried out, "Don't hurt my mommy!"

My nose began to burn as tears welled up in my eyes. What a sweet cherub! The mother's heart in me began to break. Love is sacrifice. Grant willingly laid his body across mine to sacrifice himself to protect me. His body formed a cross as he covered me. My tears began to roll down my cheeks as I remembered my prayer, "Lord, show me love!"

—TARA RYE

I'm So Excited!

"Songs of joy and victory are sung in the
camp of the godly. The strong right arm
of the Lord has done glorious things!"
PSALM 118:15

"Mom, I just had to call you! I'm so excited!"

Our younger daughter always has an adventure pending. Whether she is cleaning up after a natural disaster in Mississippi, or going to a leadership conference in Minnesota, she finds life full of fun. Her latest plan is to study in Australia for a semester.

So when she called I wondered, *What now?* This time, however, the news was not as monumental. She simply wanted me to go online and look at a Web site that displayed furniture she had purchased for her first apartment.

As I thought about it, I recalled my own excited phone calls home when I was her age and letters filled with anticipation over some adventure in my life. So many times I, too, couldn't wait to share the little and big events in my life with my mom.

Isn't it wonderful that kids can always count on mothers
when they feel the need to call home?

—LaRose Karr

Broken Balloons

"Jesus looked at them intently and said,
'Humanly speaking, it is impossible.
But with God everything is possible.'"
MATTHEW 19:26

My four-year-old climbed into my lap, her big brown eyes begging a question. The space between her tiny fingers revealed a limp red balloon she had happily batted around the last few days.

"I'm sorry, honey," I said, pointing to a gash. "It's broken. I can't fix it."

Undaunted, she exclaimed, "Daddy can!"

Though her faith was misplaced, I admired her confidence. And I was thankful for the illustration God had provided through her: God is the master repairer.

Over the next twenty years I had many "broken balloons" to bring to Jesus. The thought of my daughter holding up that floppy balloon exclaiming, "Daddy can!" helped me deal with each one.

Our Heavenly Daddy can fix all our "broken balloons."

—CONNIE L. PETERS

No Such Thing as Clones

"There are different ways God works in our lives, but it is the same God who does the work through all of us."
1 CORINTHIANS 12:6

"I guess you're just different than I am," my mom said thoughtfully. "You dream of new computers, and I dream of new curtains."

I looked up at Mom with surprise. I was nearly thirty when she said this, and I realized how different our lives were. Mom was a housewife who kept a spotless home, expressed creativity through decorating cakes and sewing, and loved taking care of kids.

I was single, loved my job, and saved my money for equipment that would help me work more effectively. My creativity came out in my work, and my house was a perpetual mess.

Mom's gone, but I still hear those words. They're reminders in my ears as I look at my own children. My kids may have some things in common with me, but different goals and dreams drive them. They are not younger versions of me.

When we know our kids are unique, we can help them find the plan God has for each of their lives.

—JGL

The Love Habit

". . . Let us continue to love one another,
for love comes from God. Anyone who
loves is born of God and knows God."
1 JOHN 4:7

"I love you," I murmured to my son, and patted his hair as I walked by him.

"I love you, too, Mama," he replied, a secure smile on his face.

The interchange took only a couple of seconds, while I walked through the room intent on another errand, and while he sat on the couch, playing his Nintendo DS. Neither of us took any time out—he didn't miss a movement of the game, and I didn't miss a step. But it added a little brick to the bridge of love connecting us.

The bridge of love between each of my kids and me isn't built of big blocks of sacrifices. Instead, it's like a Lego bridge—built of little pieces. With each touch, each kiss, each expression of love or admiration, I add a brick to the bridge and make it stronger. So I'm getting into the habit of building the bridge continually.

Expressing affection and building a bridge of love is a habit we develop in our lives.

—JGL

Mothers Mentoring Mothers

"Plans go wrong for lack of advice;
many counselors bring success."
PROVERBS 15:22

The six of us gathered around Juanita like Girl Scouts around a campfire. We were hungry for Juanita's wisdom because we all desired to be godly wives and mothers.

Juanita, an octogenarian, had raised five children. She has used the Bible as her handbook for life, and she is willing to share with us what God has taught her.

Therefore, I have spent one day a week for eight years meeting with Juanita and any other women who might show up. We discuss scripture and how we can apply it to our lives in the most practical ways possible. The most frequent prayer requests involve our children. Juanita models how to trust God with our children and turn them over to Him.

I have adopted Juanita as a spiritual mentor. As she mentors me, I am becoming the mother God wants me to be.

Seeking wise and godly counsel
helps us in our tasks as moms.

—EVANGELINE BEALS GARDNER

Don't Give Up!

"So don't get tired of doing what is good. Don't get
discouraged and give up, for we will reap a
harvest of blessing at the appropriate time."
GALATIANS 6:9

"I hate you!" my older, teen stepdaughter screamed.

Some days I'm not too crazy about you either, sweetie, I
thought. But I bit my tongue. It hadn't been easy to go from
being a childless single to a married stepmom with full-time
custody of two girls. But I kept trying to follow the mantra I
was raised with: "Do what's right, even when it's hard."

Over the years I've found I'm not alone. Moms often face
tough situations, not only with stepkids, but also with their
biological kids. When the tough times arrive, it's easy to want
to strike back or to quit. But if we hang in there through the
tough stuff, the rewards eventually come. Besides stories of difficult situations with my stepchildren, I can now also tell about
blessings and joys—like the time a few years later when that
same stepdaughter told me how glad she was that I married
her dad.

Tough times don't last forever!

—JGL

Nannie's Blankets

"But God showed his great love for us by sending
Christ to die for us while we were still sinners."
ROMANS 5:8

As babies, Erik and Karl received more than their fair share
of blankets. Fleece blankets, receiving blankets, embroidered
blankets, lacy blankets, and flannel blankets. More blankets
than either of them could possibly use.

So when my mother-in-law crocheted blankets for them, I
shook my head. That was the last thing either needed. Didn't
she understand that they were inundated? The effort wasn't
logical.

But my logic neglected love. She hooked every stitch of
those blankets with love. And to my amazement, my infant
sons could tell the difference. They treasured Nannie's blankets instantly. Karl even cried if I gave him a different blanket.
Love made all the difference.

Love does make all the difference. My boys could tell the
difference between a mass-produced blanket and one stitched
with time and care. Like Nannie's blankets, God's gifts remind
me of His love.

Love makes all the difference.

—SUSAN LYTTEK

The Best Mom for Your Kids

"I have singled him out so that he will direct
his sons and their families to keep the way of
the Lord and do what is right and just. . . ."
GENESIS 18:19

The doctors expected Vidy to die. And she knew it. Cancer was destroying her body. Vidy was ready to meet God face-to-face—except she kept thinking of her three little ones at home.

"Lord, If you have someone who would be a better mommy for my children, I'm ready to go," she prayed, "but if not, then please keep me here to raise them."

God answered Vidy's prayer, and by now she's not only raised her children, but is helping their children raise children.

I heard Vidy's story many years ago. But her prayer has always stayed in my mind. It reminds me that God places families together. God has entrusted me with each child who calls me his or her mom or stepmom. He's put them in my care for a reason. That gives me courage and confidence for those times when I doubt my abilities.

You're the best person God has chosen to raise your kids.

—JGL

He's Watching!

"The eyes of the Lord watch over those who do right;
his ears are open to their cries for help."
PSALM 34:15

"What?" my son asked when he looked up and saw me watching him. I smiled and shook my head. "Nothing."

He went back to his task and I kept watching. Soon he looked up again. "What?" he asked. "What did I do wrong?"

"Nothing. I just like watching you," I said. "You're cute. And I love you so much."

Different verses in the Bible tell us that God's eyes are on us. I used to feel uncomfortable to think of God watching me. Waiting for me to slip up and fail, I assumed.

Then I heard entertainer Mark Lowry talk about God's eyes being on us—not because he is like the traffic cop waiting to catch us doing something wrong, but because he loves us so much that he can't keep his eyes off of us. God is proud of us, fascinated with us, and probably even thinks we're cute!

*God enjoys watching us as much
as we love watching our kids!*

—JGL

Any Homework Tonight?

"Better to be patient than powerful; better to
have self-control than to conquer a city."
PROVERBS 16:32

"Hey, Mom!" My fifteen-year-old son breezed into the kitchen, dropped his backpack on the floor, and opened the refrigerator door. "I did a lot better on my geometry test. You know, it really helps when you do the homework!"

I stared at him in disbelief. How many times had I said those words? I don't call myself the Homework Police for nothing! And some days, the kids call my minivan the "Lecture mobile."

My mind flashed back over teacher conferences where I always heard the familiar refrain, "If he would just complete the daily homework . . ."

But I've taken a long time to learn lessons, too. My children aren't perfect, and neither am I. Encouraging words in a calm voice usually produce better results than another angry lecture. Kids do grow up, but in their own ways, and on their individual timetables. God has a plan for each of them—and for me.

The toughest homework assignment for this mom? Patience.

—SUE LOWELL GALLION

A Piece of Laughter

"And Sarah declared, 'God has brought me laughter!
All who hear about this will laugh with me.'"
GENESIS 21:6

I let my seven-year-old son have a friend over for the day on the condition that they play quietly in his room while I worked on a pressing deadline. But from my downstairs office, their play sounded like a roaring jet repeatedly flying overhead.

I bit down on my pen—hard—leaned back in my chair, squeezed my eyes shut, and willed for peace. *How will I ever meet my deadline tonight?* I wondered. The thunder of worry and the rumble of frustration drowned out even the din of their playtime.

A while later, they bounded into my office to ask something but stopped short and broke into giggles.

"Why so blue?" my son asked, pointing at my face.

Does my countenance show that much? I wondered.

"Mom, there's ink on your chin!"

So there was—and I laughed with them all the way past my deadline. And it was good.

Lighten your load with laughter.

—SHAE COOKE

Real to the Puppies

"You must be compassionate, just as
your Father is compassionate."
LUKE 6:36

"It may only be puppy love, but it's so real to the puppies," the instructor explained.

I was in youth ministry training when I heard this nugget of truth. Anytime you work with teens, you have to be prepared to sympathize with their heartbreaks.

Since I've been a mom, I've remembered those words many times—not just when helping my teen stepdaughters through romances, but also with my younger kids.

My son loses a rock he got from Grandpa's driveway. Yes, it's just a rock, but it was special to him. God reminds me to sympathize.

My toddler cries when the dog licks her face. Yes, the dog is just affectionate, but Elizabeth's so little and the dog is so big.

When I look at situations through my kids' eyes, and remember their ages, well, it's much easier to find mercy and compassion even about the things that may seem silly.

*As we understand our children's hearts,
the love between us grows.*

—JGL

Love Her

"My child, don't ignore it when the Lord disciplines
you, and don't be discouraged when he corrects you.
For the Lord corrects those he loves, just as a
father corrects a child in whom he delights."

PROVERBS 3:11–12

My four-year-old, Ivy, was experiencing a challenging phase: total
defiance. I tried the usual things such as rewards, serious chats,
and time-outs. Nothing worked. Her purposeful disobedience
was aimed directly at me, the classic mother-daughter battle.

"Lord, what should I do?" I prayed. "How can I help her and
myself?"

The Lord answered, "Love her."

"I do love her," I replied. No more words came.

I asked a friend what he thought God meant. "Just love her.
Be consistent with discipline, great with praise. God trusts you
to love her through this. Model your love after the best parent
ever—God."

So I loved her as best I could, giving praise when limits
were met, compassion and consequences when they were not. I
did love her through it.

Ivy still tests my patience. But with God's wisdom I trust
myself. And Ivy trusts me to be a consistent, loving mom.

Through our Lord's grace you are an awesome mother!

—SUSAN KNEIB SCHANK

This Kiss!

"What joy for those you choose to bring
near, those who live in your holy courts.
What joys await us inside your holy Temple."
PSALM 65:4

"Whee!" my son squealed. Then he danced as Princess Fiona and the ogre, Shrek, kissed. However, when I try to give him a mommy peck, he pouts and runs. I sneak a kiss as I tuck him into bed at night.

Our Heavenly Parent has a kiss for each of us. God's kiss is no peck on the cheek. Nor is it a passing invitation to temporal intimacy. This holy kiss invites spiritual completion and eternal ecstasy. God's kiss affirms, "You're my forgiven child. How I love you."

How often we scurry from God's presence like pouting ogres, letting self-centered agendas enslave our time. When we pause to ponder God in His Word, we receive a holy kiss that changes us beyond movie magic! We learn to appreciate who we are meant to be: laughing ogres turned into princes and princesses, living it up in God's holy courts.

We can bask in God's love—always there for us.

—CYNTHIA AGRICOLA HINKLE

Before We Ask

> ". . . Your father knows exactly what you
> need even before you even ask him!"
> MATTHEW 6:8

For nearly an hour, I'd heard the clunk-clunk, but paid little attention. For all I knew, the dryer always made that noise. And I was preoccupied with other thoughts. My father had gotten deathly ill while he was 500 miles from home. So my kids and I had rushed to be with him. We'd already been there two weeks, with no signs of going home soon.

"Where's my Game Boy?" my son asked.

You guessed it. It was clunking in his pants pocket in the dryer. When we pulled it out, it was fried. He sobbed, but valiantly tried to keep playing it. Since being away from home, spending hours in a hospital each day, and having a dying grandpa is tough enough on a kid, without even telling him, I got him a new Game Boy the next day—before he could even ask.

> *Just as we foresee and meet our kids' needs,*
> *God is always ready to meet ours.*

—JGL

Forgive, Then Party!

". . . 'We must celebrate with a feast, for this son of
mine was dead and has now returned to life. He was
lost, but now he is found.' So the party began."
LUKE 15:23–24

Stunned, I reread the note. "Good-bye, Mom. I've gone to find
new adventures. Don't worry. I love you. Gary."

My son had just earned his driver's license. Now, at sixteen,
he'd left home with a friend in the friend's parents' car, with all
the money he'd worked long hours after school to save.

For days my emotions swirled from fear to anger to panic
to grief. Finally, the call came from Florida, 900 miles away:
"Your son is in the juvenile center for breaking curfew." The
police had found the boys locked in the car—frightened and
not knowing what to do.

As I rode to Florida, I knew I needed to punish Gary, but
I also felt joy. He had learned hard lessons from his adventure,
including misspent savings. But, like the prodigal son, he also
knew he had a parent—and a Father in heaven—who loves
him and forgives foolish mistakes.

After we're forgiven, we can rejoice in God's love.

—BARBARA YOUREE

God Talk

"... Be very careful never to forget what you have seen
the Lord do for you. Do not let these things escape from
your mind as long as you live! And be sure to pass them
on to your children and grandchildren."

DEUTERONOMY 4:9

"Good news," I announced to my family at dinner. "One of my
best clients renewed my contract."

As I scooped up fajita fixings, I felt an internal nudge. *Is
that all you're going to say?*

This contract was a direct result of my prayers, and I knew
I should also mention that to my family to encourage them that
God answers prayers.

Recently, I'd connected with a dad who said after his kids
flew the nest, his one regret was that he hadn't been more verbal about his faith. He wished he'd praised the Lord for little
things more in front of his children. His words had resonated
with me. After all, if I want my kids to sense God as part of
their everyday lives, I need to talk a bit more about how he
provides blessings.

"You know the neat thing about the contract ... " I started,
and told them how God had answered my prayers.

*If we want God to be real to our kids, we'll talk about Him
as if He's truly part of our lives.*

—JGL

A Lesson in a Bagel

"You must each make up your own mind as to how much you should give. Don't give reluctantly or in response to pressure. For God loves the person who gives cheerfully."
2 CORINTHIANS 9:7

On Teacher Appreciation Day, I had forgotten to send a gift to school with my kindergarten son. When I picked him up, he reminded me. "Mom, you didn't get my teacher anything." Then his eyes lit up. "So I gave her my bagel! Well, not my whole bagel. I started eating it, but then remembered she needed a gift," he said proudly.

"You gave your teacher a half-eaten bagel?" I asked, mortified.

Sharing was one thing, but this was going too far. I quickly drove back to school. Embarrassed, I explained to Conner's teacher why she received a smashed bagel with tooth marks.

Holding back tears, she said, "That was my best gift because it came from his heart."

Likewise, our best gifts to our children are not found in beautifully wrapped boxes, but in the depths of our heart—our love, time, and attention.

Give your children the gift of God's love from a pure heart.

—RENEE GRAY-WILBURN

Timing Is Everything!

> "Go and gather together all the Jews of Susa and fast for
> me. Do not eat or drink for three days, night or day. My
> maids and I will do the same. And then, though it is
> against the law, I will go in to see the king. . . ."
> ESTHER 4:16

Alisha walked into the house with a smile. But it quickly turned to a scowl after I said, "Hello." Because my hello didn't stop there. It was followed by a lecture because Alisha had gone off without completing her chores first.

Later, thinking about the scowl, I suddenly remembered when I was a kid. It seemed so many times I'd barely get home from a fun evening and my mother would light into me. The happy glow would fizzle, and I'd walk away feeling my mother spoiled everything.

Doubtless, each of those lectures by my mom was deserved. But it would have been nice if she'd timed them better. That's one of the things I love about the story of Esther. She definitely had something she needed to say, but she paused and prayed, and tackled it in the right timing.

> *It not only matters what we say to our kids,*
> *but how and when we say it also matters.*

—JGL

Watered by Love

"You gave me life and showed me your unfailing love.
My life was preserved by your care."
JOB 10:12

I love plants and buy them all year round. Whenever I bring a new plant home, my family members roll their eyes and hum the death march. Although I love plants, I don't really have a green thumb. I forget to water them until they droop. However, I'm trying to remember to water them before they start to look wilted—to just automatically give them that nourishment every few days.

I wasn't born with a very green "mom thumb" either. I tend to get caught up in my work and not give my kids the attention they need—until I see their personalities, joy, or obedience start to wilt. So I'm learning to do the same thing with my kids that I do with my plants—to regularly water them with encouraging words, hugs, and attention. As I do so, I find that they move ahead freely without signs of wilting at all.

Unlike with plants, we can't overwater our kids.

—JGL

On the Back Burner

"God has given gifts to each of you from his great variety of spiritual gifts. Manage them well so that God's generosity can flow through you."

1 PETER 4:10

"I used to do oil painting, but I have put that on the back burner since I had children," my friend said with a sigh.

When you become a mother, bring all you are to it—bring your art and music, bring your love of nature and your favorite football team. You will need all of these things to build a happy, whole child.

"Sure," says the new mommy, "but, when? I barely have time to brush my teeth."

Well, a baby must sleep sometime. Keep a corner of the bedroom as "Mommy's space." An easel would fit there, or a few great books. A journal beside the baby's calendar will let you record how you are growing along with how she is growing. Designate Thursdays as sandwich night and use the saved cooking time to pursue your soul. Give the toddler a tiny paintbrush, or the teen a piece of sheet music and pursue creativity together.

Our children are not interruptions; they are traveling companions to share the richness of God's world with us.

—KARLA DOYLE

Warm and Fuzzy Memories

"Choose a good reputation over great riches, for being
held in high esteem is better than having silver or gold."
PROVERBS 22:1

My husband and I go to the nursing home in our town every
week. In our role as volunteer ombudsmen, we visit each resident and serve as advocates to see that everyone receives good
care.

Many times when we walk into a room and sit down to
visit with a white-haired lady, I will comment on what a pretty
blouse or dress she is wearing. No matter which lady we're visiting, the answer is usually the same: "My mother made it for
me."

My husband and I may smile, for we know these eighty-
and ninety-year-old ladies no longer wear the clothing their
mothers once made for them. In most cases their mothers died
years ago, and the clothes these ladies are wearing probably
came from the local department store. But many years ago their
mothers loved and cared for them, and that is what these ladies
remember.

May we create warm, fuzzy memories
in our children's minds.

—LeANN CAMPBELL

59

Rebellion Not Guaranteed

"Teach your children to choose the right path,
and when they are older, they will remain upon it."
PROVERBS 22:6

"I dread my child becoming a teenager. Teens are so rebellious."

How many times have I heard moms moan that? So I brought up the issue when I interviewed Wayne Rice, founder of Understanding Your Teenager, who has worked with teenagers for several decades. When I asked Rice how parents can prepare themselves for the rebellious years, he informed me that the stereotype that teens have to act up when they hit the magic age of thirteen isn't necessarily true.

"Kids will live up to what you expect out of them, and allow out of them," Rice said. When they're little or when they're teens, our kids will push the envelope only as far as we let them.

That gave me courage and reassurance a few years later when I began parenting a teen. I learned to keep open lines of communication and not to assume that my teens would rebel.

Our kids may go through troubled times, but as we expect the best from them, it will be easier for all of us!

—JGL

Presenting Our Children to the Lord

"Then it was time for the purification offering, as required
by the law of Moses after the birth of a child; so his
parents took him to Jerusalem to present him to the Lord."
LUKE 2:22

When Dad worked nights, Mom prayed with my brother and
me before we went to bed. But on this night, Mom had something on her mind.

"You never were dedicated in the church when you were a
baby," Mom told us. "But I still dedicated you to God. I prayed
over you when you were babies, and I asked God to guide your
lives."

I was in elementary school and didn't care what Mom had
or hadn't done when I was a baby. But years later, Mom's expla-
nation warmed my heart. I felt good to know that my Mom
followed the tradition started in Exodus 13 of parents asking
God to guide their children's lives.

Whether done formally in a church or through a simple
personal prayer like Mom did, asking God to guide our children
tells them that we want them to know God. And it's a reminder
to us that our children are on loan from God.

*We can present our children to the
Lord at any time, in any place.*

—JGL

61

God Is Bigger

"I am holding you by your right hand—
I, the Lord your God. And I say to you,
'Do not be afraid. I am here to help you.'"
ISAIAH 41:13

One bedtime my daughter asked me to leave the light on because she feared the dark.

I reassured her. "God created the whole world"—I snapped my fingers—"just like that. He's bigger and more powerful than anything. And any God that strong could certainly protect you. He is with you all day ... and all night too, watching over you."

She nodded in somber thought. "So I don't need to be afraid because God is the biggest monster of them all?"

We may laugh about her question, but as mothers, we also grapple with fear. Not fear of the dark or shadowy creatures, but monsters of a different kind. Failure. Financial problems. Career choices. Health issues. We experience the same heart-pounding anxieties as my daughter.

We can let those troubles go by remembering that God is bigger than anything we fear. We can be comforted with His assurance in Isaiah 41:13.

*God is trustworthy, faithful, and powerful enough
to help us overcome any "monsters" lurking
in the shadows of our hearts.*

—LORI Z. SCOTT

Instant Weight-Loss Plan

"Give your burdens to the Lord,
and he will take care of you. . . ."
PSALM 55:22

Do you ever get tired of carrying the weight of the world? If you're a mom, you know what it feels like to be the one who will come through with cookies for the school party, with Band-Aids for skinned knees, with dinner for a hungry family. Sometimes you get so busy and tired that you have to dig deep inside to find the energy, patience, love, and grace that the people in your life need. And you are run ragged taking care of everyone . . . except yourself.

Wouldn't it be refreshing to let someone else be in charge for a while?

Then let someone else be in charge! Accept help—from your husband, your children, your friends. Above all, accept help from God. Put down that to-do list, let the phone ring, pour a cup of tea and settle down with God. Tell him your worries. Let the weight of the world go, and feel the pounds melt away.

You can accept—even ask for—help.

—TRACY DONEGAN

When Parents Aren't Popular

"But even if you suffer for doing what is right, God will
reward you for it. So don't be afraid and don't worry."
1 PETER 3:14

"Parenting is not a popularity contest," my friend Patty explained.
As a new stepmom, I'd asked for her best advice. "Many times
when you do what you're supposed to do, your kids won't be
happy. Parenting is not about being their buddy who lets them
do anything; it's about doing what's best for them."

I think that's the wisest concept I've heard as I've just
completed ten years of parenting kids at home, and face fifteen
more years of it!

"No, I'm sorry; you can't go to Taco Bell at two a.m. with
your friends."

"No, I'm sorry; you can't eat a Popsicle for breakfast."

"Yes, you need to do your homework before you can call
your friends."

"No, you can't ride your friend's motorbike since neither of
you has a driver's license."

Of course I usually also tell my kids why I've made a certain decision—but if your kids are like mine, when they want
to do something, they don't always listen to reason!

*Take heart! God gives grace and wisdom to unpopular—but
loving—parents.*

—JGL

Father Knows Best

"And we know that God causes everything to work
together for the good of those who love God and are
called according to his purpose for them."
ROMANS 8:28

"Your work is great; this decision is financial," the VP explained.
The company hzad expanded their team by hiring me. Then
finances plunged after September 11, 2001, and several of us
lost our jobs.

I was devastated. I loved my job, and had left a great position and had relocated my family for it.

"Lord, if you're in control, you're letting this happen for a
reason," I prayed. "Will you show me the reason?"

I let some of my former clients know I was self-employed
again, and jobs started coming in. With the flexibility of self-
employment, I could take time out to volunteer at my son's
school and to enjoy my daughter's toddler years—I'd missed my
son's since I'd been working in an office.

I still miss my old job a lot at times. But then I spend an
afternoon with my kids and realize that for me, for right now,
being around my kids is the best thing. I would never have quit
my job to be with my kids, so I feel God made that decision for
me.

When unexpected things happen in our lives,
we can still trust that God is in control.

—JGL

March

Masterpiece in the Making

"For we are God's masterpiece. He has created
us anew in Christ Jesus, so that we can do
the good things he planned for us long ago."

—Ephesians 2:10

*A*ny mother will tell you what you don't want to know: at no age—from birth to young adult—can a child can be trusted with a permanent marker. I've had a teenager design a crowd-stopping graphic-arts campaign for student council president with tools no more sophisticated than red and blue felt-tipped pens and—rather than a more appropriate work surface—a beige carpet.

What about the four-year-old who created a raucous-colored mural of a house (complete with curly chimney smoke, rudimentary swing set, pine trees decorated in Christmas lights, and a flower garden to die for) upon the whitewashed wall of our living room? Unbelievably, the kid had enough creative energy left over to compose a whopper.

He pointed to his nine-month-old sister in her high chair and said with a straight, albeit marker-covered, face, "She did it."

An ambitious middle schooler of mine once used a single sheet of thin newsprint and a brown marker to create a treasure map for a party she was hosting. A conscientious child, she decided to protect the dining room table from damage by covering it with a pink damask tablecloth.

In her own defense at the ruined-tablecloth hearings, she said, "I was worried that the marker might soak through the newspaper."

But that's not all. When you're the mom of creative kids, it's never all.

We have an attic space with Sheetrocked walls that the three of them used to create a giant timeline of their lives, complete with hieroglyphics barely decipherable to the adult eye. They'd sneak in there and write cryptic notes to each other in purple, mark their heights with corresponding ages and dates in green, and—every once in a while—even leave pictorial hints about their current crushes and heartbreaks.

My husband and I have painted over a lot of stuff in our lives, but when we're old and gray and giving up this house of a lifetime, the attic walls will remain a departing testament to our family's wonder years.

Somewhere along the line, I became less frustrated with my children's regular attempts at masterpieces, and more fascinated with the masterpieces they were becoming. Walls could be updated in the color-du-jour, throw rugs could cover damaged carpets, and tablecloths could be dyed to match brown marking pens, but God's work in the hearts of my kids? That couldn't be duplicated or replaced.

One incident, though, nearly did me in, leaving an indelible mark on my soul that remains to this day.

My three-year-old daughter, Carrie, a free-spirited child whose artistic temperament I was hoping to mold— if only for the sake of my newly hung wallpaper—was one day overtaken by some primal urge to color outside the lines. Unfortunately, the lines in this case formed the title on the cover of my 1939 edition of *Gone with the Wind*.

MARCH

The volume, given to me by my beloved grandfather, was bound in muted green cloth until Carrie relieved herself of her artistic yearnings. Its elegant G was aggressively victimized by an attack of magenta. *Gone with the Wind*, its monetary value having plummeted in an instant, was now *One with the Wind*.

I stared at my treasure's new title, and then focused on my toddler's shining eyes. Somehow, I couldn't help but look into her future.

Would she grow up to be an artist? Or perhaps a pianist or a dancer? Even at her tender age, the signs were all there. Even when she colored inside the lines, she couldn't silence the song in her spirit or quiet the dance in her soul.

No matter how many priceless masterpieces she may create in her lifetime, I thought, my prayer for her is that she becomes the beautiful masterpiece of her Maker.

I took Carrie in my arms and kissed her then and felt, if only for a single moment, what it must be like to be one with the wind.

—KATY McKENNA RAYMOND

Out of the Mouths of Babes

"Always be joyful. Keep on praying. No matter what
happens, always be thankful, for this is God's will for you
who belong to Christ Jesus."
1 THESSALONIANS 5:16–18

I turned the key to start the engine of our van. Nothing—the
battery was dead. I groaned. I was having one of those weeks.

My six-year-old son's voice broke the silence. "Will we be
stuck here forever, Mom?" He was genuinely alarmed.

"No, buddy," I responded wearily. "Mommy will call the
tow-truck man and he will get the car going."

Though not entirely convinced that we would ever escape
the Safeway parking lot, he relaxed a little at my words of reassurance.

Twenty minutes later, the tow truck arrived and we were
on our way. I still wallowed in gloom as we left, but Joseph was
overjoyed. He broke into spontaneous praise, singing, "God is
so good!"

My heart was instantly lifted. In my son's short life, this
was a true crisis and he remembered, in his childlike way, to be
thankful in all things.

*We may not know what each day will bring
to us, but we can find something to praise
God for, no matter what happens.*

—LISA VITELLO

71

Giggling in a Powder Wonderland

"[There is] A time to cry and a time to laugh.
A time to grieve and a time to dance."
ECCLESIASTES 3:4

They had been quiet for way too long. Where are they and what are they up to? I wondered.

I checked the living room ... no toddlers. *Hmm.*

Then I heard their giggles. I ascended the stairs.

What's this? I followed a dusty white trail. *Oh my goodness, it's everywhere!* The familiar fragrance of Johnson's baby powder greeted my nose.

There stood my boys, in our bathroom, frozen in a powder wonderland, wide-eyed, staring at me through powder-covered faces.

I took a deep, cleansing breath. To my amazement, I relaxed. Giggles surfaced from within, giving life to my weary soul. The boys hadn't been defiant—just creative. I ran for the camera.

Sometimes I get so focused on the tasks at hand, I forget to relax. Even God relaxed after six busy days of creating our world, and perhaps he even giggled.

*Ask God to help you relax today
and even enjoy a giggle or two.*

—CAROLYN BYERS RUCH

The Blessing That Keeps Blessing

"You will be blessed with many children and productive fields. You will be blessed with fertile herds and flocks."
DEUTERONOMY 28:4

"I can't wait until my kids are in school so I can get things done," one mom laments.

"I can't wait until he can drive himself all these places," another mom moans.

"When she's on her own, she'll understand real life," another mom predicts.

I listen to these moms and relate as I look at my toddler—the girl is high maintenance. Sometimes I end the day feeling I haven't gotten anything done. She's always interrupting me: "Mommy, I want this!" Or she sobs to me, "Mommy, the dog ate my hot dog."

Sometimes she pesters me to hold her while she watches *Barney*, or she keeps running to me with little hugs and interrupting my train of thought to say "I luss you!" or to cover me with sticky kisses.

Maybe I'm not in such a hurry for her to grow up and stop being a pain after all.

Kids are a pain or a source of joy, depending on our focus.

—JGL

When Yelling Can't Be Heard

"And after the earthquake there was a fire, but
the Lord was not in the fire. And after the
fire there was the sound of a gentle whisper."
1 KINGS 19:12

I saw red. Five-year-old Brandon's bicycle was in the driveway
again. I stomped into the house, yelling his name the whole
way.

He met me in the hallway. "Brandon," I roared, "put your
bicycle away, right now!" My voice reverberated off the walls.

Brandon's knees bent slightly and he wavered like a bird
ready to take flight, but his feet didn't move. I waited. Still he
didn't move. I couldn't believe it. My anger subsided as curiosity
took over.

I lowered my voice. "Why aren't you doing what I said to
do?"

"I couldn't hear you," he said. "Your eyes were too big."

"I'm sorry." I quietly repeated my instructions. Brandon ran
to obey.

God's voice thundered when His people needed to fear
Him so they wouldn't willfully disobey Him. But like Brandon,
Elijah became sidetracked. God spoke to Him in a gentle whisper and directed him back on course.

*A gentle voice, rather than loud yelling, often effectively
produces desirable behavior changes.*

—CAROL HATHEWAY SCOTT

Necessities of Life

"Lazy people want much but get little, but those who
work hard will prosper and be satisfied."
PROVERBS 13:4

"So how do you help Cynthia remember to do her chores?" I
asked the seasoned mom. I'd only been married a few months
and my stepdaughters balked at the chore routine.

This mom fixed her steely blue eyes on me and announced,
"My daughter does not *do* chores."

I later realized they have a housekeeper and Cynthia is an
only child and a debutante.

On the other end of the scale is my friend Pat. She has
four kids and works full-time. She does all the housework alone
because she feels too guilty to make her kids do chores.

Most of us fall in the center. And most of our kids will
have to work for a living. So it's good to get them in the habit of
work when they're young. We now have a chart listing chores
that our kids mark off as they complete them. Then they earn
privileges, like going out with friends, for doing their chores.
Even though they won't admit it, they feel a sense of accomplishment when they do their chores. And I rest assured that
we're helping build their future success.

*God honors work so much that he had chores
for Adam to do—even before the Fall.*

—JGL

A Father Answers

"When they call on me, I will answer; I will be
with them in trouble. I will rescue and honor them."
PSALM 91:15

"Why did God let Dad die?" ten-year-old Jonathan asked for
what seemed like the hundredth time since Gordon died of
pancreatic cancer.

Exhausted from grief, I prayed for wisdom.

"You know, one time your Dad was mad at God." I told
Jonathan how a death in Gordon's family had made him want
to leave his faith. "God told Dad he could go through his grief
alone and be miserable, or walk through it holding His hand.
Dad chose to walk through it with God."

Explaining that Jonathan also had a choice, I left him
alone to pray.

"God spoke to me," Jonathan told me later that night. "He
said He healed Dad for one summer. I guess He listened to my
prayers."

Tears came to my eyes. Unlike Gordon, pancreatic cancer
patients rarely go into remission. I smiled and thanked God for
His answers and for that wonderful summer.

God gives us wisdom when we ask.

—ALICIA GOSSMAN

The Second Mile

"If a soldier demands that you carry his gear for a mile,
carry it two miles."
MATTHEW 5:41

One of my biggest challenges is fitting exercise into my crammed schedule. I found hope, though, when I realized how long my driveway is. I discovered walking eight laps on it would equal a mile.

One morning, as I completed my eighth lap, my husband decided to join me. Rather than moan at having already accomplished my goal, I chose to do the extra mile to enjoy his company.

So many times in motherhood we are also required to go the extra mile. When we do so, these miles end up being the times that we enjoy our greatest fellowship with the Lord, as we feel His grace and strength carry us.

Just as the second mile of walking is where you burn the most fat, so the second mile of mothering is where you bear the most fruit.

*The second mile provides the greatest
satisfaction and reward.*

—MARIBETH SPANGENBERG

The Ultimate Stain Remover

"'Come now, let us argue this out,' says the Lord.
'No matter how deep the stain of your sins, I can
remove it. I can make you as clean as freshly
fallen snow. Even if you are stained as red as
crimson, I can make you as white as wool.'"
ISAIAH 1:18

The day started with our toddler spilling a bottle of indelible emerald ink on our white carpet. Later the puppy chewed up a sippy cup, leaving milk and shredded plastic all over. Spilled glasses of water. Cherry Popsicle pieces melted on the wooden floor. Knocked-over plants. And the grand finale came as I headed for bed and found dark piles of incontinence from our ancient Dalmatian all across our white bedroom carpet. Followed by an encore of more water spilled by my son and a gross potty chair to scour. A typical day in our home.

How I wish I had someone to clean up the nonstop messes in our house! As I cleaned the potty chair, I thought of all the messiness of life—and of how glad I am that God is always willing to clean up our messes.

*Do you have a mess in your life? Turn it over to God today.
He can handle it.*

—JGL

"Sure!"

"Happy are those who obey his decrees and
search for him with all their hearts."
PSALM 119:2

"Sure!" my son usually chirps when I ask him to do something
like feed the cats or help me with something or even assist his
baby sister. He makes it sound like he's delighted I've asked
him.

How refreshing that can be—especially on the days when
his little sister is whiney and his big sister is surly. His "Sure!" is
a bit of verbal sunshine in my life and makes it so much easier
when I know I'm not going to have a fight trying to get a kid
to obey.

My son's "Sure!" also inspires me. How do I respond when
he or his sisters or my husband asks for help? I'm guessing they'd
all find it refreshing if I act willing and cheerful, instead of
grudgingly. How about when God asks me to obey Him? Am I
going to be cheerful about it? Sure!

God loves a cheerful, obeying person, and
everyone loves a cheerful helper!

—JGL

Trust That Melts a Mother's Heart

"When everything is ready, I will come and get you,
so that you will always be with me where I am."
JOHN 14:3

"Stay in the car. I'll get the costume," I yelled.

I raced inside and grabbed the bright yellow bird costume covered with feathers plucked from several feather dusters.

I drove off and asked, "James, why didn't you tell me we didn't have it with us?" Silence hung in the air.

"James, answer me!" Nothing.

"James got out at home," Michael said.

"Why didn't anyone tell me this?" I demanded.

"You didn't ask."

I drove to school and dropped off my other children. Darlene's lips quivered. "How can I be little bird without my big bird?"

My heart melted a bit. "I'll go get the big bird," I promised.

She trotted off, dragging her costume.

I sped home, picked up James, and asked, "Were you scared when we left you behind?"

My heart finished melting when he said, "No. You came back for my costume, so I knew you'd come for me."

Your child learns trust by watching your actions.

—KAREN H. WHITING

Keeping Our Minds on Him

"You will keep in perfect peace all who trust in you,
whose thoughts are fixed on you!"
ISAIAH 26:3

"Shh! Be still," I whispered to my elementary schooler wiggling at my side. I bit my lip, fervently hoping she hadn't distracted anyone.

I took my responsibility as a mother seriously. When I was small, I had not been allowed to move, make noise, or otherwise misbehave in church. And now I held my daughter to those same standards Therefore, I sat rigidly in church, hearing little the pastor said, focusing on my daughter's behavior. I felt it was my job to make sure those around us who needed to hear the gospel were not distracted.

Then one day I realized I had become spiritually undernourished. I was so busy watching my daughter that I didn't hear the songs or the scripture or the pastor—or the Lord speaking to me through him.

During the next church service, I participated in the service, attending to my daughter if she disturbed me. However, I left other people's concentration up to God.

Let's not be so worried about our children's
behavior that we miss God's words to us.

—IMOGENE JOHNSON

The God Who Says "Yes!"

"You want what you don't have, so you scheme and
kill to get it. You are jealous for what others have,
and you can't possess it, so you fight and quarrel to
take it away from them. And yet the reason you don't
have what you want is that you don't ask God for it."

JAMES 4:2

"Can I go to the mall?" my seventeen-year-old asks.

"Sure," I answer.

"I can?"

"Is there a reason I shouldn't let you?" I say.

"Well, no," she says as she trots off to get ready.

So many times she acts so shocked that I'll let her do something she wants to do. I'm careful about only saying no to her
requests if I have a real reason to do so. And I've been that way
for the ten years I've been her full-time stepmom, so it both-
ers me when she automatically expects me to be an ogre and
squelch her fun.

The last time she made a request with the "bet you won't
let me" attitude, I thought of this scripture. How many times
do we have a "bet you won't let me" attitude with our heavenly
Father—maybe even to the degree that we won't even ask?

Never hesitate to ask for favors or
blessings from the Father who loves you.

—JGL

Safe in His Hands

"'I asked the Lord to give me this child, and he has
given me my request. Now I am giving him to
the Lord, and he will belong to the Lord his
whole life.' And they worshiped the Lord there."
1 SAMUEL 1:27–28

Talk about preachers' kids being rebellious! Eli was God's priest, and his sons, also priests, had a horrible reputation. They flagrantly dishonored the God they were supposed to represent. And Eli let them get away with all of it.

If I'd been Hannah, I would have thought twice about handing my son over to Eli to raise, considering his sons. But Hannah had promised her son to God, and she doubtlessly knew in her heart that Samuel belonged in the temple.

It's a good thing she trusted God with her child—he came out just fine. In fact, he was the spiritual leader to the Israelites for many decades.

At times our kids are going to encounter bad influences—even in good places. We can't shield them from everything. But if we follow God's guidance with our children, we can rest assured that when situations are out of our hands, they're still in God's hands.

Whenever God clearly leads our children,
he will also protect and provide for them.

—JGL

Power to Change

"And now, may the God of peace, who brought again
from the dead our Lord Jesus, equip you with all you
need for doing His will. May He produce in you, through
the power of Jesus Christ, all that is pleasing to Him. . . ."
HEBREWS 13:20–21

"Turn that music down! Clean your room! Get your homework done!" My teenagers turned a deaf ear to my commands.

I retreated to the family room and reflected on my own teenage years. I had often longed for my parents' encouragement and companionship, but their distaste for my preferences created a gulf between us. I resented their criticism. A tear rolled down my cheek. Did I want my children to feel that same resentment toward me? I closed my eyes and whispered a prayer. I needed a change of heart, an attitude makeover.

I walked over to the closet, pulled out a board game, and knocked on their bedroom door. They turned down the music and I smiled, "Anyone up for Monopoly? And bring that CD so we can listen to it while we play."

I couldn't do it on my own, but I knew with God's grace I could change.

Every day we can become more and more like Him.

—GINNY CAROLEO

The Rewards of Praying for Our Children

"But when you pray, go away by yourself, shut the door behind you, and pray to your Father secretly. Then your Father, who knows all secrets, will reward you."
MATTHEW 6:6

I walked into the house in tears, greeted by my fourteen-year-old son. I blurted out to him the outcome of the evening's marriage-counseling session between my estranged husband, the counselor, and me.

"I don't think things are going to work out between Dad and me, but please know that I'll always love you, no matter what happens," I told him.

Mark hugged me. His love was evident in the strength of his embrace. "Mom, I know you're going to get through this. Your faith in God is strong. Even if the worst happens, trust God," he said.

I have steadfastly prayed for my son for years. And in that moment, I felt I was seeing proof that God had heard and answered. I caught a glimpse of the character of the man he would become and thanked God for the blessings of persevering prayer.

Never give up praying for your children. God will answer in His timing, showing that He heard every word.

—ELISA YAGER

Good Things

"The Lord will give you an abundance of good things in
the land he swore to give your ancestors—many children,
numerous livestock, and abundant crops."
DEUTERONOMY 28:11

"No! You can't be pregnant!" my husband exclaimed. As the
weeks passed, he felt no better about it. "I just can't tell my
mother!" he moaned.

Though I wasn't upset about having another child, I
understood a bit of how he felt. He was fifty-two and his mother
thought he was neither the age, nor had the finances for another
child. After all, he already had three.

Mark finally told his mother, and she was more supportive
than he expected.

Now my husband doesn't even remember his dismay that
we were having a child. Instead, he adores our toddler. I think—
maybe because he is older—he takes advantage of enjoying her
more than he did his older kids when they were young.

Scripture tells us that children are a good thing. Let's
remember to thank God for these good things he's given us.

*When's the last time you included your
children among the blessings in your life?*

—JGL

A Glimpse Inside

"Because he bends down and listens,
I will pray as long as I have breath!"
PSALM 116:2

"And then blah, blah, blah. And then blah, blah, blah . . ."

My son is a jabberer. He didn't start talking until he was nearly four and hasn't stopped since. He has a wild imagination that devises intricate plots.

I'm not a talker. I like quiet. Sometimes it's hard to give him my full attention. My eyes glaze over or I answer abruptly. Then I see the pain in his eyes, focus on him, and get him talking again.

At times I've wished he were a little bit quieter. But I'm learning to thank God for my son's many words. For as he talks, I get a priceless opportunity to look into his heart and mind. I get to understand him better than I might if he were quiet. I'm learning to be thankful that he doesn't know how to shut it off—and shut us out.

May our goal be to listen to our children as patiently,
lovingly, and faithfully as God listens to us.

—JGL

In My Daughter's Eyes

> "Then I observed that most people are motivated
> to success by their envy of their neighbors. But
> this, too, is meaningless, like chasing the wind."
> ECCLESIASTES 4:4

My daughter sat on the sofa reading while I was watching television. Suddenly she looked up. "You know, Mom, in the world's eyes, you and Dad aren't very successful."

I smiled at my daughter and waited for her next statement, knowing what she would say.

When Dennis and I decided to have children, I'd vowed to be open and honest with them. I've always answered the hard questions truthfully—even when doing so revealed things in my past I'd rather they didn't know. But rather than causing my children to think less of me, my honesty helped me to earn their respect. It also allowed them to talk with me about the difficult issues in their own lives.

"But, in God's eyes, you are." Her words were a joy to hear!

*In the world's eyes I may not be successful,
but in my daughter's eyes I am.*

—MICKI ROBERTS

Use It, Don't Lose it

> "So they come pretending to be sincere and sit before
> you listening. But they have no intention of doing
> what I tell them. They express love with their
> mouths, but their hearts seek only after money."
> EZEKIEL 33:31

My husband rummaged through the spices. "Where is the red pepper?"

Since I had just used it in a casserole, I knew its exact location. "In the pantry, middle left-hand shelf, next to the plastic bags."

It was a different situation when my daughter wanted to brush our dog's hair. "Where's the brush?"

I had not groomed the dog for a long while, and couldn't remember where I'd put the brush. A week later I found it stuffed beneath the kitchen sink.

In life, God's truth is like my lost-and-found situations. As mothers, if we intentionally use God's truth regularly to practice kindness and love, then when we need it, these qualities can be easily found in our character. But if we don't use God's truth, the qualities that come with it are quickly lost and forgotten … and only after much seeking can we reclaim them.

> *Don't just listen to God; be intentional*
> *about doing what He tells you to do.*

—LORI Z. SCOTT

Let's Go to the House of the Lord

"I was glad when they said to me,
'Let us go to the house of the Lord.'"
PSALM 122:1

I memorized Psalm 122:1 when I was quite young. And it was true for me; I loved going to church. Good thing, because we were there whenever the doors were open. I remember lazy summer Sunday evenings before air-conditioning, when we felt the breeze through open windows and locusts provided background music for people telling their testimonies. And missionary meetings, where I saw slides of people in other countries learning about God. Prayer meetings, where I listened to others take their needs to God. Sunday school—where I won little awards for memorizing scripture verses.

Now that I'm a mom, I'm amazed at how faithfully my mom took us to church. Especially since my dad wouldn't go. A woman going to church without her husband was an oddity back then. It must have been really tough for her to be consistent. But it made an incredible difference in my life.

Getting our kids to church is, in the long run, worth any hassles or inconveniences!

—JGL

Oops

"So think clearly and exercise self-control.
Look forward to the special blessings that
will come to you at the return of Jesus Christ."
1 PETER 1:13

"Oh, I hate that dog," I grumbled. The Dalmatian is old and has always been half deaf. Those two facts get her a lot of sympathy. But she's also the stupidest dog my husband and I have ever encountered, so no wonder I finally snapped.

Unfortunately, my kids heard me say those words. The problem? They lack a sense of balance.

I was told in one parenting class that parents should especially watch what they say and do—because what parents do in moderation, kids tend to do in extreme or excess. If they see us do something or hear us say something once, they think it's okay to practice all the time. If I say I hate the dog once, they say it regularly. If I lose my temper and act inappropriately once, they see it as a license to perform that behavior.

*In that quick moment when a little voice says
"Maybe you shouldn't . . . " it helps us maintain
control when we realize little eyes are watching.*

—JGL

A New Creation

"What this means is that those who become Christians
become new persons. They are not the same anymore,
for the old life is gone. A new life has begun!"
2 CORINTHIANS 5:17

"How will the mums grow again?" my five-year-old son asked.

I had just announced plans to plant two pots of wilted
mums sitting on our front porch. Their new home would be a
flower bed in the backyard.

"Oh, they'll grow," I reassured. "But we may not see them
grow until spring."

I came to this conclusion after two other pots of mums,
which also appeared lifeless in their flowerpots, came back to
life after being placed in that flower bed. When the snow had
melted and spring had officially come, I noticed a startling visi-
tor in the flower bed. In the middle of lifeless tangled stems and
leaves was a tiny speck of green. It wasn't a new weed . . . it was
the first growth of what would become large bursts of beautiful
yellow flowers!

*Are you open to wherever God places you as a mom, or are
you choosing to remain in the same old pot?*

—SHANNA BARTLETT GROVES

He Rejoices over You

"For the Lord your God has arrived to live among you.
He is a mighty savior. He will rejoice over you with
great gladness. With his love, he will calm all your
fears. He will exult over you by singing a happy song."
ZEPHANIAH 3:17

"Jesus loves me . . ." my daughter sang while swinging in our backyard. My husband and I joked about the set of lungs she had. She was definitely making a statement to the whole neighborhood!

As I watched her, I remembered when I was also four years old. I was walking in our garden singing praise choruses with gusto. I recalled the warm sunshine and God's presence surrounding me as I sang. I realized He was pleased with me, and had probably been singing along with me!

Ever since that revelation, I have wanted my daughters to understand the concept that God delights in them. He watches over them and feels pride in the women they are becoming. I want to help them be aware that they can experience God's pleasure. They can be sure that their Creator is singing a special song just for them.

Meditate on the fact that God sings for joy over His children!

—EVANGELINE BEALS GARDNER

Caught–Not Just Taught

"So I ask you to follow my example and do as I do."
1 CORINTHIANS 4:16

There's a difference between my teen stepdaughter and my toddler. My oldest thinks she's a princess—and my youngest knows she is. So for the past three years, the two have had a subtle rivalry. At times my teen has been mean to my toddler when she thinks I'm not looking.

I haven't said much. I've just continued to treat my toddler like a little one should be treated—with love and protection.

Then this year our teen underwent a transformation. Suddenly, she's treating the toddler lovingly, like a big sister enjoying her little sister.

Another interesting facet is how this has affected my young son, who's between the girls in age. Suddenly he is kinder to his little sister, too. He's carrying her around and caring for her tenderly instead of treating her like a pest. No one has said anything to him—he's just picked it up from watching me, and now his big sister.

So many actions and attitudes are
"caught" rather than "taught."

—JGL

Finding Rest

"Then Jesus said, 'Come to me, all of you who are weary
and carry heavy burdens, and I will give you rest.'"
MATTHEW 11:28

"Mrs. Littleton, your kidney stone is huge. We'll give it a chance
to come out on its own, but we'll probably have to go in and
remove it," the doctor explained. My family was 1,000 miles
from home, visiting my husband's mom when I'd ended up in
the ER.

I have a confession: I kind of liked being in the hospital.
The meds numbed the pain, so I napped most of the time. No
messes to clean. No fighting kids. No work beckoning. Nurses
bringing me meals and even waiting on me a bit. Almost a
vacation! A kidney stone was almost a small price to pay for
two days of peace and rest!

It's hard for us moms to find rest for our bodies. Perhaps
that's why it's so important to take our burdens to Jesus—so he
can at least give us rest for our souls and rejuvenate us.

Thankfully, God promises us rest when we need it.

—JGL

MARCH 26

God's Grace and a Sister's Advice

"These older women must train the younger women
to love their husbands and their children . . ."
TITUS 2:4

I carefully unwrapped the blue blanket from around my precious newborn. My heart pounded as I checked every tiny toe and fragile finger. I stroked his soft skin, and ran my fingers through his fine, fuzzy hair. I wondered how I would take care of this tiny being curled on my lap.

I pondered the thought that my older sister gave birth six times. I suddenly saw her in a different light. I envisioned her as a woman with great wisdom.

Maybe she could help me! I thought.

I picked up the bedside phone. As I dialed her number, I felt relieved God had placed experienced women in my life, to help light the new path ahead of me. With God's grace, and my sister's advice, I felt ready to embrace the new season in my life.

*Our faithful Father places others in our lives
with the knowledge and skill to teach us.*

—ANNETTEE BUDZBAN

The Prayer of a Child

"Keep on praying."
1 THESSALONIANS 5:17

My daughter, Anna, is eleven years old and has autism. She functions at the level of a toddler.

Anna prays. She wants to pray before meals and snacks, and when she has second helpings, and when she gets a drink. She wants to pray in the car before we leave the driveway. From time to time, she will stop whatever activity she is doing, fold her hands, and ask to pray. I often see her praying by herself, and we never miss bedtime prayers.

One night she asked to pray again after bedtime prayers. I asked her what she wanted to pray for. She said, "Thank you, Jesus." I repeated it after her. "Died on the cross," she continued. It took all my self-control to repeat her prayer without bursting into tears.

Anna never forgets to pray. Oh, would that be said of me!

God longs to hear from us.
May we learn to have a praying heart.

—PAM HALTER

The Powerful Words

"Confess your sins to each other
and pray for each other. . . ."
JAMES 5:16

"My spiritual gift is groveling," my friend said. I can relate. I want to be a kind, sweet-tempered, patient mom. But my desires get buried under an avalanche of stress, and I end up ill-tempered, impatient, and sometimes downright mean. Not to mention a bad example to these kids I'm trying to train to be godly!

What's a mom to do? I've taken a lesson from my friend. I've learned to swallow my pride and say those powerful words, "I'm sorry" and "Will you forgive me?" and "I was wrong."

I've also learned to confess my sins to my kids—because they know them anyway—and to ask them to pray for me.

I still work at being a good example by doing what's right. But I've learned when I'm wrong, if I want my kids to find God's forgiveness, I have to own up to the sins in my own life.

Confessing and praying for each other—
isn't that what family's all about?

—JGL

Rewards of Your Labor

". . . Be strong and courageous, for your
work will be rewarded."
2 CHRONICLES 15:7

It was one of the richest moments in my life. My young friend, who works twenty hours a week, told me, "I want to have a baby so I can quit my job and stay home. I don't like working."

And now, if you've finished laughing, you can be proud that I kept a straight face—even though my young friend seriously thinks the only thing involved in having a baby is sitting around holding the child while you watch TV.

We moms know better than anyone—even dads—just how much work it takes to raise a family. As you know, it's a never-ending task and if something happened to you, your husband would have to hire at least two other people to handle everything you do alone. It's exhausting and often discouraging. But know that God's words to the men of Judah in 2 Chronicles 15:7—who stuck it out even when facing insurmountable odds—also hold true for you.

*Keep your eyes open for God's rewards,
and know they will come!*

—JGL

The Bubble Principle

"But when the Holy Spirit controls our lives,
he will produce this kind of fruit in us: love, joy,
peace, patience, kindness, goodness, faithfulness,
gentleness, and self-control. . . ."

GALATIANS 5:22–23

The beautiful spring day beckoned to us. Kaitlyn opened her bubbles, took out the wand, and blew as hard as she could. Splat! went the bubble solution onto the ground. Kaitlyn looked to me for help.

"If you blow gently, you'll make more bubbles and they will travel farther," I explained.

She took the wand and blew ever so gently. A multitude of small and large bubbles danced into the wind. Kaitlyn and her sister squealed and ran after them.

As I saw Kaitlyn's success, I realized this lesson also applies to training my children. When we blow too hard, we often cause a huge burst . . . usually into tears! But when we blow with gentleness, we give them the power to go a greater distance.

> *Our children need our loving instruction*
> *and gentle wind to carry them into the*
> *blessed life that God has created for them.*

—CARMEN SCHROEDER

The Safe Place

"The Lord is my rock, my fortress, and my savior; my God
is my rock, in whom I find protection. He is my shield,
the power that saves me, and my place of safety."
PSALM 18:2

I had only met my neighbor once when she brought her toddler
into our yard to play with my toddler. As the little girls ran
between the swing set and the trampoline, I enjoyed getting to
know this sweet younger woman.

At one point in our conversation she started to reveal
something about her daughter's bedtime. It sounded like little
Susie seldom made it to dreamland before ten p.m., but as soon
as the words were out, Andrea faltered and her expression told
me that this information had slipped out inadvertently.

"Don't worry," I told her. "This yard is a safe place. Your
secret's safe with me—besides, our family is just as bad!"

She relaxed and kept chatting. I realized that all of us
moms need a safe place—someplace we can go and someone
we can tell even what we consider to be shameful secrets.

Besides havens we can find on earth,
we can find a safe place in God.

—JGL

APRIL

PLAYING PROMISE GAMES

"But let your 'Yes' be 'Yes,' and your 'No,' 'No.' For
whatever is more than these is from the evil one."
MATTHEW 5:37

$\mathcal{M}$om, will you play a board game with us today?" My sons, Erik and Karl, asked one Saturday morning.

"Sure," I replied automatically. "Later."

But I really wasn't thinking about my boys or their request. My husband, Gary, and my father-in-law had just finished remodeling our family room. We needed to get everything back in place and organized. I had papers to grade, too, and an assignment due the following week. On top of all that, the mountain of laundry had grown so high you could probably ski down it. I scrambled the eggs and sighed. They were active boys. Certainly they would forget what they'd asked me to do.

Gary and I were figuring out where to put the pictures when Karl came up to me again. "Mom, will you play Monopoly with us? Erik promises to try a new way so he won't cream us."

I barely turned to look at him. "Not Monopoly, Karl. It takes too long. You and Erik pick something else."

"But you will play with us today, right Mom?"

"Yes, later. When everything's done." Then I handed Gary the drill and went back to hanging pictures.

Erik found me on the computer grading papers after lunch. "When do you think you'll be able to play a game with us?" he asked.

I sighed loudly. "I don't know. But when everything's done, I promise."

"Could I play computer games while we wait?"

I seized that tidbit. Surely computer games would keep the boys occupied enough, and long enough, that I could finish my work. "Sure, Erik. That would be fine."

Focusing on the paper I was grading, I mumbled, "How could she ignore so many of my corrections?"

At dinnertime, the boys found me hurriedly clearing piles of clean and folded laundry off the dining room table so we could eat.

"After dinner, Mom?" Karl asked.

"What?" I shook my head trying to understand his verbal shorthand.

"A game, remember?"

"Oh," I hedged. "Maybe."

"Maybe?" asked Erik. "But you promised."

"Well, we have that movie to watch. We have to return it tomorrow." I saw their faces fall in unison. "Maybe we can play something while we watch the movie."

I let it drop there, and the evening continued with the same busyness. The phone rang, the dryer beeped, thousands of little things claimed my attention.

Suddenly, it was time to put the boys to bed. Gary and I prayed with them. Time for my nightly kisses! As I leaned toward Karl, he avoided my arms.

"What is it?"

"You never played with us," he said accusingly.

"I'm sorry. Some days are like that." So I wrestled a hug from him and went to bed.

The next day was Sunday. Church uplifted and encouraged me. I expected the same from the Bible class that followed. After all, we were studying the Beatitudes.

Our teacher wrote "Work, Friends, Family" on the whiteboard. We had to tell how and when we had lied or had considered lying under each category. I even offered a few answers. Then Jamie spoke up. "We can lie to our kids by making promises we don't intend to keep."

God instantly replayed the previous twenty-four hours in my mind. Ouch. I hadn't just been too busy to play; I had lied to my boys about ever intending to play. I vowed silently to agree with scripture and let my yes be yes and my no mean no.

The boys occupied themselves on Sunday. But Monday, as I homeschooled them, they asked again if I would play a board game with them.

I swallowed and made certain I answered honestly. "We have a lot of schoolwork left and then errands to run. If it rains, though, I promise I will cut the errands short and play a game. I'll even let it be Monopoly."

There wasn't a cloud in the sky when I said this. And only a 20 percent chance of rain forecasted. But shortly after dinner, it began to sprinkle, then to pour.

"Monopoly, Mom?" asked Erik.

"Get the game," I said.

—Susan Lyttek

Foolish Mom or Wise Mom?

"Only fools say in their hearts, 'There is no God.'"
PSALM 14:1

I remember I first read, and decided to memorize, Psalm 14:1 as a young adult. I believed in God with all my heart, and knew that only fools would pretend He didn't exist.

I kept in close contact with God for years. Then I got married and became an instant 24/7 stepmother. Soon my life was filled with chaos, which only increased as two more kids were added to our family.

I'm not sure at what stage I realized that much of the time I was acting as if God didn't exist. Sure, I still said he existed and knew He did—but I sure didn't act like it. I rarely found time to enjoy my relationship with him. And I forgot to turn to him first when I had needs. I was living like a fool—not acting like I believed in God and his mercy, omnipotence, and power.

Being a wise mom means acting on what we believe.

—JGL

Never Alone

". . . For God has said, 'I will never fail you.
I will never forsake you.'"
HEBREWS 13:5

"I don't like it here! I miss all my friends!" My daughter cried angry tears into her pillow. My heart broke as I saw her pain over our relocation.

I remembered the same kind of tears when she was four years old and her favorite stuffed animal lost its tail. We found the tail, and I sewed it back on. Problem solved!

This time I couldn't fix the situation. Instead, I could only sympathize and pray for her. Hugging her, I told her I understood her pain. I reminded her that I loved her. Most of all, I prayed and reassured her that she was not alone—God is always with her.

Before long, my daughter made friends and began to enjoy our new home. I was grateful to God for the new joy she expressed. I was especially thankful for the opportunity to remind my daughter that she can always turn to God.

God is our faithful friend.

—GINNY CAROLEO

The Wonderful World of Children

"Then God looked over all he had made, and he saw that
it was excellent in every way. . . ."
GENESIS 1:31

"Got another one!" I cried triumphantly as I scooped the little grasshopper into the jar.

I never would have dreamed that I would ever be outside catching grasshoppers. But a few weeks earlier, my seven-year-old, Gardner, and I had gotten a leopard gecko. The gecko didn't like canned food but gobbled up grasshoppers we bought at the pet store. So I decided to take advantage of the grasshoppers in our pesticide-free yard. Gardner wouldn't catch them alone, so together, we learned how to wait patiently and then scoop them up.

Since then, we've adopted a dwarf hamster, a teddy bear hamster, and fish. These are pets I never had when I was a child, so I'm fascinated and learning, right along with my son. He gets new pets to love and learns responsibility. And I get to share intriguing glimpses of God's handiwork with my son.

*Whether pets or in other areas, children give us
a wonderful reason to expand our horizons!*

—JGL

Going to Jesus for Our Children

"A leader of the local synagogue, whose name was
Jairus, came and fell down before him, pleading
with him to heal his little daughter. 'She is about to
die,' he said in desperation. 'Please come and place
your hands on her; heal her so she can live.'"

MARK 5:22–23

"Mommy, I bouncing!" Our two-year-old giggled as she jumped on our bed.

"Elizabeth, stop. You'll get hurt," I told her, my words interrupted by a *smack!* as she rammed into the edge of the bedside table. I ran to her and held her tight against my heart as she screamed.

Already, a purple egg-sized lump filled her tiny forehead. "Oh, Jesus, be with my baby!" I cried.

I continued praying nonstop as we raced to the ER. The ER route wasn't new—our son had been born with a heart problem, at one he'd rammed staples through tiny fingers, at two he'd nearly died from eating medicine. I'd taken him to Jesus in prayer many times and had fervently taken his older sister to Jesus in prayer during her turbulent emotional times. Now I repeatedly begged Jesus to heal and help my precious baby.

"You're lucky," the ER nurse told us. "It's on the surface and she'll be fine."

*In life-threatening situations and in everyday life,
thankfully, we can take our children to Jesus.*

—JGL

Buck Up!

"For I can do everything with the help of Christ
who gives me the strength I need."
PHILIPPIANS 4:13

"You made us tough. You didn't baby us or let us whine about things. You told us to 'Buck up and get through it.'"

My reaction to my grown son's statement was to wonder if I had failed him as a mother. I'm not the best of nurses, and I don't like whining. So, had I failed in some way to show compassion to my two sons when they were growing up?

Then I remembered all the times my heavenly Father told me to "Buck up and get through it." Making me responsible for the outcome didn't mean God didn't love or care about me. On the contrary, He was preparing me to face adversity with resolve.

I didn't abandon my sons when they needed me, but I expected them to do their part in getting through the tough times. God expects no less from His children.

God is always available when we need him,
and He gives us the strength to do our part.

—KAREN MCKEE

Watch Your Step

"Dear brothers and sisters, pattern your lives after mine,
and learn from those who follow our example."
PHILIPPIANS 3:17

"Watch your step; everyone else does," the sign in front of the church said. As I drove by, I grumbled about morally challenged politicians and celebrities who made the news because of dishonest dealings, divorces, and illegitimate babies. But then I had a second thought—if others were watching my steps as the world watched celebrities', didn't I have a golden opportunity to set a good example? Didn't that mean I could show a life patterned after Christ's?

Emulating Christ can be simple. We can show His love through little things, like listening to a child's fears or providing an after-school snack.

Now, I am happy to have my steps watched. I can try to show kids and the world at large what the life of a Christian should be.

What small things can I do to set
Christ's example for my kids?

—KIM SHEARD

The Value of a Friend

"The heartfelt counsel of a friend is as sweet
as perfume and incense."
PROVERBS 27:9

"The doctor says I'm depressed," my mother said. I knew that confiding tone and felt terribly afraid.

My mom was a godly woman who had her share of problems. One of her biggest problems was that she didn't have a friend to confide in. So from the time I was about eight, Mom often told me her woes, from health issues to marriage challenges and other adult topics that petrified me. I would feel panicked and scared, like she wanted me—a child—to solve her adult problems. So I didn't know what to do whenever she got that confidential tone. Sometimes I just listened. At other times, when I felt too rattled, I made an excuse to leave the room and play with my Barbies.

Women are made to be relational and to talk about their problems. But as we moms talk about the things that distress us, we need to remember our children's ages before we make them our sounding boards. Yes, we need to get our worries out of our systems, but our burdens might be too heavy for young shoulders.

*One of the best things a mom can do for
her kids is to stay emotionally healthy by
building a support system outside the home.*

—JGL

Hokey Bunnies and Creative Messages

"So commit yourselves completely to these words
of mine. Tie them to your hands as a reminder,
and wear them on your forehead. . . . Write them
on the doorposts of your house and on your gates."
DEUTERONOMY 11:18, 20

It was one of the goofiest things I've seen. Two stuffed bunnies sat on a little platform. When you pressed one bunny's paw, outdated organ music started and the big bunny moved as if he were talking. In his grandfatherly voice, he told the story of Easter—the story of Jesus dying on the cross.

After I'd listened, I walked on. It was hokey, and priced more than I wanted to spend. But then I returned and listened to it again. I'd been asking God to show me ways to help the kids see beyond the candy and eggs. So I picked up the last hokey bunny off the shelf.

The creators of the hokey bunny apparently know more about kids than I do. My toddler loved it. She listened to it again and again. And I was just thankful that my child was hearing about Jesus.

We can use creative means to teach our kids God's truth.

—JGL

Blankets and Babies

"Be humble and gentle. Be patient with each other, making
allowance for each other's faults because of your love."
EPHESIANS 4:2

I was snuggled into my spot on the sofa, crocheting a soft baby
blanket for my cousin who was expecting soon.

"I love the yarn," said my son. "It's so soft."

"Feel it." I rubbed part of the lavender blanket against his
cheek.

"You're spending a lot of time on it."

"It does take quite a bit of patience to make a blanket, but
my cousin will need even more patience with her new baby."

"Why's that?" he asked.

"Well, babies take lots of work," I said.

"Yeah, they cry and fuss a lot. And have disgusting diapers."

I nodded. "Plus, they need to be fed and held. But even
though they have these faults, we still love them dearly."

"I bet I've got faults too, but you still love me, right?"

"Of course. I've got plenty of love for you!" I wrapped the
blanket around him and gave him a big squeeze.

Be liberal with your patience today.

—KARIN LINDSTROM

Making Bold Claims

"And she made this vow: 'O Lord Almighty, if you will
look down upon my sorrow and answer my prayer and
give me a son, then I will give him back to you. He will
be yours for his entire lifetime, and as a sign that he has
been dedicated to the Lord, his hair will never be cut.'"

1 SAMUEL 1:11

Many of us have dedicated our children to the Lord. But Hannah went a step further: she boldly made promises for Samuel. Hannah not only promised never to cut his hair, but she also promised he would follow those guidelines.

When I read that, I thought, *How can she make a promise for her son? What if he doesn't feel that way?*

On the other hand, maybe we Christian moms today don't claim enough for our kids! I don't mean we should promise God that our children will be pastors, but perhaps we should claim our children for the Lord in the sense that we assume they will love and serve Him. And if we raise them on that assumption, maybe our kids will indeed stay true to God.

Parenting carries no guarantees—God gave our children their own wills. But as far as our influence goes, let's make bold spiritual claims for our kids.

*What spiritual claims are you
making for your children today?*

—JGL

Learning to Love

> "But anyone who does not love does
> not know God—for God is love."
> 1 JOHN 4:8

Have you ever found it difficult to love someone who has suddenly been thrust into your life? Good news. You can learn to love them with God's intervention.

Let me explain how that has worked in my life. When I remarried, I realized my new husband was truly a gift from God. However, at first, I had difficulty loving and accepting his son.

I asked God to give me the ability to love Steve as He did. One afternoon as I observed Steve playing, I realized that he was so much like his father. He walked like my husband and had many of his mannerisms. Then I realized that Steve was simply an extension of my dearly loved husband. I can't explain the love I felt for him that moment except to say that God moved in and gave me Steve as my own child.

Need to love? Love! You can. Just ask Him!

—ANN VARNUM

Thank God for Runny Noses

"For even I, the Son of Man, came here not
to be served but to serve others, and to
give my life as a ransom for many."
MARK 10:45

I sigh as I wipe yet another runny nose. The flu season visits my home again, and I realize my motherhood dreams left out certain graphic details. I never wrote a fourth-grade essay entitled, "I Want to Be a Nose-Cleaner and Bottom-Wiper When I Grow Up."

But the discharge is real and must be removed gently by loving hands. Jesus has removed worse stains from me, and I'm learning to thank God for strange reminders of His grace. Those runny noses keep me from obsessing over my own problems. Like Jesus, who healed a blind man with mud and spit, I must reach every day beyond my immediate interests to take care of the needs of helpless little ones.

But I am also grateful to know that children grow quickly and can soon wipe their own noses and other body parts. Some days, I can only take so much humility.

*I can demonstrate the servant
heart of Jesus in the lowliest tasks.*

—LYNNETTE P. HORNER

Whose Fault?

"'Who told you that you were naked?' the Lord God asked. 'Have you eaten the fruit I commanded you not to eat?' "'Yes,' Adam admitted, 'but it was the woman you gave me who brought me the fruit, and I ate it.'"

GENESIS 3:11–12

"Lord, it's these children you've given me," I grumbled. "How can you expect me to be a good, patient, kind, godly mother when you've given me kids who are so rambunctious and gouge on every nerve I have?"

I had just acted anything besides patient and kind with my kids. They'd bothered me while I was trying to concentrate and something in me had finally snapped.

Now, as I sighed to God about my failure, my words reminded me of what Adam had basically said when God confronted him with his sin, "Not my fault, Lord. In fact, it was that woman *you* gave me who caused it."

Was I, like Adam, blaming my sin on everyone else? Sure, most kids will always find a way to vex their parents. But it helps us get over it and get on with life when we accept responsibilities for our own actions.

Accepting responsibility for our actions is the first step to finding God's mercy—and His grace.

—JGL

Things Are Subject to Change

"You will show me the way of life, granting me the joy of your presence and the pleasures of living with you forever."
PSALM 16:11

Early one morning while I was dressing for work, my daughter called. "Mother," she began, "I am so sorry for my bad attitude and for all the bad things I've said or done."

"Well," I started, "what have you done?" I assumed she was referring to some recent occurrence.

"I had no idea how bad I was, and now, I'm getting paid back!" She explained that her own little girl was behaving much in the same way as she had done when she was a child.

I laughed. "Payback is hard, isn't it, sweetheart?" We both laughed then, for you see, my daughter is now my closest confidante.

Who would have ever believed that my "rebellious" teen, who often had made me question my own sanity, could today be such a supporter of her mother? It is still a miracle to me that after just a short few years have passed, my daughter esteems me as being the epitome of wisdom, charm, and grace.

So, if you are experiencing major stress right now, doing battle with one of your teens, cheer up—it will not always be like this. Just keep trusting God . . . pray always for your offspring . . . and wait!

No matter what we face in life, things are subject to change.

—ANN VARNUM

What We Can Count On

"O Lord, God of Israel, there is no God like
you in all of heaven or earth. You keep your
promises and show unfailing love to all who
obey you and are eager to do your will."
1 KINGS 8:23

Don't you wish you had $1 for every time you've heard some-
one say "Nothing is certain in life except death and taxes"?
And parenting can be one of the most uncertain ventures we
undertake!

Thankfully, as we maneuver this unmapped course, we do
have something that is certain: God and his promises.

What are some of those promises?

God promises to love us. No matter what we do, he still
loves us—He feels for us that love we feel for our children—
that sacrificial, unending love.

God promises to take care of us. Nothing will happen to us,
or our families, that he's not in control of. He promises to provide
for us not just in this life, but for all eternity.

God promises his presence. He promises to guide us
through mothering minefields—to give us wisdom when we
ask, and strength, and emotional support so we can, in turn, be
steady, dependable moms our kids can count on.

Even when death and taxes are long gone,
God's love, and a mom's love, are still unchanging.

—JGL

A Time for Everything

> "There is a time for everything, a season
> for every activity under heaven."
> ECCLESIASTES 3:1

The moving van had just pulled away from our driveway, when we realized our Scotty dog, Baron, had run off. So our family jumped into the car, rolled down the windows, and began calling his name.

From Daddy's window: "Baron! Here Baron!"

From Mommy's window: "Here Baron!"

From 3-year-old Holly's window: "Here Baron!"

Then, from 4-year-old Laura's window we heard: "Doolah! Here Doolah!"

I turned and looked my precious child in the eye. "Honey, what are you doing?"

"I've decided I don't like the name Baron. I want to change his name to Doolah."

What a classic memory—changing a name at a time like that. We did manage to find Baron, who recognized the name being called from three of our four car windows.

Timing is everything when we're making any kind of change. We moms need to seek God's wisdom and direction, for His timing is always perfect.

We can count on God's timing.

—SANDI BANKS

Let God Grow Your Children

"My job was to plant the seed in your hearts, and Apollos watered it, but it was God, not we, who made it grow."
1 CORINTHIANS 3:6

I recently bought my daughter a gardening kit. Carefully, she planted zinnia seeds in her pot, placed her treasure in a sunny location, and watered it regularly. But initial excitement soon turned to frustration after days of seeing only dirt. Then one day it happened.

"Mom! Mom! My flowers are growing!" Cayla exclaimed. Overnight, several of her seeds had sprouted.

It's easy for us moms to get frustrated when, after diligently planting seeds of righteousness in our children and watering those seeds with prayer, we don't see green sprouts emerging through the dirt. It's easy to wonder where we went wrong. But we have to remember where our job ends and God's begins. He promises that, if we are faithful to sow seeds and provide regular watering, He will be faithful to bring increase. Then one day—sometimes overnight—it will happen. Our "pots" will be filled with beautiful flowers.

We can entrust our children to the Gardener's care.

—RENEE GRAY-WILBURN

Ready, Aim, Release!

"Children born to a young man are like
sharp arrows in a warrior's hands."
PSALM 127:4

My father died this year. Although he is gone, his influence isn't. My father taught me many good things—like service, a strong work ethic, and loving others. But his influence doesn't end with me; I've passed many of my parents' values, beliefs, and practices on to my children. A parent's influence is felt for years.

A pastor of mine felt this verse indicated that influence. "Children are like arrows because we can shoot them out farther than we'd ever go," Bud Long explained. "As we raise godly children and they eventually go out into the world, they make a difference in their sphere of influence because of the way we've trained them. Through our children, we multiply our faith and have a broader influence for righteousness on the world."

As we live for Christ, and instill godly values in our children, our children are arrows of light hitting the target of a dark world.

What traits will our children take out into their worlds?

—JGL

Why Did the Chicken Cross the Road?

"A glad heart makes a happy face; a
broken heart crushes the spirit."
PROVERBS 15:13

One Saturday after a busy week, my daughter and I relaxed on
the deck and took turns making up lame jokes based on things
we spotted around us.

"Why do leaves sway in the breeze?" I asked.

Meghan wrinkled her nose. "Because they don't know how
to dance?"

Laughter bubbled up in us and spilled over like soda pop.
It felt good. We hadn't smiled much recently. Our schedules
had kept us rushing here and there, causing fatigue, general
grumpiness, and stress.

"My turn. Why don't dogs like hammers? Because they
don't like the pound!"

And so we passed an hour, giggling with wild abandon,
remembering gladness.

As mothers, I think often we approach life with somber
seriousness. How tedious! Perhaps we should smile more and
worry less. Perhaps Proverbs 15:13 will remind us about the
astounding joy that stems from God arriving to live with us in
our hearts!

It's no joke: God loves us and exults
over us with a happy song!

—LORI Z. SCOTT

The Toughest Job in the World?

"The Lord gives his people strength.
The Lord blesses them with peace."
PSALM 29:11

"Mommy, mommy, mommy!" my toddler cried for the twentieth time in ten minutes.

"Mo-om, aren't you even *listening* to me?" my third grader chimed in.

I sighed, lifted my hands from my computer, and turned to my kids. As I took care of their needs—*again*—I realized how much I missed working in an office. An office where no one calls your name twenty times in ten minutes or needs you nonstop.

Being a stay-at-home mom is the hardest job I've ever had. The hours are more demanding than at an office. I have to manage several people's schedules. The physical labor is much more demanding (oh, for a custodial staff to come in at night!). The emotional stuff is much more intense. It wears me out *way* more than working in an office ever did.

How do stay-at-home moms—and working moms—survive? I think the secret lies in knowing we can't do it on our own.

*When the going gets tough, remember
where your strength comes from.*

—JGL

Wings to Fly

"Oh, what a wonderful God we have! How great are his riches and wisdom and knowledge! How impossible it is for us to understand his decisions and his methods!"
ROMANS 11:33

After giving us one last hug, our oldest daughter boarded the plane for a year of study in Venezuela. My heart twisted as she walked through a door that was taking her so far away. I worried about every little thing that might happen. Letting her go was a tearful experience, but the right decision. The plane flew her there, but I gave Melanie her wings by trusting both God and my daughter. She came home more fluent in Spanish, which led to her employment as a teacher. She also met a wonderful man in Venezuela, who, two years later, became her husband.

Giving our children wings to fly toward their God-promised plan takes faith, courage, and strength. Had I not allowed Melanie to fly toward hers, I would not have a wonderful son-in-law or a gorgeous three-year-old granddaughter with jet-black hair and midnight-blue eyes!

Even when we may not understand His decisions, God's plan for us and our children is always the best plan.

—KAREN HESLINK

The Power of Music

"Praise the Lord, for the Lord is good;
celebrate his wonderful name with music."
PSALM 135:3

I've always loved music. As a teen, I played the violin and sang in a couple of performance groups. After high school I sang in a couple of traveling groups and a church choir. Music erased the tension from my life and was my outlet for stress.

Then I became a stepmom, and my stepdaughters covered their ears and howled when I sang or played music I liked. Before long I didn't even hum anymore. I also became a grouchier person around the house.

But recently I'm relearning the power of music. When I need an energy boost, I crank the stereo. When I'm frustrated, a few praise songs put everything back into perspective. I become a much more balanced mom and don't feel so overwhelmed by the tasks at hand. And my younger children love singing with me.

Music has been mentioned in the Bible since Genesis 4. Maybe it's one of the tools God gave us to help us maintain joy and emotional balance in our lives.

Handling the challenges of motherhood
is easier when you have a song in your heart.

—JGL

Luxury Homes

"Sell what you have and give to those in need. This will store up treasure for you in heaven! And the purses of heaven have no holes in them. Your treasure will be safe—no thief can steal it and no moth can destroy it."
LUKE 12:33

We were on our way to church when I saw a billboard: "Luxury Homes from the 300's." The thought of buying a "luxury home" has great appeal. Perhaps we tend to subconsciously assume that if our lives are going well enough to afford a luxury home, our lives will automatically be flourishing in other areas, too. For instance, if I had a luxury home, my marriage might be better, my child's grade-point average higher, and, of course, getting to that exercise class would be unnecessary because I would already have my life all together!

But I've learned I need to be careful not to long for things that we just can't have right now—such as a luxury home. So many times I set the tone for my kids' attitude about possessions. As I am satisfied with my old vehicle and nonluxury home, it sets an example for them to be satisfied with their games and toys.

A satisfied heart is contagious!

—KARLA DOYLE

Shelter in the Storm

"Don't be afraid, for I am with you. Do not be dismayed,
for I am your God. I will strengthen you. I will help you.
I will uphold you with my victorious right hand."
ISAIAH 41:10

When I saw the plywood fly past the window, I knew it was time to join my husband and kids downstairs. My stepdaughter, sobbing her heart out, huddled close to me for the first time in her life, while my son was hidden in my husband's arms. I cracked lame jokes to try to take their minds off the roar above. Finally the sirens ended. When we exited the basement, we saw the tornado's path. We lost only trees, but yards away, complete homes were destroyed.

Since then my young son panics each time tornado sirens sound. The last time was while we were in Home Depot. "We're going to die!" he sobbed as I tried to make light of the matter and led him to the store's designated area.

"It's okay," I told him. "I'm with you."

I can't promise my son that the tornadoes won't come, or that we won't suffer damage. But I can promise to be there for him as much as humanly possible and to provide safety in any way I can.

God can be our shelter in all the storms of life.

—JGL

Our Children's Other Parent

"Who can find a virtuous and capable wife? She is
worth more than precious rubies. Her husband
can trust her, and she will greatly enrich his life.
She will not hinder him but help him all her life."
PROVERBS 31:10–12

"I just don't love your father anymore," my mother said sadly.

I looked up in shock. I knew my parents fought a lot—
when Mom was angry with me, she often said, "Oh, you're just
like your father." At other times, she accused me of loving Dad
more than I loved her. I often felt pulled between them.

But still, these were strong words for an elementary school
child to hear and I lived in terror that my parents would split up.

Somehow my parents made it through their tough years
and ended up together forty years. And I wasn't married too
long before I learned that all marriages have their tough times.
Maybe we can't shield our kids from all of our spats. But perhaps the key is to also make sure children see the good times
together. Sometimes being a good mom means being a good
wife. That may mean biting our tongues when we're aggravated
with our husbands (or even ex-husbands). They don't need to
worry about the two people they love most getting along. Our
kids deserve—and need—better than that.

*What can we do today to help our
children respect and love their father more?*

—JGL

Little League Choices

"'For I know the plans I have for you,' says the Lord.
'They are plans for good and not for disaster,
to give you a future and a hope.'"
JEREMIAH 29:11

Jay was very handsome in his gold-and-green Little League uniform. We have the photos to prove it. But we had a problem. He watched almost all of the games! When one of the sponsor's wives got the drift that I wasn't thrilled, she asked me, "Have you been unhappy with the team this year?"

I replied, "We do not think eight-year-olds learn to play baseball by sitting on the bench." For the next dozen years, our son played baseball, but in leagues where all players played at least half of the game.

As a college student, Jay had the chance to choose his sport. He chose baseball. Pitching skills allowed him to letter his freshman year. He lettered all four years. He was the only one from that first Little League team to have a career at the college level.

We can't always judge success by an initial experience.

—ZETA COMBS DAVIDSON

Building Good Character

"Don't be fooled . . . for 'bad company
corrupts good character.'"
1 CORINTHIANS 15:33

We didn't know much about Alisha's friends, but I didn't have a good feeling about the bunch she'd been hanging out with lately. And I was distressed that she didn't connect with other kids in our large church or the Christian kids at school.

I didn't know what to do. I had no definite reason to keep her from seeing her friends. But her dad and I began to pray that God would control her friendships.

A few weeks later, Alisha recommitted her life to Christ. Turns out my instincts had been right about those friends— she'd been drinking and trying pot with them. But when the focus of her life changed, the friendships just naturally ended. God brought strong new friends into her life who helped her grow spiritually.

I learned my lesson, too. Like we did with Alisha, we've put our younger ones in church programs and other places where they'll meet good friends. We talk to them about appropriate friends. But we also do the most important thing: pray about their friends.

*Since friends are more influential than
anyone except parents, it's definitely a
matter for consistent, persistent prayer!*

—JGL

Does God Have a Favorite Color?

"Give thanks to him who made the heavens so skillfully.
His faithful love endures forever."
PSALM 136:5

"Mom, do you have any scissors?" my eight-year-old daughter asked.

Scraps of paper, glue sticks, markers, a red pen, and recent photographs stretched across the table.

"Let's see," I said, digging through our art tub. I found Popsicle sticks, ribbon, silk flowers, stickers, and broken crayons. "I don't see any. Why don't you check your room?"

While she was upstairs, I admired her scrapbook pages. Soon she returned with her scissors.

"I really like this page," I told her.

"I used purple because it's my favorite color," she explained.

"God is an artist, too," I reminded her. "You can tell just by looking at the sky. I wonder if He has a favorite color."

Later, I stood beneath a tree and gazed at green leaves with sky blue peeking through them. It made me want to praise and recognize God for His amazing love and creativity.

God's beauty and love will last forever.

—KAREN WHITSON

The Habit of Saying "Yes"

"If you sinful people know how to give good gifts
to your children, how much more will your heavenly
Father give good gifts to those who ask him."
MATTHEW 7:11

"Tell your children yes every chance you get," my mentor, Vidy Metsker, always taught. Her words often come to my mind—especially when I'm on the verge of just saying no for no real reason, such as when my child wants to have a friend over. I might be tempted to say no just because I'm tired—instead of realizing if my child's occupied, I'll get a break. Or I might say no because something inconvenient may be involved, like picking up the friend, which would take about five minutes and would give my child hours of happiness.

If I operate on the premise of saying yes whenever possible, this makes me think the matter through. I determine if I really have a reason to say no and am more consistent with my kids.

It also helps my kids learn that I care about their desires.

*When we say yes consistently, our kids are more likely to see
God as one who cares and says, "Yes!"*

—JGL

Walk with Me

"I will walk among you; I will be your God,
and you will be my people."
LEVITICUS 26:12

"I missed going for a walk with my daughter yesterday," my friend Sally lamented. "I had some things I wanted to tell her."

"Something important?" I asked, concerned.

"Oh no, I was just looking forward to talking with her about nothing in particular."

"Well, what happened?" I asked. "Why didn't you go?"

"Nothing really happened," Sally said. "Kayla just said she didn't want to walk with me."

We sat for a moment in silence.

"I wonder how many times I've done that," Sally said.

"What do you mean?"

"Jesus has invited us to have a relationship, a daily walk, with Him. But sometimes my actions or attitudes say, 'No, Lord, I don't want to walk with You today.'"

Ouch, I thought. How true of me, too.

"I wonder what I've missed," Sally mused. "I wondered what He would have told me those times if I had walked with Him."

Just as He healed the paralyzed man in Mark 2:1–12,
Jesus enables us to walk with Him.

—DIANNE E. BUTTS

MAY

HANG ON TO YOUR HAT!

"Whatever happens, dear brothers and sisters, may the
Lord give you joy. I never get tired of telling you this.
I am doing this for your own good."
PHILIPPIANS 3:1

arenting. What a ride! Sometimes a joyride. Sometimes one of those downright scary trips. I had five kids in seven years. Talk about a wild ride! It's been a constant adventure, with plenty of ups and downs. But even when I felt a bit nauseated, I've never wanted to leave the parenting amusement park.

And amusement? There's been plenty of that. One of my teen boys, for instance, came upstairs yesterday with a look on his face that said he had something significant to announce. He made some exaggerated opera-type motions with his arms, then he burp-yelled the words, "I have the pow-er!"

No kidding. One solid belch.

I tried not to be amused, really I did. Couldn't help it. We all laughed for a good five minutes. Then I wiped my laugh-tears, told him it was *not* funny and that he should have better manners than that. The Mom Handbook requires me to make those disclaimers. That way, none of the blame for my kids' manner deficiencies comes back on me. Then I laughed for five more minutes.

My sixteen-year-old daughter wiped her own tears and said, "And you don't have a girlfriend right now?"

I said, "He could if he wanted to. It's not like he doesn't have the pow-er."

Don't tell my kids, but if I could've belched the last statement, I would've. I just don't have the power.

One of the things I've learned from my children is that I need to hang on to the power of laughter. Do you think we get the idea that laughter is irresponsible, childish, or that it's a little disrespectful to God? But God created us with a sense of humor—and it wasn't an accident. It creates endorphins, helps boost our immune system, and has all kinds of healthy effects on our bodies. Proverbs 17:22 says it! "A cheerful heart is good medicine" (NIV).

It wouldn't surprise me one bit to find out that our Father was tickled with the things that tickle us. Every time we laugh at the appropriate things and at the appropriate times, I can imagine him laughing too.

Granted, parenting is serious business. We're supposed to shape these mannerless creatures into productive members of society and spiritually mature contributors to God's kingdom in just eighteen or so short years. But no one said we had to do it alone. And no one said we had to do it without giggles.

When the parenting is said and done, I'm guessing we'll regret very few of the times we've chosen to laugh. In fact, I find those are some of our sweetest family memories.

So have fun on this parenting ride. Keep hands and arms inside the ride at all times, and remain seated until it comes to a complete stop.

—RHONDA RHEA

An Empty Love Cup

"No one has ever seen God. But if we love
each other, God lives in us, and his love
is brought to full expression in us."

1 JOHN 4:12

One morning Julie's four-year-old son had been in trouble many times and none of her discipline methods had worked. Julie was at her wit's end as she prayed, "Lord, please show me what to do."

An idea popped into her mind. Willing to try it, she knelt down, looked into her son's eyes, and said, "Honey, is your love cup empty?"

His lower lip began to quiver as he whimpered, "Uh-huh."

She gathered him in her arms and sat down on the couch for a long snuggle. That was the end of his naughtiness.

This is so like our heavenly Father. He disciplines those He loves as proof that we are His children. But, He also wants to fill our hearts with His love, knowing that receiving His love will change our behavior.

As a mother, we have the privilege of portraying
God's heart to our children.

—MARGARET WILSON

God's Greatest Masterpieces

"You formed the mountains by your power
and armed yourself with mighty strength."
PSALM 65:6

Colorado is one of my favorite places to visit because it's full of God's masterpieces. In February, I enjoyed his work in the Garden of the Gods. And nothing was as praise-inspiring as attending a conference in the middle of the Rockies in May! I was admiring those beautiful mountains when I should have been watching where I was going. Suddenly, I landed splat on the pavement in front of those lovely peaks. I limped through the conference in agony, and back home, I couldn't even move without excruciating pain. So I tried to stay off my feet and let my kids run errands for me.

As I sat on a white couch in the not-so-spectacular vista of Kansas City, I noticed another masterpiece of God's—those three kids running around the house. Each is different, each has a distinct personality, each has gifts and abilities. Each is truly a work of art.

Our children are among God's most awe-inspiring work!

—JGL

Divine-Colored Glasses

"The Lord looks down from heaven and sees
the whole human race. From his throne he
observes all who live on the earth. He made their
hearts, so he understands everything they do."
PSALM 33:13–15

When I was young, I often heard the phrase, "looking at the world through rose-colored glasses." It means to view everything as rosy, positive, more vibrant. How we look at the world does affect how we think, our attitudes, and how we affect others. This is especially important for moms, since our kids take their cues from us.

Perhaps we need to ask God to help us put on "divine-colored" glasses and see the world through His eyes. If we looked at the world with God's perspective, we'd understand others better. We'd have more patience. We'd act and be wiser. If we learned to look at the world through His eyes, we'd feel and express love more.

We can't put on literal glasses, but we can ask God to show us more of the world as He sees it. If we do so consistently, it's bound to change our attitudes . . . and our lives.

God is willing to help us see the world through His eyes.

—JGL

Joy Blooms

"Yet I still belong to you; you are holding
my right hand. You will keep on guiding me with
your counsel, leading me to a glorious destiny."
PSALM 73:23–24

Teenage insurgence collided with menopausal hormones as my son and I fought. Fresh into single parenting, I teetered on an emotional balance beam. How could I set healthy boundaries, yet assure him of my love? Almost nauseous from the terrible words we had thrown at one another, I wondered how to restore trust.

Then I remembered that God was holding my hand. I didn't have to figure it out in one day. God would show me how to parent my son, and how to ease him into manhood through the tunnel of teenage independence.

That afternoon, I drove into the school parking lot and saw the familiar blond hair. He slid into the passenger seat and handed me a fistful of flowers. "Here," was all he said.

I caressed the dandelion and the chickweed, and planted a kiss on his emerging beard.

"Thanks, honey," I said. "I love you, too."

Even the hard times can bloom into joy.

—R. J. THESMAN

Always in Style

"And the most important piece of clothing
you must wear is love. Love is what binds
us all together in perfect harmony."
COLOSSIANS 3:14

"Mommy, don't forget my purse!"

My daughter *click-clack*ed out of the minivan in her glittering plastic Cinderella mules and hot pink tights, her striped knit dress barely visible under the sequined lavender mermaid costume. A beribboned Easter hat and white patent leather purse completed her outfit.

If we see anyone we know, surely they'll realize she dressed herself, I thought. In the grocery store, she greeted other shoppers with a proud smile.

"What a gorgeous hat," one lady said.

"Did you pick that out yourself?" another woman asked. My daughter nodded happily.

In the check-out line, she received more compliments. I thought of the matching outfit I had suggested. Fashion disagreements between us will be inevitable as she grows. But on this day, warm smiles and friendly words from kind strangers admiring her unusual attire made this shy little girl's day. And they made mine, too.

My fashion statement today is my smile.

—SUE LOWELL GALLION

Night Watch

"I will lie down in peace and sleep,
for you alone, O Lord, will keep me safe."
PSALM 4:8

"Mom, what kind of watch does it say?" my son asked as I flipped the TV channels.

"It said we're under a thunderstorm watch, sweetie," I explained. I didn't tell him the other channel showed a tornado watch. Meteorologists predicted the storms would arrive in our area in the middle of the night.

When I let the cat in at midnight, I felt the blasts of hot southern air. And a few minutes later, I heard the strong, cold northern winds that would challenge the warm winds. I couldn't sleep, although the rest of the family slumbered peacefully. I finally realized why I was awake—nighttime tornados are rare, but when they do come, sleeping through sirens is a concern. So I was keeping watch.

"Lord, I think I'll let you handle this one. Please wake us up if something happens," I prayed. Surprisingly, I fell right to sleep and woke up in the morning refreshed.

*At times we need to just rest assured
that God is watching over our families.*

—JGL

Our Primary Ministry

> "And so, since God in his mercy has given
> us this wonderful ministry, we never give up."
> 2 Corinthians 4:1

My friend Sally is my ideal of a Christian who serves. I met her twenty years ago when we sponsored her sons' high school Bible club together. Her care expanded beyond the teenagers. Even when she was working full-time, she took time to help people. She has taken care of her elderly neighbors; she walked through the valley of death with cancerous friends; she takes meals to friends who are going through tough times.

And now that she's retired, there's no stopping Sally! One day when she came by my house to borrow a kettle—she was taking several large pots of chili to the local mission—I said, "Sally, teach me how to do good works. I want to serve like you."

She gave me a warm smile and said, "Kiddo, you have your hands full with your own ministry right now—those kids of yours."

Never underestimate the value of the
ministry you have in your own home.

—JGL

Following the Vision

"The Lord says, 'I will guide you along the best pathway
for your life. I will advise you and watch over you.'"
PSALM 32:8

Our son decided to make a career change in midlife. He had a
vision, a dream. He believed the Lord was leading him to enter
the pastoral ministry. Sure, I wanted him to answer God's call
on his life, but what about his wife and children? How would
they manage financially, adding the cost of seminary to the
ordinary bills requiring payment each month? It was then that
he reminded me of his grandmother's saying, "God won't lead
you where His grace can't keep you."

Craig was right. God had led him to this point in his
life. God would continue to care for him and his family. Craig
trusted God with his future. God's grace would keep him as he
began this new journey of life.

> *When God provides a vision, he also
> provides the resources for that vision.*

—VIOLA RUELKE GOMMER

Can You Hear Me Now?

"The quiet words of a wise person are
better than the shouts of a foolish king."
ECCLESIASTES 9:17

Years before cell phones, I had a bag phone, an awkward, heavy
contraption that hung from my shoulder like a purse. One day
while loading my children into the car, I inadvertently pushed
auto-dial, calling the house phone, and our answering machine
picked up. We were running late, but the kids were intrigued
by something in the yard and delayed getting into the car. I
screamed at them to hurry up, and my words were recorded on
the answering machine.

When I listened to the messages, I was mortified to hear
how I sounded. I sank to my knees, asking God to forgive my
unnecessarily harsh words. I realized my children needed to
hear words of encouragement and quiet instruction rather than
shouting from a shrew. God gently reminded me He is infinitely
patient with me, speaking with a loving voice, and I should do
the same with my children.

Think how you sound to others before you speak.

—CANDY ARRINGTON

A Father's Comfort

"God blesses those who mourn,
for they will be comforted."
MATTHEW 5:4

While she was in high school, our teen left home. I didn't know what to do. So I started asking other parents if they had dealt with a prodigal child and had advice.

Over the next few months, dozens of parents shared their experiences—many so much more difficult than ours. One mom told how her son killed himself. Another told me how she raised her unmarried prodigal child's daughter—and is now raising the unmarried grandchild's daughter.

My heart wept as I heard the anguish in parents' lives. But most of these moms also shared stories of hope, for in their pain, God had become more real to them and to their children.

Our teen didn't return home, but God worked in both of our lives. My sorrow diminished as he intensified my love for her and showed me that despite not making the best choices, this independent girl was becoming a delightful adult.

God weeps with us during the tough times
of parenting and gives us hope for the future.

—JGL

Sunshine in Seattle

"God has made everything beautiful for its own time..."
ECCLESIASTES 3:11

I picked up the phone and heard my daughter softly weeping.

"I took Aaron in for his two-year-old checkup today," she said, "and the pediatrician says he needs to be checked for autism."

We grieved when the doctor's suspicions were confirmed, not realizing what a delightful gift this child would become. Though he's a little different from most, he's exceptionally bright, has a terrific sense of humor, and sports a smile that—his mother tells him—makes the sun shine for her.

As with many autistic children, he has an affinity for numbers and dates. Early one morning five-year-old Aaron bounded out of bed and into his mother's room.

"Mama, it's May fourteenth! Happy Mother's Day!"

Reluctantly, she opened her eyes.

"Oh, but it's raining!" Aaron moaned when he peeked under the window shade and saw a typical Seattle drizzle.

"But," he said, flashing his million-dollar smile, "I know how to make the sun shine."

Some of God's best blessings come
wrapped in unexpected packages.

—SHARON SHEPPARD

The One Who Wants to Help

"Suddenly, a man with leprosy approached Jesus.
He knelt before him, worshiping. 'Lord,' the man
said, 'if you want to, you can make me well again.'
Jesus touched him. 'I want to,' he said. . . ."
MATTHEW 8:2–3

"Lord, if you want to, we know you can reach our son," the mother prayed. As I listened, I thought of the story of the lepers, and the words from this verse—"If you want to . . ."—came to my mind.

When the leper reached Jesus, he came straight to the point, saying, "If you want to, you can make me well again."

Jesus didn't say, "Let me think about it." Or, "Okay, let's talk about this."

Instead, He instantly said, "I want to. Be healed."

What a joy I find when I realize that Jesus says these same words to moms in every parenting situation. If we say, "Lord, will you help me have more patience?" He says, "I will. I want to." If we ask Him to protect our children on the band trip, He says, "I want to."

And I knew He was also answering this mom's prayers—even if she didn't see the results at the moment.

*When we ask for His help, Jesus answers, "I'd love to"
—no hesitations, conditions, or refusals!*

—JGL

Better Than Breakfast

"But Martha was worrying over the
big dinner she was preparing."
LUKE 10:40

"Mommy!...Mommy!...Mommy, mommy, mommy, mommy,
MOMMMMYYYYYY!!!!!"

I quickly worked to place bowls and spoons on the table,
trying desperately to tune out my daughter as she followed me
around the kitchen. "Breakfast is almost ready honey," I said,
grabbing a box of cereal and a jug of milk. "Just give me *one
more minute!*"

Her yelling grew more insistent. "Mommy! Mommy!
Mommy!...MOMMYYYYY!"

"What? What is it!" I finally shouted, losing my temper.

"Mommy," she said quietly, extending her tiny hands.
"Hug?"

It's amazing how tasks like setting a breakfast table or rushing out the door can seem so important. So many distractions
consume our focus and keep us from hearing the message God
has for us. That's why it is so important to take the time from
our busyness to stop and listen. If we don't, we could miss out
on the greatest blessings of our lives.

Put down your plans and let God surprise you with His.

—KATHERINE CRADDOCK

Waiting on God's Promises

"Then the Lord did exactly what he had promised."
GENESIS 21:1

"Mommy, you promised we could go to the park. When? Let's go!"

My son isn't patient when I've promised to do something. He wants my promises fulfilled immediately. So sometimes, he learns about waiting.

Abraham was one of those in the Bible who had to wait. God had promised him a son, but years passed and he and Sarah were still childless.

Finally, Abraham tried to make God's promises come true—he impregnated his wife's maid, planning that he and his wife could raise the child.

What a mess that ended up to be as Abraham's family ended up in arms!

Waiting on God is tough in every area of our lives but especially in parenting situations such as when we ask God to build something, like gratitude or patience, in our children. But it's necessary to keep believing He'll do what He promises.

When we're waiting on God, we have
to trust that His timing is perfect!

—JGL

Time for Wonder Woman!

"Pride goes before destruction,
and haughtiness before a fall."
PROVERBS 16:18

I collect vintage wind-up watches and am watching a fun one on eBay: a Wonder Woman watch. I want it to wear on days when I have a million tasks and am zooming through them.

Most of us moms have a Wonder Woman mentality. We have a lot to do, and we faithfully try to be all things to all people.

But, we all also know the downside to this. A little thing called exhaustion. Add high blood pressure and bodily rebellion. Short tempers and bad attitudes, maybe?

If you're like me, you sink under the weight of Wonder Woman expectations because you're too proud to send an SOS. Honestly, many times I sink not because help is not available, but because I insist that I can do it all.

We need to cut the Wonder Woman mentality. But I think I'll still get the watch to remind me of who I'm *not*!

*Don't be shy to ask for assistance—
and when a helping hand comes along, take it!*

—JGL

Laying Down Our Lives

"We know what real love is because Christ gave up
his life for us. And so we also ought to give up our
lives for our Christian brothers and sisters."
1 JOHN 3:16

My husband and I exchanged amused glances. Our daughter,
Amelia, sitting between us, considered it a tragedy for us to be
sitting in a high school principal's office on our twenty-fifth
wedding anniversary.

Fortunately, the serious problem of marijuana being found
in her locker during a police dog search was easily remedied. It
was not hers. The culprit, a friend of Amelia's locker partner,
confessed.

Later that day, I remembered the verse God gave me when
Amelia was a toddler: 1 John 3:16. The Holy Spirit had whispered to me, "That is your life's verse as a mother."

I knew instantly that I was to lay aside job offers and stay
home to be a full-time mother to my little girl.

I was so grateful that I obeyed His leading, because during this crisis, I had not even wondered if the drugs belonged
to Amelia. I knew her friends, her schedule, her hobbies, and,
most importantly, I knew her heart.

*Our obedience to God affects His
blessings to us and to our children.*

—EVANGELINE BEALS GARDNER

Run to Me

"Save me from my enemies, Lord;
I run to you to hide me."
PSALM 143:9

"Mommy, help me!" Elizabeth cries as she hides behind me.

Our huge black lab is only a year old, but she's already figured out who's the easiest target when it comes to getting "people food." Zoey tends to follow Elizabeth around, hoping she'll drop food. And at other times, Zoey is prone to trying to steal the food right out of Elizabeth's hand. So when Zoey gets that hungry look in her eye, Elizabeth runs to me for protection. In fact, anytime Elizabeth feels threatened by anything in life, I'm likely to find her behind me.

Kids don't have the corner on the market when it comes to being afraid. How many times do we moms feel pursued or threatened—by the creditors at our door, by the overwhelming tasks we must juggle, by the very demands of motherhood. Maybe we should take a lesson from our children and run to God when the ominous appears.

*God is big enough, and more than willing,
to protect us from whatever threatens.*

—JGL

Unstring Before You're Unstrung

"And he will give you all you need from day to day if you live for him and make the Kingdom of God your primary concern."

MATTHEW 6:33

In ancient times when warriors fought with bow and arrow, they found the best way to keep their bows tight was to unstring them at night, giving the wood a chance to relax. When they restrung them again the next morning, they were better, tighter instruments.

That's not bad advice for moms, either. There never seem to be enough hours in the day to meet the demands put upon you. When we continually pour from ourselves into others, we're like a pitcher that will eventually run dry. For me, the best way to unstring my bow and refill my pitcher is to start my day alone with God. It might mean getting up earlier or turning a blind eye to dirty dishes and clothes. But it's always worth it when He replenishes me and gives me the energy and the wisdom to meet the demands of a new day.

If you have nothing left to give, stop and
spend some quiet time with God so He can fill
you and remind you how much you mean to Him.

—MIMI GREENWOOD KNIGHT

When Children Go to War

"Give all your worries and cares to God,
for he cares about what happens to you."
1 Peter 5:7

My baby boy—a Marine, a father, a husband—went to the war front again, the third time in his career. He wasn't a father the first time.

I think about ancient days when young David picked up his slingshot to defend God's people from Goliath. Surely his mother cried, "He's just a boy—too young to do battle."

I confront God: "Waiting is hard. My heart aches. Do you care?"

My husband holds me while I cry. "Honey, Eddy has been trained well. He's an excellent leader, and best of all, he walks with his Lord."

I remember my friend whose teenage son died in a car wreck coming home from mountain climbing.

God comforts me as I consider the uncertainty of our tomorrows.

Today, with love, I call my friend who survived after her child's death, and I call my daughter-in-law who waits in faith.

Mary watched her son die on a cross—then God raised Him from the grave and peace lives within us forever.

—Liz Hoyt Eberle

Meet My Friend

"Inside the Tent of Meeting, the Lord would speak
to Moses face to face, as a man speaks to his friend.
Afterward Moses would return to the camp, but
the young man who assisted him, Joshua son of
Nun, stayed behind in the Tent of Meeting."
EXODUS 33:11

My children weren't very old when they came home from Sunday school with pictures and crafts that included the words, "Jesus is my friend."

We raise our children to believe that Jesus wants to be their friend, but our kids aren't the only ones Jesus wants to befriend. Way before Jesus was born, God proclaimed Himself as a friend to people. While Adam and Eve enjoyed Eden, God actually chatted with them daily. I don't imagine they discussed lofty theological concepts. Apparently, God just liked being with them and talking about everyday stuff.

Sometimes it's hard for us to imagine, but God wants to be our friend, too. He doesn't just tolerate our company, He enjoys us. He likes not just being our advisor, but our companion.

What better way to help our children see that Jesus wants to be their friend, than to let them see that Jesus is our friend, too.

Enjoy God on a personal level—and let Him enjoy you!

—JGL

You're the One

"God, who calls you, is faithful; he will do this."
1 THESSALONIANS 5:24

My husband, an airline pilot, was describing a harrowing landing. His voice was matter-of-fact. He didn't even seem impressed by what he'd done.

"How do you have the guts to land a plane with 130 lives in your hands?" I asked.

Then it dawned on me: he knew that out of those 130 people, he's the most qualified person for the task. It's his job and he's equipped to do it.

As a mom, you do something even scarier every day. You raise kids. How do you have the guts to mold and shape something as fragile and precious as a child?

I'll tell you: You're the one. Out of billions of people on this planet, God chose *you* to be mom to your kids. You're the one most qualified for the job. He's called and equipped you and no one else can do what you do.

You're the mom God chose for your kids.

—BECKY FULCHER

Waiting for God to Act

"Be still in the presence of the Lord, and wait patiently
for him to act. Don't worry about evil people who prosper
or fret about their wicked schemes."

PSALM 37:7

One of the saddest days of my life was when my two children
went to live with their father. I had fought this for years, but my
children were old enough to choose.

I cried, but relief never seemed to come. One day my friend
gave me this advice: "Ann, those children don't belong to you.
God only allowed you to be His administrator over them. He
can look after them better where they are than you can in your
own backyard."

God did protect my children. My son became a member of
the Fellowship for Christian Athletes at the new school, and
my daughter had a wonderful teacher who regularly shared
Bible truths with her.

Letting them go was the best thing I ever did. They saw
what life was like on their father's side of the fence and have
returned to live with me, bringing an added maturity with them.
God taught me how to give up and how to receive again!

We can trust God even when we don't know His purposes.

—ANN VARNUM

Training for Response

"I discipline my body like an athlete,
training it to do what it should. . . ."
1 CORINTHIANS 9:27

After watching ten minutes of flip turns, my children's swim coach threw up his hands in frustration. "Do you know why we're working on flip turns? Because you still aren't doing them right! You think, 'It's okay to breathe before flipping in practice, I won't do it in a meet!' Or, 'I don't need to waste energy streamlining off the wall in practice, I'll do it right in a meet!'"

"I got news for you guys. If you don't do it right in practice, you won't do it right in a meet, either. When the pressure is on, your body will do what it's trained to do."

To me, the coach's comments hit home in the spiritual sense as well. If we practice relying on God and habitually pray, when a crisis comes, we'll do what we trained to do: trust God.

Practice patience and learn endurance; practice kindness and learn compassion; practice love and become genuine.

—LORI Z. SCOTT

All You Need

" . . . My gracious favor is all you need. My
power works best in your weakness. . . ."
2 CORINTHIANS 12:9

On any given day, by the time the clock strikes nine a.m., I'm
already frazzled by the number of titles I've worn: mommy, short-
order cook, maid, finder of lost shoes and misplaced homework,
chauffeur, and employee. Spreading myself too thin can leave
me drained, doubting my own abilities, and questioning if I am
giving my best, especially to my children.

Paul asked God to remove his weakness three times, and
God's "no" answer brought him much comfort.

Even before I acknowledge my many flaws, God's power
is available to me. Despite my self-doubts and my tendency to
meet everyone else's needs before my own, God's Word lets me
know He is by my side, every step of the way.

His gracious favor and His power are all I truly need.

—MISTY FONTENOT

More Than Flowers

"And may the Lord our God show us his
approval and make our efforts successful.
Yes, make our efforts successful!"
PSALM 90:17

Prompted by a small yard bouquet my daughter, Allison, enthusiastically thrust into my hands earlier that day, I quizzed her at bedtime.

"If you could be any flower, what flower would you be?" I asked.

Anticipating a simple answer, I waited.

"I want to be whatever you want to be," said Allison. Innocent four-year-old eyes looked intently into mine. Her blond hair fanned out across the pillow.

"Really?" I said.

She nodded thoughtfully.

I kissed Allison goodnight and pondered my role. I marveled at my influence in her life. That night I felt like a rose, but I've had my share of dandelion days.

I prayed for wisdom to slow life's frenzied pace, for patience to nurture, and for love to gently direct my child's path.

Since then, whenever my daughter skips toward me grasping a yard bouquet, I'm reminded of my impact on her life and the One who will see me through.

Sometimes the simple things in motherhood speak the loudest.

—ELIZABETH HEY

A Bumble Bee and a Mother's Plea

"Praise the Lord; praise God our savior!
For each day he carries us in his arms."
PSALM 68:19

"Luke, leave that bee alone; it's going to sting you," I cautioned.

My three-year-old continued chasing the bee, swatting at it as it buzzed busily around the flowers in my garden.

"Luke, stop it! The bee will hurt you."

He ignored my plea once again.

A thought shot through my mind. *Fine. If you get hurt, don't come crying to me.*

Then came God's whisper: "I'm not like that, Carolyn."

Immediately I understood.

I wonder how many times I disregard God's loving warnings in my own life and later find myself crying out to Him, "Lord, please help me. This hurts!"

He never retorts, "I told you so. Don't come whining to me." God reminded me of His loving character that day in my garden. And I want to be a mother who, like Jesus, never turns her hurting children away... no matter what.

God's arms are always open to His children, at any time and for any reason . . . no matter what.

—CAROLYN BYERS RUCH

Eternal Encouragement

"May our Lord Jesus Christ himself and God our
Father, who loved us and by his grace gave us eternal
encouragement and good hope, encourage your hearts
and strengthen you in every good deed and word."
2 THESSALONIANS 2:16–17

Opening the door, I greeted my daughter, Joanie, who was cry-ing. Over coffee a few minutes later, she blurted, "You know Susie graduated last night."

"How'd it go?" I asked.

"We've waited years for this. But afterward, with everyone so proud and excited hugging their children, we couldn't find Susie! Finally, we spotted her talking with our friends. She hadn't even looked for us first!"

"That hurt," I said.

"I cried all night. And I wrote a poem about baby robins learning to fly away."

I read her poem and then told her, "I hurt when you flew away."

"I guess all mothers do," she said, wiping her eyes.

"Yes, but God helped you express your pain. This poem has God's love in it. You can write, Joanie!"

She hugged me. "Oh, thank you, Mom."

When a child or friend hurts, God can give us words to bring her hope and new purpose.

God's compassion is always with us.

—LUCY WOODWARD

Those Who Have Gone Before

"By faith these people overthrew kingdoms, ruled with
justice, and received what God had promised them.
They shut the mouths of lions, quenched the flames of
fire, and escaped death by the edge of the sword. Their
weakness was turned to strength. They became strong
in battle and put whole armies to flight."
HEBREWS 11:33–34

Every Memorial Day, Mom cut her roses, peonies, and irises.
Then we drove to a large cemetery in Mom's hometown, leaving flowers on the graves of her mother and brothers. A few
blocks away, we'd search endless rows of white military headstones for her father's grave. Our next stop was a stark hillside
where Dad's family was buried.

The day might bring tears, but it would also bring memories, laughter, and reminders of the joy of living. Those who
were buried only a few yards away were not forgotten. And our
parents told us the stories of their lives.

Hebrews 11 is the Bible's Memorial Day celebration. The
writer led his listeners in remembering those who lived in
faith. As they remembered, they were challenged, inspired, and
strengthened.

We don't need to wait until Memorial Day to
remember, and teach our children about,
the great lives of those who have gone before us.

—JGL

God Calms the Storms

"He calmed the storm to a whisper and stilled the waves."
PSALM 107:29

While I watched the weather on television, my hands trembled. My three grown children live in various parts of Georgia. The storms that had produced damaging tornadoes the day before were roaring across our state. Even though my children are now grown, I still feel those protective motherly instincts.

When the children were little, I could hold them close. When they were teenagers, I could insist they stay at home. Now that they are grown, I can only pray that God will protect them during the storms of life. I uttered a prayer for them and went back to work, realizing I could do nothing else.

At some point in every parent's life, we have to stop depending on ourselves and trust God to take care of our children. Isn't releasing control to God the perfect solution to calming not only the storms, but also our parental nerves?

God is truly the Master of the wind.

—NANCY B. GIBBS

An Endless Supply of Love

"Dear friends, since God loved us that
much, we surely ought to love each other."
1 JOHN 4:11

The young missionary was home from her station in China, ready to return as soon as her second child was born.

As we talked about her experiences, I recalled that I'd heard the Chinese government forbade more than one child per family, and asked, "Does anyone give you a hard time for having another baby?"

"Yes, but not because of the one-child rule," she said. "They don't want more than one child. They don't understand how parents could love a second child as much as they love the first. They can't conceive that their love would stretch that far."

I think of parents who have more children than I do—and love them all as much as I love mine. Thank God that our love for our kids is like a magic pitcher—the more love we pour out, the more we have.

God's love stretches, too—to cover each of us.

—JGL

Spreading Out

> "[Jabez]was the one who prayed to the God of Israel, 'Oh, that you would bless me and extend my lands! Please be with me in all that I do, and keep me from all trouble and pain!' And God granted him his request."
> 1 CHRONICLES 4:10

I can't resist a plant sale! So when I saw the two-for-one deal, I chose two gorgeous begonias that were outgrowing their pots.

I immediately repotted one, but then ran out of potting soil. So I put the other one aside for another day . . . which stretched to two weeks. Meanwhile, the repotted plant thrived. The other poor plant didn't excel at all. In fact, it started to die.

The principle is the same with our kids. Sometimes we moms want to keep them safe in the little pots—after all, it's a big, scary world out there. But we have to give them room to grow, to expand their experiential lands. That doesn't mean we turn them loose, but it does mean we help them make their worlds a little bigger so they can spread their roots and flourish. If we don't, they shrivel.

> *A wise mom helps her kids find*
> *new ground to expand their roots.*

—JGL

JUNE

FOR BETTER OR WORSE— JUST LIKE MOM

"He remembered us in our weakness.
His faithful love endures forever."
PSALM 136:23

here are my keys?" my son shouted. He shuffled papers, checked under stacks of laundry, and roved from room to room while his words gained intensity.

"I can't believe it! Keys don't just get up and walk away," he practically screamed. "Where are they?"

"Please stop it. You're acting just like me," I told him with a wince.

He laughed, and it diffused the situation. But although he thought I was joking, I wasn't. Watching my son and listening to his words, I'd felt like I was looking in a mirror that reflected me in my son's body and voice.

Once upon a time I thought that cowlicks, pug noses, and just plain weird toes were the things my children inherited from me. And the "healthy" thighs and troublesome waistline I passed on to my daughter. I often notice these physical traits we share—usually after we have a bowl of ice cream loaded with chocolate syrup!

A double photo frame sits in our living room. It holds a picture of my youngest son and my husband when they both were ten years old. I display them together as black-and-white proof that they must, indeed, be related. The remarkable resemblance leaves no doubt.

If only family likenesses were just skin-deep. But after twenty years of motherhood, I know family traits and characteristics transcend the physical. I first suspected this when we were a family in the fast lane of five small children. Often impatient, hurtful words shot from one child to another. Or frustrated tones ruled when someone did not meet another's expectations. Unfortunately, these harsh words sounded all too familiar—too much like their mother's.

Later, having three teen drivers, I received even more humbling reminders of my own inappropriate behaviors. My daughter said the next time she was stopped for speeding she would ask, "Can I just claim heredity as my defense?"

When my children sinned, acted unbecomingly, or spoke harshly, though I knew they made their own choices, I also saw the seeds I had sown. Over the years, guilt overshadowed my mothering. I seemed to fail on so many issues. How often did I wish I had been more patient? I nagged myself because we should have had more family devotions. I should have played more with my kids. Had I been too lenient in their dress codes and social lives?

Over the years I had sought God's wisdom many times. I longed to be a good example for my kids. Though often I sensed God's guidance and was able to respond to it with positive results, I continued living with a nagging sense of never living up to my expectations. Then I had an eye-opening discussion with some other moms.

We were all talking about the difficulties of raising teens—clothing choices, bodily noises teen boys are prone to, lack of communication skills, immature social relations, and other common behaviors. I admitted that my household experienced some of these challenges.

After I spoke, though, one mother quickly informed us that her children were not allowed to act like that and, in fact, she strove to keep her family from such "worldly" actions. Her words cut to my heart. It seemed as if my failures were now multiplied and magnified for the entire world to see.

Later, as I reflected on our conversation, tears stung my eyes. Through my tears, I prayed, and experienced what would become a turning point away from the guilt I carried. "God, you know I've always wanted to be a good example for my kids. But you, of all people, know how I've failed at times. You know my weaknesses."

Then the Holy Spirit led me to God's comforting truth. Before I knew what I was saying, I confidently declared, "But, God, *you* can make up for every one of my weaknesses as a parent. I'm asking you today to fill in the gaps where I've failed. Thank you that when I am weak, *you* are strong!"

The simple truth that God can make up for my failures has relieved mounds of guilt in my life. Maybe I'm still not always the example I want to be for my children, but I know I have a big God who covers me with His grace. And I rest in the assurance that my children's heavenly Father stands in the gap for my children with His protection and guidance.

We'll always have the family likenesses of pug noses and strange toes. And as God continues to work in my life, I'm looking forward to the day when my children act like me—and it's a *good thing*!

—KAREN MOREROD

God on the Dock

"When you go through deep waters and great trouble, I will be with you. When you go through rivers of difficulty you will not drown!"

ISAIAH 43:2

Terror tightened its noose around my throat as I peered into the murky bay. Why had I taken my cousin's dare to jump from the dock and swim to shore? The water looked so cold and forbidding!

I had an advocate, though. Mother was my greatest cheerleader in everything I attempted. "You're strong! You're a great swimmer! Piece of cake!" she crooned.

The icy water snatched the breath from my lungs. My heart beat wildly, and I struggled against panic.

"Don't give up! You're almost there!" All other sights and sounds faded. I was aware only of Mother calling encouragement. At last I was in her warm embrace.

Our Lord, too, assures and reassures us all along our way, sustaining our spirits and cheering us on to the shore. There He stands, beaming, with arms open wide, waiting to welcome us with a hearty "Well done!"

We mirror God's love and devotion when we give our children encouragement and support and when we give them confidence, which helps them achieve otherwise unattainable goals.

—SUSAN ESTRIBOU RAMSDEN

Pool Boys and Pure Lives

"How can a young person stay pure?
By obeying your word and following its rules."
PSALM 119:9

"Oh, look. I've shocked the innocent newlywed," Jill said with a derisive laugh.

I blushed. I was fixing VBS treats at church with a group of moms when Jill made a suggestive comment about her pool boy—years before *Desperate Housewives* came on TV and a year after I'd gotten married.

My temptation to sin may not be lusting after pool boys, but even as we try to instill purity in our children, each of us moms faces our own temptations. Psalm 119:9 isn't just important for young people, it's also especially important for moms—for our kids see the ways we handle temptation. They note if we make excuses to do wrong, or if we stand strong. And they often follow the example we set.

So how can we moms be pure? The same way our kids can—by learning and reading God's word so we can maintain a close relationship with Him.

*A wise mom maintains a pure life by reading, studying,
and following God's Word.*

—JGL

Following His Lead

"Jesus replied, 'If I want him to remain alive until
I return, what is that to you? You follow me.'"
JOHN 21:22

"But Karen lets her kids watch those movies," my kids whined
when I vetoed some videos I felt were inappropriate. "She's a
good mother, and she's a Christian."

"I don't care what Karen does—she's not responsible for
you; I am," I answered.

I thought of John 21:21–23. Jesus had just given Peter some
news about his future. Instead of talking to Jesus further about
his own life, Peter pointed to John like a squabbling child and
said, "Well, what about him, Lord? What's going to happen to
him?"

Jesus basically said, "Don't worry about him. You follow
me."

There's a lot of pressure in this world for us moms to con-
form to other people's standards and convictions—both tighter
and laxer than ours. But when it comes to raising our kids, we
parents have to set down the rules and guidelines as we feel
God is leading us; not as anyone else dictates.

Be strong in your beliefs, mom, even when others don't agree.

—JGL

Trusting God's Choices

"The Lord is good. When trouble comes, he is a strong
refuge. And he knows everyone who trusts in him."

NAHUM 1:7

From the time my children were born, I prayed for their future
mates. I was shocked when my son, Trant, told us he had asked
Karen to marry him. She was older than he was and already had
two children. She was definitely not my choice for my son's wife.
I begged God to end the relationship. I heard only silence.

Then, one day after church, my son and his bride-to-be
walked in. I spotted the insecurity and fear in Karen's eyes. As
she rose so I could hug her properly, my arms wrapped around
her and the greatest flow of pure love came from me to her. She
felt it, too.

All of this happened almost twenty years ago. I now know
God did give my son the right mate. Why does it take us so long
to trust Him, and the way He chooses to answer our prayers?

Take that "leap of faith" to believe His choice is always best.

—ANN VARNUM

Looking at the Heart

"End the wickedness of the ungodly, but help
all those who obey you. For you look deep
within the mind and heart, O righteous God."
PSALM 7:9

Nicole was our child who liked to be different from the mainstream. She often wore goth clothes, although she wasn't goth. She reached out to kids at school who looked different from the crowd. She liked guys with unruly haircuts and stubbled chins.

After Nicole moved away from home, we got interesting reports on the phone. She dyed her bright blond hair coal black. Soon she got a tattoo. Then she and her husband got matching tattoos.

I wondered if I should worry. But then we went to see Nicole. She had purple hair that weekend. And her husband's goatee matched it.

But Nicole's smile was the same, and her eyes shone clean and bright. Her home was way cleaner than mine and tastefully decorated. Tattoos, purple hair, piercings, whatever. She was still the same friendly, smart, creative girl. I realized I had nothing to worry about.

May God help us keep our focus on our children's hearts,
not the outer appearances!

—JGL

Try–and Try Again

> "We have worked wearily with our own hands to
> earn our living. We bless those who curse us.
> We are patient with those who abuse us."
> 1 CORINTHIANS 4:12

I sat at the sewing machine and guided the material. As soon as I finished sewing the waistband on, I would have a new skirt. But when Mother looked at my crooked stitching, she shook her head and handed me the seam ripper.

Each time I picked out a stitch and sewed the waistband again, Mother would look at it and shake her head. By the time I got it right, Mother and I were weary and the waistband was nearly worn out. But I learned two valuable lessons: how to sew a straight seam and perseverance. Later, I would use both to teach my daughters, and then my grandchildren, to sew.

Mother could have stitched that waistband onto the skirt in a couple of minutes. But a mother's task is not to do everything for her children; it is to teach them. Though we grow weary in our work, Mother taught me that it's important to do the job right.

When nothing seems to work, try one more time.

—LeAnn Campbell

No More Leftovers!

"The poor will eat and be satisfied. All who
seek the Lord will praise him. Their
hearts will rejoice with everlasting joy."
PSALM 22:26

"Mama, you can have it," Elizabeth says, thrusting an ice-cream cone in my hands that she'd begged for five minutes earlier. She explained, "I don't want it."

I've learned from experience that it doesn't do any good to say, "You wanted it; now eat it." Then she furtively tosses it in the trash.

So I usually put the unwanted item in the refrigerator. And I end up eating a lot of leftovers for my meals. Nothing is wrong with leftovers, but they do get tiring! It's nice to have fresh, tasty food cooked just for me sometimes!

I wonder if God ever gets tired of leftovers. So often we get busy and give him the leftovers of our time, our energy, our attention, and affection. Thankfully, he does take our leftovers, but he would probably appreciate it—and it would be good for us, too—if we started giving him more of our fresh fare.

Let's make our time with God a priority instead of a leftover!

—JGL

Little Love Steps

"Do nothing out of selfish ambition or vain conceit, but
in humility consider others better than yourselves."
PHILIPPIANS 2:3

I remember well when our grade-school children, Karen and
John, chattered at supper and each told about the day—at the
same time.

"John, you're talking on top of me!" Karen said.

"But it's my turn!" he shouted.

"Stop!" their father called, waving his hands.

"I have a plan," I said as I reached for a baby ceramic duck
on the nearby counter. "When this fellow is in front of your
place, talk all you want for five minutes and no one will inter-
rupt." I slipped the duck in front of Karen and she told about
her spelling bee at school.

Like taking "baby duck steps," our children gradually
learned to honor each other by listening. As a mother I prayed
for God's love to fill our home and for our children to be able to
express what was important to them. In time, the unnecessary
ceramic duck just waddled away.

Express God's love by carefully listening.

—CHARLOTTE ADELSPERGER

Sandpaper People

"It is I who makes the green tree wither."
EZEKIEL 17:24

"I never want to speak to my toxic mother again!" shouted Maggie. "She is as coarse as sandpaper and rubs me the wrong way."

Maggie is a respected journalist, the mother of two young daughters, and my therapy client. Maggie's mom is a retired schoolteacher who wanted her to become a doctor instead of a journalist. Her mom constantly questions Maggie's writing, parenting, and housekeeping skills.

A big part of Maggie wanted to sever all ties with her mom. Another part felt guilty as she knew that her mom was aging. In therapy we slowly uncovered that she never felt "good enough" in her mom's eyes. Maggie eventually chose to embrace whom she had grown to be and to separate this from her mother's expectations.

The dynamics of mother-daughter relationships can be challenging, but as we accept our differences with our moms, we can be moms who enjoy our own moms.

Sandpaper people polish us!

—RANI MOODLEY

When Others Build on Our Foundation

"Because of God's special favor to me, I have laid the foundation like an expert builder. Now others are building on it. But whoever is building on this foundation must be very careful."

1 CORINTHIANS 3:10

"My mom never liked Shirley," Lisa told me. Shirley was an older woman who had been Lisa's spiritual mentor and had a huge impact on her life.

I understood. I'd had a couple of older women who'd been my mentors and dear friends, and my mother wasn't crazy about them either, even though she didn't know them.

I finally figured she felt a bit jealous. She probably resented that I spent time with these women and realized they knew more about what was going on inside me than she did.

It's only normal that, as our children start leaving our nests, God brings other mentors and friends into their lives. It's part of growing up.

And it's also yet another matter of parenting prayer for us. As our kids branch out, we can pray that God will bring the right mentors into their lives to carefully build on the foundation we've laid.

*No matter how close a mentor is,
he or she can never replace a mom.*

—JGL

185

I'm Sorry!

"Prove by the way you live that you have really
turned from your sins and turned to God."
MATTHEW 3:8

As I walked into the closet, I could have died. Everything that
had been hung on the lower bars and folded on the shelves was
now on the floor.

"Elizabeth!" I hollered.

Elizabeth came and realized I'd caught her.

"I sorry," my toddler said readily.

Later, I found a pile of beads and realized Elizabeth had
taken scissors to some necklaces. I scolded her, and she looked
at me solemnly and said, "I sorry, Mama."

"Don't do it again!" I directed. But a half hour later, I found
another pile of beads.

So many times our kids are certainly sorry they've upset
us, or truly sorry they've been caught . . . but they're not really
repentant. I tell my older ones, "If you're truly sorry, you won't
do it again!"

When we do something wrong, it's not enough to just say
we're sorry, but true repentance means being sorry enough that
we change our behavior.

True repentance means we're sorry enough to change.

—JGL

What Are You Afraid Of?

"But when I am afraid, I put my trust in you."
PSALM 56:3

"No, don't close it, Mommy. I'm scared!" five-year-old Sam yelled. He'd outgrown his fear of thunderstorms and monsters in the closet, but now he was afraid of having the bathroom door closed at bath time.

During that cold winter, our drafty house didn't retain heat well, and Sam froze each time he got out of the tub.

Finally one night we reached a compromise, and I closed the door halfway.

Thirty minutes later, I heard Sam muttering in the bathroom. Curious, I crept to the door.

"When I am afraid, I put my trust in you. When I am afraid, I put my trust in you..." Over and over Sam repeated his memory verse from his kindergarten class.

How wonderful to know God's Word can comfort our little ones with little fears as well as adults with grown-up worries.

What are you afraid of?

—CINDY HVAL

The Compassion of a Child

"When darkness overtakes the godly,
light will come bursting in. They are
generous, compassionate, and righteous."
PSALM 112:4

"It's okay, Grandpa." Little Elizabeth was less than two years old, but she was a girl with a mission. She put all of her effort into pulling her little yellow plastic chair right up to Grandpa's knees, where he sat in the burgundy easy chair.

Grandpa had been on depression medication since his stroke and the bouts of crying were normal. Of course, Elizabeth didn't know that. She only understood that her adored Grandpa was sad. So she patted his knees, her big blue eyes wide with compassion. Then she ran and climbed up on the yellow divan, not climbing in Granny's lap as usual, but reaching behind Granny for a facial tissue.

Elizabeth ran back to her grandpa and handed him the Kleenex. As he clumsily wiped his eyes, she again took her post on the plastic chair, patting his knees and saying, "You be okay, Grandpa."

And she stayed there all evening until Grandpa felt better.

May God give us all the compassion of a loving child.

—JGL

Improving Our Focus

"Fix your thoughts on what is true and honorable
and right. Think about things that are pure
and lovely and admirable. Think about things
that are excellent and worthy of praise."
PHILIPPIANS 4:8

In my morning exercise walk through our lovely apartment
grounds, one day I only saw the weeds around the flowerbeds
and shrubbery. Impulsively, I pulled a tall weed and tossed it in
the trash. On the next round, though, I realized that same area
held beautiful little bushes.

Suddenly, I was ashamed. As Philippians 4:8 tells us, we
are to focus on the good, not on the bad. Goodness and beauty
are much more pleasant. If we're too busy concentrating on the
bad, we miss the good.

It's the same when we relate to our husbands or children.
Each person has wonderful qualities, yet something makes us
automatically focus on negative qualities. Then we stew about
how to tell them. It's not our job to change them. God calls
us to focus on the good things about others. Why don't we put
more energy into doing that?

Keep focused on God's beauty in others.

—SALLY R. DANLEY

Out of Danger

"He led me to a place of safety;
he rescued me because he delights in me."
PSALM 18:19

"If we were home in Missouri, I'd think those were tornado clouds," I muttered to my baby in the backseat. But we were in the North Carolina Outer Banks, where I didn't think they had tornadoes.

"Let's go inside the store anyway," I told my son.

As I spoke, a cloud dropped a wide brown tail to the ground a few blocks away. I jumped out of the car into the pouring rain to open the door by my son. It was locked. As I unlocked it and wrestled with his seat belt, I felt as if the seconds were going in slow motion. I was consumed with one thought: to get my child to safety, no matter what it took. I finally got him free and we dashed into a store—to look and see that the tornado had dissipated.

Repeatedly, scripture compares God's love for us to our love and care for our children. Do you feel threatened? He cares about your safety even more than you do.

Trust God to keep you out of the path of danger today.

—JGL

Floating in His Embrace

"The eternal God is your refuge, and
his everlasting arms are under you."
DEUTERONOMY 33:27

Olivia struggled to release herself from my grasp. "Let me go, Mama! I can swim by myself!" She watched as her friends, who wore life vests, paddled around her. She wiggled and kicked and pushed against my arms, trying to launch into the deep water of our community pool.

We had forgotten her life vest and she was indignant at being held "like a baby." She couldn't swim, but that didn't matter one bit to my self-confident three-year-old!

How like my strong-willed daughter I have been, I thought. So often I have believed that I knew best and could swim dangerous waters without God's support.

As I mature spiritually, I am learning to ask the Lord before plunging into the deep end of life. I don't struggle as often against His guidance, but instead seek the comfort and security of His everlasting arms. There, I know, I will never flounder or sink!

*How much more secure we are when we trust and
release ourselves to God's tender love and guidance.*

—SUSAN ESTRIBOU RAMSDEN

The Fathers in Our Lives

"And because you Gentiles have become his children,
God has sent the Spirit of his Son into your hearts, and
now you can call God your dear Father."
GALATIANS 4:6

Dad's roommate motioned to me. Though he could hardly talk, he painfully whispered, "You take great care of your father. It's good to see that."

Dad was in rehab after a stroke, pneumonia, and a heart attack. We'd celebrated Father's Day in this hospital. I spent many painful hours each day watching him struggle, so the roommate's words encouraged me.

"I love him," I explained. "He's a great dad."

I'd been raised to appreciate my dad. Father's Day was a big deal for us. Dad wore a gold cardboard crown and relaxed on a hammock, listening to the ball game on the radio while we brought him iced tea.

Part of being a good mother is trying to spoil my husband on Father's Day, too, and encouraging my kids to focus on celebrating how terrific their dad is. If I teach them to do this now, I hope they'll always show appreciation for their father.

Take some time out today to help your kids celebrate the fathers in your lives—including your heavenly Father.

—JGL

Knowing Where to Look

"We do not know what to do,
but we are looking to you for help."
2 CHRONICLES 20:12

"I couldn't believe you didn't go ballistic," Alisha told us.

"I didn't go ballistic because I was in shock," I explained.

We were totally surprised when we discovered our "good teen" Alisha had been drinking away from home.

We grounded her, but as I looked at the root of her behavior, I thought, *she needs a purpose in life, God. She needs to see just how great it can be to serve you.* We had no idea how to help Christianity become real to her, and this verse became my prayer.

Then my kids and I spent a day helping some friends who run a Christian youth camp getting the camp ready. Without my prompting it, the directors invited Alisha to help at the children's camp. Two weeks later, she came home a changed person, ready to make her faith her own instead of following Jesus just because we did.

*When we don't know where to look for help,
we can start by looking to God.*

—JGL

Pregnant and Panic-Stricken

"... Do not lose heart or panic."
DEUTERONOMY 20:3

The pregnancy strip turned pink! Pushing forty, I cried angry tears, dreading number five!

My worried husband called my friend Debbie. "Please come over and calm Pam!"

With an armful of maternity clothes, Debbie appeared. I sobbed, "We have no maternity insurance." *God must be punishing me,* I thought.

God proved my notion false. Whenever I squawked about putting on more pounds or about impending dirty diapers and late-night feedings, Debbie swaddled me with encouragement and prayers. Her friendship was God's way of lavishing His love upon me. God also led me to a top-notch resident's clinic offering reduced fees. Hundreds apply, but only twenty new patients get selected each month. I was chosen!

Anna, now fourteen, constantly dispenses joy. Recently, she wowed me with a dozen yellow roses. "Mom," she bubbled, "I love blessing you!"

I'm learning that God loves blessing me, too—even in my shortcomings!

God's love shows no boundaries.

—PAMELA ENDERBY

A Little Bit of Growth

"For wisdom will enter your heart, and
knowledge will fill you with joy."
PROVERBS 2:10

"How about some scrambled eggs?" I asked Elizabeth as I pulled out the skillet.

"Mommy, I want to help," she demanded.

"No, Liz, you're too little."

But she was insistent. "You can't let a three-year-old help you make eggs," my logical mind insisted.

"Oh, why not try it?" another part of me said, even though I was mindful of messes.

Elizabeth had already pulled her chair up to the counter. And she wanted to be part of every stage. She cracked the eggs and gave them to me to break into the bowl. Then I taught her to gently stir the eggs and milk—she didn't even slosh them out of the pan! She loved adding salt and pepper. She even helped stir them while they were cooking, understanding that she needed to stay away from the burner. She did a great job—and I learned not to underestimate my kids!

The only way our kids grow in wisdom and knowledge
is by trying new things.

—JGL

A Gossip Betrays a Confidence!

"A gossip goes around revealing secrets, but those
who are trustworthy can keep a confidence."
PROVERBS 11:13

As Ola and I sat telling stories about our children, our laughter
rang through the house. We told each other tales of woe, discipline, and antics.

Suddenly, I saw a body flash through the door down the
hall. With all of our kids playing outside, I hadn't thought anything of our gab session. But I started to think about it when I
heard the hurt voice shouting, "I can hear you!"

Ola and I froze, giggling like schoolgirls caught doing
something wrong.

Ola whispered, "You should go to her. I will leave."

I sheepishly walked into Mikayla's room. She was sobbing.
"Mom, you tell us not to talk about people! Why are you allowed
to talk about us?" she asked.

Reproach gripped my heart as I realized I had betrayed
her confidence in me! "Oh God, forgive me!" I silently cried.
"Please help me guard her trust!"

Loose lips sometimes sink our children's hearts.

—TARA RYE

Focusing on Faith–Not Fear

". . . I know the one in whom I trust, and I
am sure that he is able to guard what I have
entrusted to him until the day of his return."
2 TIMOTHY 1:12

I was sick. Yet another man had kidnapped, raped, and killed a child. I felt overwhelmed with rage, grief, and especially fear.

Fear because our cute toddler draws a lot of attention every time we go into a store. And we live on a very busy corner, so I've been petrified someone would grab her if she even stepped outdoors.

As I fought waves of anxiety that day, I prayed, "Lord, I know hundreds of people who've raised children with no problems. I can't live in fear like this."

"Give her to me," God seemed to say.

"Lord, I can't," I cried. "She's my baby."

"She's mine, too," he replied.

I thought of 2 Timothy 1:12 and entrusted her to him that day. I still keep a careful eye on her. And I have to entrust her to him again sometimes. But I'm beginning to focus on his faithfulness instead of fear.

> *Real faith means putting our most*
> *precious treasures in God's hands.*

—JGL

Ten Little Words

"But Mary quietly treasured these things in her heart and
thought about them often."
LUKE 2:19

Skits and fun songs over, our pastor began a "What do you like
about children's camp?" discussion.

My nephew snuggled beside me, clearly enjoying his first
camp. Such a sharp contrast from his life before coming to
live with me! Adjustments hadn't been easy. Twenty-eight and
single, I'd suddenly become a substitute mother. Memories from
the past difficult year rushed over me: joys, yes, but interspersed
with so many heartaches.

God, give me strength to go on, my heart pleaded.

The pastor said, "I'm going to thank God now. You may,
too, if you like." He paused. "Thank you, Father, for the beautiful sunset over the Bay." A flood of childish sentence thank-
yous followed.

My nephew whispered his first public prayer: "Thank you,
Jesus, for letting me come here with Colleen."

I heard no more. God had used ten little words to show me
He would give whatever I needed to keep on keeping on. He
did—for ten more tumultuous years: years my nephew now says
were the best of his life.

> *God has special blessings that help*
> *Moms do the job. He has given them.*

—COLLEEN L. REECE

When a Child Is a Child

"It's like this: When I was a child, I spoke
and thought and reasoned as a child does. But
when I grew up, I put away childish things."
1 CORINTHIANS 13:11

"Wait a minute," I commanded as my eight-year-old son and I walked across the parking lot. I'd noticed a big glob of dirt right inside his ear.

He stopped and I flicked the dirt out of his ear with my fingernail. Gardner grabbed his ear and hollered like he was being scalped.

"For heaven's sake, stop acting like a child," I said.

He stopped his noise and turned to me.

"But, Mom, I am a child," he quietly explained.

There are other times when I need to remember my son is only a child. Like when he hasn't mastered certain virtues, such as self-control and patience. Or when I forget how fragile his emotions and self-image are. Sometimes I expect too much of him, forgetting that he's only been on this earth eight years. Our children are in a constant process of growth, but we need to remember, kids are still just kids.

Children aren't just miniature adults,
emotionally or in any other way.

—JGL

Prayer SOS

"Confess your sins to each other and pray for each other
so that you may be healed. The earnest prayer of a
righteous person has great power and wonderful results."
JAMES 5:16

I was feeling totally overwhelmed. I had way too much to do
and too little time to do it in. I was having work problems and
teen problems and health issues were wiping me out.

"What am I going to do?" I wondered as I sat at the computer. "There's no earthly way I can make it."

No, there was no human way, but I've always heard that
God delights in doing the impossible for us. Prayer was in
order.

Unfortunately, I didn't even feel like I could focus to pray.
But I remembered that I had praying friends. I sent an SOS
prayer request to a half-dozen people who'd prayed for me occasionally in times past. Immediately, they answered. They even
did a round-robin prayer for me using e-mail, with each writing a prayer and hitting "reply to all" so they were all praying
together. Before long, I began to feel God's power.

*Are you facing tough situations at home, at work, personally?
Send out an SOS for prayer.*

—JGL

Heavenly Acceptance

"How great is the love the Father has lavished on us,
that we should be called children of God."
1 JOHN 3:1

"I can't do this! It's not perfect! I'll never get this right!" my
seven-year-old son screamed, and threw his handwriting paper
on the floor.

How many times I've had those same anguished thoughts:
*God, I failed again. I lost my temper with the kids. I'm such a bad
parent. I'll never be perfect.*

But does God really expect us to be perfect?

When my son fell apart, I told him no one looks for perfection from him, but for growth in his life. I try to help him
accept himself and see the strengths God has given to him.

I love my son regardless of his ability to perform. Isn't that
how the heavenly Father loves us? He knows our potential and
will push us. He knows our weaknesses and will tutor us.

I need to forgive myself for my imperfections. God doesn't
expect or demand perfection. He loves me just because I'm His
child.

*God's arms aren't on His hips in condemnation
but rather outstretched in love.*

—STACY ROTHENBERGER

Enjoy the Journey!

"So don't worry about tomorrow, for tomorrow will bring
its own worries. Today's trouble is enough for today."
MATTHEW 6:34

Like a seasoned pilot, my husband ran through his final check-
list: "Luggage stowed?"

"Check."

"Snacks?"

"Check."

"Kids buckled in their seats?"

"Check, check, check!" chorused our three children. Daddy
announced, "We are cleared for takeoff."

Thus began our seven-day car trip. Before we hit the inter-
state, our five-year-old whined, "When're we gonna get there?"
My husband answered, "Estimated time of arrival for stop number one is twelve o'clock."

This announcement set off complaints. With their eyes
only on the final destination, our children would fail to enjoy
the journey and its wonders.

That's when the flight crew, aka Mom, stepped in to help
them focus on fun, songs, travel games, and mapping our progress.

I can't blame the kids for just wanting to get there. I do the
same thing as a mom. Often I fix my eyes on the next milestone
in my children's lives, instead of delighting in the trip of mothering opportunities.

Enjoy the journey of mothering, not just the destination.

—VICKI TIEDE

Serving a Banquet of Love

"He brings me to the banquet hall, so
everyone can see how much he loves me."
SONG OF SOLOMON 2:4

"What do you want for your birthday dinner?" Mom asked. She was a brilliant cook. And she liked to show us her love by using her skills to make a birthday banquet for us each year.

Usually I chose her mouth-watering meatloaf. My brother usually chose her crispy pan-fried chicken.

We always had birthday cake, too. Mom made these from scratch and she enjoyed figuring out how to decorate them to reflect our interests. One of my cakes was decorated like a stack of records. My brother's cakes included one shaped like a football. Dad got a bowling pin–shaped cake one year. When I got older, Mom even created a cake to look like a computer and keyboard.

My kids don't have it so well. I'm not a good cook. And I can't decorate a cake to save my life! But I can use my other skills to let them know they're special and I love them.

Every mom can find special ways to say "I love you."

—JGL

Empty or Full?

"For it was I, the Lord your God, who
rescued you from the land of Egypt. Open your
mouth wide, and I will fill it with good things."
PSALM 81:10

My car's temperamental gas gauge reads inconsistently. When I fill my tank, I can't ever tell how much gas I have because the red stick measures differently from one moment to the next. Sometimes I'm running on gas fumes, and I don't even realize it!

The gauge of motherhood measures that way, too—up one moment and down the next. We're up when we have time for bubble baths, a good book, or lattes with a friend. We're down when we face fatigue. And fatigue looks like an insurmountable mountain of laundry, tastes like leftovers, sounds like self-absorbed children bickering, smells like another dirty diaper, and feels like just another day of motherhood.

God may not rescue us from the "land of laundry," but He promises to fill our motherhood tank daily so our gauge always reads full. We just need to ask—and then open our hearts wide.

We weren't meant to run on spiritual fumes.

—JAMIE BIRR

Respect and a Bit of Grace

"For the Lord God is our sun and our shield.
He gives us grace and glory. The Lord will withhold
no good thing from those who do what is right."
PSALM 84:11

I shared with my friend, Heidi, a painful event in my life. I told her I felt I had let my family down for leaving a great paying job for one with less compensation. Heidi knew I had been struggling with a verbally abusive boss.

Rather than sympathizing with me, Heidi remarked that I was setting a great example for my six-year-old daughter. I didn't understand. How could quitting my job and putting my family's finances in jeopardy be a great example?

Heidi explained that by having the courage and integrity to stop allowing myself to be mistreated I was showing my daughter it is okay to expect respect. Heidi helped me remember that we are made in His image and each of us deserves to be respected. I was looking for a pity party. Instead God, and Heidi, gave me grace.

Our kids will value themselves the way we value ourselves.

—SUSAN KNEIB SCHANK

JULY

MOTHERHOOD: NOT FOR WIMPS

"Yet I am confident that I will see the Lord's goodness
while I am here in the land of the living."

PSALM 27:13

When I was a little girl, I often left my tea parties and dollies at home for days at a time to trek through the wilderness with my family. My father was an adventurer, and though he fathered three girls before his little boy was born, he was determined to teach his family the way of the woods. My mother and two sisters and I, and later, our little brother, trekked through some of the same areas where my father hunted big game such as elk, deer, bear, and even a record-sized cougar.

Our survival on these trips depended upon our ability to ride horses, hike for long distances, carry packs, and be quiet when we felt like complaining. I don't remember the first time my dad told me the words "Be tough, be brave." Probably after I fell off the back of a horse or slipped down a little gully as we hiked. But I heard the words a lot through my growing-up years, and it wasn't until I was a mother that I realized their significance.

In my mind, my life contained two separate parts: the soft part and the hard part. The soft part was at home, "playing mommy" and having tea parties—an essential skill for mothering to be sure. The hard part was going out into the "real world" and showing how tough I could be. (I didn't realize at the time that the woods are not a part of the "real world" any more than tea parties are!) Both parts came together when it was time to become a real mom.

When my first son arrived four and a half years into my marriage, I still thought my tea-party-mothering philosophy would work. My son's strong will proved otherwise. Our tea parties were a bust.

Two years later, I became pregnant again. When we went for the sonogram that would tell us whether to prepare for a girl or a boy, the sonographer puzzled for a long time. She turned the screen slightly away from my husband and me and little two-year-old Seth, who had come to "see the baby on TV."

"The doctor will come in and take a look. She'll be in after a few minutes."

For a moment, I didn't realize that something was wrong.

"Is it a girl or a boy?" I asked.

"I can't tell," she said. "There is no amniotic fluid around the baby. I can't tell what's what."

I am an RN, but still the reality escaped me. "What does this mean?"

"You'll need to talk to Dr. K."

Within that hour, our doctor gave us the news that the baby I had carried for eighteen weeks held very little chance of survival, and sent us for an immediate visit with some obstetricians specializing in high-risk pregnancies. We sat in their office and cried as they gave us the news.

"You have a one-in-ten chance of having this baby alive. Not a normal baby, any baby."

Be tough, be brave.

Long days and nights in the OB ward followed.

A card hung over my bed. It said, "Look to God, and praise Him with me now, that He will know we worship Him not for our circumstances, but for who He is."

Thirteen weeks before his due date, Mark came into the world. He cried. So did everyone else. My mom was there, telling me in her own way that now was just the beginning of the tough times—and telling me to be strong.

Baby Mark was transported to a children's hospital while I remained in the hospital where I'd given birth. That night, the children's hospital called to tell us Mark was dying. Because my hospital wouldn't discharge me in the middle of the night, my husband went to our baby alone, while I whispered screams to God.

"Save my baby, Lord! You brought us all this way. I beg of you, save him!"

God carried Mark through that night, and many more nights when his life hung in the balance.

One day, we brought Mark home. Eventually, we weaned him from the monitors, oxygen, and therapy. I held to 1 Peter 1:7 through all of this. Part of it says, "These trials are only to test your faith, to show that it is strong and pure." I found new ways to apply "Be tough, be brave." The daily work of kindness and gentleness replaced the survival mode we had come to accept.

And then, I discovered that I would have another baby—almost exactly on Mark's third birthday. What a relief when everything progressed normally after our previous trials. We finally enjoyed tea parties and long stories in the rocking chair and walks through the neighborhood. The week I was due with our third son, we celebrated Mark's birthday, and I blocked half of the camera shots with my big belly.

A couple of nights later I awoke in the dark. I was bleeding. The next three days followed in a blur. A rush to the hospital. A crying doctor. No crying baby. Relatives and loved ones. A sweet little boy's face in a tiny casket. A funeral.

Mom and Dad came from their home in the mountains. We didn't talk much, but Dad looked me in the eye and squeezed my shoulders in a way that I knew exactly what he meant. *Be tough, be brave.* More trials, more strength, more purity, according to 1 Peter 1:7. The words were difficult to accept in those early days after our loss. But one day I found Psalm 27:13: "Yet I am confident that I will see the Lord's goodness while I am here in the land of the living." The verse confirmed for me that bravery was not just for special occasions, and not only for wilderness times. God's goodness would provide the source of the strength I needed to continue as a good mom each day.

Today my house is full. I have two living boys, and two little girls. We fish, hike, and have tea parties. Some days take more bravery than others. But I rejoice knowing that the trials came, and will come, to teach me what I needed to know about motherhood all along. His jobs are not for the faint of heart. Be tough, be brave, not for your own glory but for God's. Beyond the wilderness, a tea party awaits.

—ANITA LYNN RAMSEY

On the Road Again

"We prayed that he would give us a safe journey and
protect us, our children, and our goods as we traveled."
EZRA 8:21

Summertime! Like many Americans, we hit the road every
summer to travel halfway around the country (in different
directions) to visit grandparents and get my stepdaughter to her
maternal family's house. My husband and I sometimes attend
a professional convention together in the summer—and make
a family trip out of it. And once in a while we go somewhere
just to be tourists!

Summertime isn't our only travel time; our family tends to
travel more than most. But somewhere along one of these journeys, we've started a simple family tradition. Before, or right
after, Dad pulls the car out of the driveway, we pray together.
We pray for safety on the journey, for rest at the destination, for
our kids as they tolerate ten- to twenty-two-hour drives, for the
people we're going to see or business we're doing, and we even
ask the Lord to bless us with relaxation and fun.

*This summer, as you head out, don't forget
to ask the Lord to ride or fly with you!*

—JGL

Managing a Joy-Filled Home

"Give me happiness, O Lord, for my life depends on you."
PSALM 86:4

Much of life with my eight-year-old son is spent in our car, or with me as his task manager. He dutifully checks off daily chores and completes homework before running outside to play with neighborhood buddies. He rarely asks me to play tennis with him anymore or even to spend time with him.

One summer evening he asked me to walk to the park to play tennis. I readily agreed. Ten minutes into our game, he said, "Mom, you look really happy. Like a girl or something."

I laughed and told him I felt like a girl. It was good to play with him. This was the most joy-filled moment we'd had together in quite a while.

Too often I let days pass by without finding time to play with my children. I'm too busy managing their tasks and obligations. But you know the old saying, "The family that plays together stays together!"

Manage to find playful, joyous moments
each day with your children.

—HEIDI SHELTON-JENCK

In Search of Independence

"For you have been called to live in freedom—
not freedom to satisfy your sinful nature, but
freedom to serve one another in love."
GALATIANS 5:13

My oldest stepdaughter was the Patrick Henry of our family. "Give me liberty or give me death!" seemed to be her motto. I tried to teach her that responsibility brings added freedom, but she still felt squelched and couldn't wait until she turned eighteen and was a legal adult.

She was still in high school when the big eighteen arrived. A couple of days later, she was bewildered. "But I don't feel any different. Nothing's changed," she moaned.

A week after that, she left home in search of that freedom.

From that experience, I learned to keep aware of my kids' need for independence. From the cradle on, they seek to find their own way—otherwise, they'd never grow up! Part of the way I can serve my children in love is to not only respect that need, but to also help my children meet that need at their different ages and life stages.

Independence is a gradual process we can
help our children walk through.

—JGL

Land That We Love

"Then if my people who are called by my name will
humble themselves and pray and seek my face and turn
from their wicked ways, I will hear from heaven and will
forgive their sins and heal their land."

2 CHRONICLES 7:14

I wonder who first said, "Why should we serve a king who's in
another country and doesn't even know what's going on here?"

Someone had to say it for the first time, even if several
thought it. Perhaps a colonial dad mulled over the thought
with his kids. Then perhaps he talked to a neighbor or friend,
and his kids said something to their friends. Next thing you
know, most of a whole new country is up in arms, clamoring
for freedom.

And aren't we thankful!

It only takes one person praying, talking, and working to
eventually start a revolution and change a whole country.

Are you talking with your family about our country? Are
you teaching them to pray for government leaders—whether or
not you agree with them? And, of course, prayer and works go
hand in hand. Who knows what kind of revolution could begin
with your family!

*We can teach our children to be good citizens by
teaching them to pray for and care about our nation.*

—JGL

Stones of Remembrance

> "In the future, your children will ask, 'What do these
> stones mean to you?' Then you can tell them..."
> JOSHUA 4:6–7

I've been fascinated with stones since I found my first agate. I have some nice fossils, agates, petrified wood, and more. I also have an ordinary stone that stands out above the others. It is not worth much money but is precious to me and is always on display.

During my daughter's teenage years, when she seemed a bit wobbly in her faith, our family enjoyed a day at a beautiful creek. We spent the afternoon getting wet, eating, and playing tag. But the best part came the next day. She gave me a flat stone from the creek on which she had written the Ten Commandments. It was her way of saying, "I remember what I've been taught. I'm making my own decisions, and I will choose how I will live, but I remember."

After that, whenever I was concerned about her, I had my "stone of remembrance."

> *Look for the stones of remembrance,*
> *which can encourage as well as instruct.*

—MERILYN MILLIKAN

Youthful Words of Faith

"Don't let anyone think less of you because you are young.
Be an example to all believers in what you teach, in the
way you live, in your love, your faith, and your purity."
1 TIMOTHY 4:12

I didn't want to discourage my stepdaughter, but while we drove across town, I had to tell her, "Your dad's really concerned about whether we can afford one of these colleges you're looking at." We talked for a few minutes and then she said naturally, "Well, if God leads me there, I guess he'll provide somehow."

I nearly wrecked the car. She'd never really expressed her faith as a strong part of her everyday life. I knew she'd recommitted her life to Christ, but wow! This was a big change!

In the following weeks, several times my stepdaughter spoke firm words of faith. And even more surprising than hearing the words come out of her mouth was their effect on me. For a while I'd been just coasting in my own spiritual walk. Before long I was being encouraged and challenged by this faith-filled seventeen-year-old myself.

Go ahead—show your kids 1 Timothy 4:12 and let your kids be a spiritual encouragement to you, and thank them for it.

—JGL

Pats of Encouragement

"They encourage one another
with the words, 'Be strong!'"
ISAIAH 41:6

What am I doing? I wondered as our burgundy Toyota wagon sat in unmoving beach traffic.

I'd just spent a week with my fiancé, his children, and his extended family. It was a whole new world for me, and I'd enjoyed the fun of the beach home his family rented every year. But I'd also felt a bit overwhelmed by my fiancé's brilliant siblings and his two young children.

Am I making the right choice by getting married? I wondered. I turned my head to look out the window so Mark wouldn't see the confused tears sliding down my cheeks.

Just then, a tiny hand reached up from behind and comfortingly patted my shoulder, as if to remind me that I wouldn't be in this alone. Not only would God help me adjust, but my stepchildren would, too. We'd all adjust together—and ten years later, we're still giving each other pats and words of comfort and love.

*Thank goodness that God gives us encouragement
from our families.*

—JGL

Celebrate the Dance of Life!

"You have turned my mourning into joyful dancing. You have taken away my clothes of mourning and clothed me with joy, that I might sing praises to you and not be silent. O Lord my God, I will give you thanks forever!"
PSALM 30:11–12

The cabin doors opened, spilling campers into the field to search for waiting parents. It had been a long week of separation. My heart raced as I spotted my daughter and waved. She dashed toward me. Our embrace turned to a dance of joy celebrating our reunion. The two-hour ride home was filled with her eagerly telling me stories about new friends, swimming, hiking, crafts, and the camp food. I treasured her every word. We laughed as we sang old camp songs together off key. What a gift it was to have her with me again. I missed her so.

The Lord's arms are always open to each of his children. His ears are ready to hear our stories. If we stray from him he is overjoyed to welcome us home, saying, "I have missed you, my dear child."

Take time to celebrate life . . . your life!

—VIOLA RUELKE GOMMER

The Game of Encouragement

"So encourage each other and build each
other up, just as you are already doing."
1 THESSALONIANS 5:11

"Mommy, I got sixty thousand points!" my son cried. I was talking with his father, so it took me a minute to focus. But then I realized he'd been playing our vintage pinball game, which he's finally tall enough to operate.

"Whoa! I don't know if I've ever gotten that high!" I said. "Here, let's play together and see who gets the highest score."

He was, of course, game for the competition. I pulled the release and started flipping the flappers on the machine. *Ding! Ding!* My score was climbing perilously close to his record.

He started shouting—I assumed he was shouting in grief that I was catching up to him. But no, I listened to the words: "Way to go, Mommy! Keep it up!"

My competition-loving son was more interested in seeing me do my best than in being able to brag that he beat Mommy. Wow! What a lesson for all of us!

When we cheer each other on, we're all winners!

—JGL

Fin Chagrin

"The horses are prepared for battle,
but the victory belongs to the Lord."
PROVERBS 21:31

Five minutes before swim practice, my daughter started crying. "I forgot my fins!"

I assured her, "I'll zip home and get them for you."

So while she dipped, I zipped over four sets of railroad tracks and 157 potholes. Screeching into my driveway fifteen minutes later, I grabbed her fins, and then reversed the whole process back to the pool.

The maddening part was, after all my effort, the actual using of the fins lay in the coach's hands. And coach never did use them that practice.

My escapade reminds me of Proverbs 21:31. Like getting horses prepared for battle, we pray for our children and otherwise do all we can to equip them to face the world. But their success lies in God's hands. Ultimately, God carries them through each circumstance. Our preparation, His victory.

Actually, it's not a bad deal. At least there aren't any railroad tracks to cross.

Be prepared, but trust God for the victory.

—LORI Z. SCOTT

Becoming a "Why"s Mother
Experiences, Experiences!

"It is good for people to eat, drink, and enjoy their work
under the sun during the short life God has given them."
Ecclesiastes 5:18

"That cost less than ten dollars," my husband announced as he
slammed the car hood.

"You're good, honey!" I told him.

"Well, I'd never have thought I could fix it if you hadn't
suggested it," he said. But he still swelled a bit with pride over
learning to do the simple car-maintenance task himself instead
of hiring a mechanic.

When Mark was growing up, he wasn't encouraged to
think he could fix anything, so I encourage him and praise him
in this area.

This has also taught me to encourage our kids to try to fix
things with their hands. Our teen daughter is getting pretty
good at using tools, and our elementary-age son is already
finding satisfaction in completing manual tasks. It's not just a
matter of being mechanically minded; it's a matter of helping
them learn to *try* new things instead of assuming they can't do
something.

One of our joys can be guiding our kids
to try new experiences.

—JGL

My Son's Forgiveness

"Where is another God like you, who pardons
the sins of the survivors among his people? You
cannot stay angry with your people forever,
because you delight in showing mercy."
—MICAH 7:18

"Where's my Boy Scout cot?" My teenage son asked me. He dug
through the closet, but he couldn't find his green canvas cot.

"Here it is." I pulled out what I thought was the cot. It was
green canvas on a metal frame, and at first glance it looked like
the Boy Scout cot. I handed it to my son and he shook his head.
We unfolded it and discovered this canvas contraption was a
piece of exercise equipment that had belonged to my mother-
in-law.

Then the truth hit me. I had intended to donate the exercise equipment to a charity auction, but I apparently gave away
the wrong thing. Now my son's cot was gone.

My son had every right to be upset over my careless mis-
take. But instead of being angry, he said, "It's all right, Mom."

*Mothers make mistakes—what a blessing it is to
hear their children say, "It's all right, Mom."*

—LeAnn Campbell

Outnumbered, Outsmarted, and Overwhelmed

"Trust in the Lord with all your heart; do not
depend on your own understanding. Seek his
will in all you do, and he will direct your paths."
PROVERBS 3:5–6

I became the mother of four boys, all born within the first six years of my marriage. With toddlers, life was hectic, but I stayed in control.

It changed in prepuberty years. My darlings drove me to distraction. If I reprimanded one boy for mischief, the other three would burst in with a crisis like, "Mom, we were playing with the magnifying glass in the backyard and now the grass is on fire!"

After the emergency, the boy was gone, and I forgot why I was scolding him. I was outsmarted—*again*! It happened too often. I felt overwhelmed.

Finally, I cried, "Lord, my kids are getting away with murder. Please help me get back in control."

Proverbs 3:5–6 popped into my head. I repeated it every day. Things changed. Together, *God* and I outnumbered and outsmarted my mischievous sons, and they have become fine, responsible young men. Thanks be to God!

When we earnestly ask the Lord for help,
He never lets us down.

—DIANA L. JAMES

Bringing Forth Life!

"Encourage those who are timid. Take tender care of
those who are weak. Be patient with everyone."
1 THESSALONIANS 5:14

My older teenage son approached me with an adventurous summer vision—to climb a dangerous mountain, gallivant around
Europe, and camp for a week in the Oregon wilderness. I could
have "slammed on the brakes" and screamed "No!"; instead,
I felt honored that he trusted me with his "crazy-ideas" and
brought them to God in prayer.

As moms, we can develop a child's desires . . . or destroy
them; we can encourage a God-given purpose . . . or pinpoint
all the ways an idea will never work. We can be a child's greatest coach and cheerleader . . . or a most-daunting opponent. As
women, we birth babies and nurture children; and we also have
a soul designed to "bring-forth-life" and to "nurture" dreams.

My son reached that mountaintop, wore out a EuroRail
pass and brought home some fabulous photos. And best of all,
he's eagerly fulfilling God's plans, too!

With God's help, let's bring forth life.

—ANN DUNAGAN

Take Care!

"For the whole law can be summed up in this one
command: 'Love your neighbor as yourself.'"
GALATIANS 5:14

When my child was born, one of my clients sent a gift—but
unlike most people who gave clothes and baby items, this was a
different kind of gift. It was a mom's care package—wonderful
soaps, lotions, and other items for me to use to pamper myself.
My client knew that when moms feel good, they take good care
of their kids.

Several scriptures tell us to love our neighbors as ourselves.
People interpret this differently. "To love neighbors as ourselves
means we gotta love ourselves first" some chant. Others counter, "Loving ourselves is not usually a problem. We need to just
focus on others."

Moms are usually too busy taking care of their kids to
debate the issue! As we express love for our kids every day, we
also need to remember: we have more energy to pour love into
our kids if we take care of ourselves.

*Moms need to take care of themselves
to keep those love tanks filled!*

—JGL

Waiting for Rescue

"You are my strength; I wait for you to rescue me,
for you, O God, are my place of safety."
PSALM 59:9

"Thank you," I said to the lifeguard. As I sat in the warm sand at Hanauma Bay, my body shook.

While I snorkeled near the beach, I grew distracted at the beauty and moved beyond the safe area. As I surfaced, large waves sucked me into their grip. I choked on the salty water. I was exhausted and tempted to give up. But then the lifeguard rescued me.

On the airplane ride home, I thought about another life-threatening problem—my son's battle with alcohol addiction. I couldn't rescue him, but I knew the One who could.

As we call out to God for others, He sees their need and is ready to rescue them and move them to the safety of His care. That's exactly what He did for my son. It's been nearly five years since he chose to reach out and accept the hand of rescue that God so freely offers to all.

With God's rescue comes a place of safety.

—CHARLOTTE KARDOKUS

Praying Like a Mantis

> "Pray at all times and on every occasion in the power
> of the Holy Spirit. Stay alert and be persistent in your
> prayers for all Christians everywhere."
> EPHESIANS 6:18

It was the biggest praying mantis we had ever seen! My son found it in our backyard and placed it in a large bug jar. Our family studied it throughout the afternoon. It appeared to be studying us in return! "Why is he always praying?" my daughter asked. I explained that the insect is called a praying mantis because it usually holds its front legs as if praying. Another of my children responded, "Oh, he's just making sure he is always ready to pray."

We set the praying mantis free later that day, but the lesson of his "praying" stayed with me. Throughout the joys and struggles of parenting, this incident reminded us to always be ready to pray. I offer my heavenly Father thanksgiving, and ask for wisdom and strength through my prayers. He, in return, is always ready to listen and to supply everything I need.

> *What better approach to parenting
> than to pray like a mantis?*

—JERI REDMAN

What's in Your Mouth?

"And I have put my words in your mouth. . . ."
ISAIAH 51:16

As Elizabeth looked up, puddles formed in her blue eyes. Then her face scrunched up and she began to cry.

"I'm sorry, baby," I said, biting my lip and wishing I'd bitten my tongue. I picked her up and held her close.

"Scary, Mommy," she sobbed.

"I scared you by yelling at you?" I asked. She rubbed her teary eyes and nodded.

We all have our weaknesses, but mine is certainly my mouth. Sarcasm. Anger. Criticism. Harshness. And in this case, yelling instead of instructing.

There may not be an antidote for poisonous words, but perhaps Isaiah 51:16 has a vaccination to prevent runaway mouth disease: "And I have put my words in your mouth. . . ."

Perhaps those of us whose Achilles' heel rests in our mouths need to start each day with a specific prayer: "Lord, please put your words in my mouth today so I only speak as you'd speak."

If we ask God to put his words in our mouths more, maybe we'll have a foot in our mouths less.

—JGL

Grow Deep

"But I am like a green olive tree thriving in the house of
God. I trust in God's unfailing love forever and ever."
PSALM 52:8

My four-year-old son planted an apple seed in the shadow of
my neighbor's apple tree. Though he tended it devotedly, the
tree was sickly from the beginning. It put all its energy into
growing tall.

When Erik came to me with a pained look, I knew the tree
had died. I told him to imagine it looking up at the big apple
tree and saying, "That is what I am. I'm going to grow big and
make apples just like that tree." So it used its strength to grow
up and neglected the strength it needed to grow in and down.
It neglected its roots.

"Do I have roots?" he asked.

"Inside you. You need to learn and grow from the inside, so
you can grow big and strong outside."

Satisfied, Erik asked for an apple. Another seed would go
in the ground soon. My boy's roots were growing.

Dig your roots deep in God and allow him to nourish you.

—SUSAN LYTTEK

Flying Lessons

"Like an eagle that rouses her chicks and
hovers over her young, so he spread his wings to
take them in and carried them aloft on his pinions."
DEUTERONOMY 32:11

"Mama, what's she doing?" Olivia asked. We had watched this eagle tend her young one for weeks, bringing him bits of meat in her talons. Now she gave a shrill cry and swooped over her nest.

"I think her baby is about to get the ride of his life!" I told her.

The eaglet climbed onto his mother's wing and held on with tiny talons. Soon, his mother fluttered her wings, flipped upside down, and shook him loose, dropping her young one onto an air current.

"Oh, no!" Olivia cried. "He's gonna die!"

The mother circled her panicky fledgling, caught him on her wing, and began the process again. Over several weeks, he became strong enough to stay aloft.

God does the same for His people! He asks that we step out in faith and hold firmly to His promises, even when things look impossible. When we trust Him, we will soar!

The Lord provides for us and watches over us like a mother eagle, and He will never let us fall.

—SUSAN ESTRIBOU RAMSDEN

Reconciliation Begins at Home

"So if you are standing before the altar in the Temple,
offering a sacrifice to God, and you suddenly remember
that someone has something against you, leave your
sacrifice there beside the altar. Go and be reconciled to
that person. Then come and offer your sacrifice to God."
MATTHEW 5:23–24

"I asked our youth pastor to invite Meghan to church this week,"
Allison told me. Allison and her teen, Meghan, had fought,
and Meghan had moved in with her dad. Months later, Allison
was still upset over Meghan's words and hadn't talked to her.
But now Allison's church was having a special teen night.

"Allison, it's not the youth pastor's responsibility," I gently
pointed out. "Why don't you call Meghan."

"But her words were so unacceptable!" Allison said. "And
she's never cared to call me, her own mother."

"Yeah, but she's a kid," I reminded Allison. "She doesn't
know how to apologize. She needs you to show her how to
mend broken relationships."

Allison eventually called Meghan and the two cried
together and made up. Now you'd hardly ever guess that they
had spent months not talking together.

*Sometimes reconciliation begins at home—even while our
children are still in our homes.*

—JGL

A Snake in the Garden

"Now the serpent was the shrewdest of all
the creatures the Lord God had made. 'Really?'
he asked the woman. 'Did God really say you
must not eat any of the fruit in the garden?'"
GENESIS 3:1

If I vacuum it, within minutes it is littered with Legos, leaves, and Cheerios.

If I cook it, an instant later it will vanish. If I wash it, it won't stay clean for long. I live in a house of growing boys.

It seems there's a snake in my garden. His name is Discontent. He rears his head and whispers, "You're unappreciated. Why bother?" If I listen, his poison seeps into my home and stifles joy.

But the antidote is as simple as an old song. I count my blessings. I name them one by one: health, home, husband, and children.

My work, repetitive though it may be, is not unnoticed. The dandelion bouquet on my kitchen table is a tribute to the cookies I baked. A crayon drawing on the refrigerator depicts me wearing a crown, surrounded by hearts. My kindergartner thinks I'm a queen!

The serpent, silenced, slithers away.

Have you checked your garden for snakes lately?

—CINDY HVAL

Memory Prompts

"The tassels will help you remember that you must obey
all my commands and be holy to your God."
NUMBERS 15:40

Can you imagine models in *GQ* or *Elle* or other fashion magazines wearing tassels on their clothes? But tassels were all the
rage in Israelite households. Why? People wore blue tassels to
remind them to obey God.

Can you imagine trying to get your Christian teen to wear
something with *tassels* on it?

But the basic idea is sound—visual items can often serve
as reminders for us, like people who tie strings on their fingers
to help them remember something.

My visual memory method is hanging scripture artwork
in my house. My goal is not only for the photos or plaques to
remind me of truths about God, but also for them to help my
children naturally learn the scripture verses on the artwork.

You may not want to wear tassels, but consider using visu-
als to teach God's truths to your kids.

*Anything that prompts us to think of
God is good to have around!*

—JGL

The Power of a Popsicle

"Yes, you will be enriched so that you can give even more generously. And when we take your gifts to those who need them, they will break out in thanksgiving to God."
2 CORINTHIANS 9:11

Just outside the supermarket, I struggled to place my toddler in the cart. "Mommy," she sobbed, trying to wrap her legs around my pregnant belly.

"I know you're tired," I begged. "But I can't hold you."

I started to panic. Our church youth group was arriving at my home any minute; I had to finish shopping.

A woman walking past stopped.

"Here," she said, smiling and ripping open a box of Popsicles. "This should help." Gratefully, I handed the treat to my daughter, thanking God for this unexpected provision.

As moms, sometimes our only interactions take place at grocery stores, gas stations, or within our own homes. That day, I was reminded that I don't have to work in a soup kitchen or relief organization to bless others. Sometimes the smallest acts of kindness—a smile, holding open a door, or even sharing a Popsicle—can result in thanksgiving to God.

How can you share God's blessings to you
with someone else in need?

—KATHERINE CRADDOCK

A Tomato Tornado

"Then he stood up and rebuked the wind
and waves, and suddenly all was calm."
MATTHEW 8:26

Out my kitchen window, I saw the sky turning an ugly black-green color. The huge sycamore trees in the backyard bent at alarming angles.

"Timothy, Ben, come on *now!*" I yelled as tornado sirens started screaming.

We scrambled for the basement.

As I turned on the television, my three-year-old son asked, "What's happening, Mom? Is a tomato going to hit our house?"

I stopped and looked at my sweet child. "No, honey, a tomato is not going to hit our house."

How funny, in the middle of this storm, I imagined a big, ripe, red tomato falling from heaven. I started laughing, and felt a peace in my spirit. "We'll be OK, Ben, God's here."

Perhaps you are experiencing a storm in your life right now. Perhaps you're bent in an uncomfortable angle. Perhaps the sky seems dark. Remember Jesus. Now focus again on the last words of this verse: "All was calm."

*In our life storms, this is who Jesus is. Peace, protection,
complete calm.*

—JENNIFER WHYMAN

Who's on Your Prayer List?

"Rise during the night and cry out. Pour out
your hearts like water to the Lord. Lift up your
hands to him in prayer. Plead for your children
as they faint with hunger in the streets."
LAMENTATIONS 2:19

My friend Rhonda works with special needs teens in a public
school, and she considers this position a huge privilege. "Some
kids in my class will do well in society," she explained to me,
"but for some of them, this is as good as it gets."

But once a child is in Rhonda's classroom, he or she is not
only in Rhonda's heart, but is also on her prayer list. "Some of
them come from really tough situations," she said. "Every child
deserves to have someone pray for them. So if these kids don't
have anyone else praying for them, at least they have me."

Rhonda's words made me stop and think: how many chil-
dren's names are on *my* prayer list? I regularly pray for my kids, but
what about their friends from school? What about the neighborhood kids who ring our doorbell at midnight and run? How about
the teens who regularly serve us at our favorite restaurants?

Perhaps the best way we can affect our world
is to pray for children we encounter.

—JGL

The Favorite Parent

"Honor your father and mother. Then you will live a long,
full life in the land the Lord your God will give you."
EXODUS 20:12

"I love you Mommy, but I love Daddy more," my son explained.

I smiled. His words didn't bother me at all or cause one
twinge of jealousy. For one thing, I knew he was likely to
change his "favorite parent status" in a few hours or the next
day. "Favorite parent" is a title that is gone with a whim.

I'm pleased when my son loves his father. His words told
me I was doing a good job in at least one thing: teaching my
children to love and respect their father.

Part of respect is something that is just learned as our children grow up with us. But another part can definitely be taught
by our supporting our spouse in his dealings with the kids, and
by saying good things about him and letting the kids know why
we respect their father.

When we teach our kids to honor their dad,
some of that respect also falls back on us.

—JGL

Multitasking

> "Put on salvation as your helmet and take the
> sword of the Spirit, which is the word of God."
> EPHESIANS 6:17

Millinery. You don't hear that word often. Moms wear a variety of hats. One of my favorite hats is the chef's toque. We express our love by feeding friends and family. The sunbonnet we wear as the gardener. Blooms and vegetables reward our efforts. The sports cap we wear as coach and cheering section for the T-ball superstars and soccer players. The pillbox hat we wear as homemakers. We scrapbook and clean. The ten-gallon hat we wear as we ride out to defend the accused offspring. The hard hat we wear as we enter the career building. We dodge debris as we clamber up the corporate ladder. The tiara we wear as the romantic partner of our prince charming. Not always riding the white horse, he rescues the damsel-in-distress just the same.

The most important hat we wear is God's helmet of salvation. As God's warriors we achieve ultimate success.

Our greatest value comes through our relationship with God.

—SUSAN PARIS

A Short Chapter

> " Enjoy what you have rather than
> desiring what you don't have."
> ECCLESIASTES 6:9

"I'm glad that stage is over," the man said to the young couple walking into the restaurant. The father carried a baby in a bulky car seat while the mother struggled with an equally large diaper bag.

I watched the scene, thinking how soon that stage would end. How often had I said the same thing? One more dirty diaper, another sleepless night, more money spent at the doctor's office, or another intimate moment with my husband interrupted by a wailing child. How could someone so little require so much sacrifice?

"It's a chapter in your life," my mother would say, her face filled with understanding.

I looked at the infant in the carrier. My oldest had just finished kindergarten and my baby would soon start preschool. A lump formed in my throat.

"Don't say that." The young mother frowned at the man.

Yes, I nodded. The chapter's too short.

When we realize how quickly chapters are over, it changes our whole perspective.

—ANGELA WELCH PRUSIA

God's Smallest Tools

"The leading priests and the teachers of religious law saw these wonderful miracles and heard even the little children in the Temple shouting, 'Praise God for the Son of David.' But they were indignant and asked Jesus, 'Do you hear what these children are saying?'

"'Yes,' Jesus replied. 'Haven't you ever read the Scriptures? For they say, 'You have taught children and infants to give you praise.'"

MATTHEW 21:15–16

In *Lighten Up!* author and comedian Ken Davis tells about the first well-paying secular convention he was booked to speak at. By the time he was called to the platform, half the audience was plastered. He didn't know how he'd regain control. But then his toddler saw him on the stage and ran to him. She begged to sing into the mic and the patrons called for him to let her. Not knowing what else to do, Davis held his little one while she sang, "Jesus loves me."

After his daughter went back to her mother, Davis delivered his speech and it was well received. After the session, people flocked to him. However, they didn't want to talk about his speech, they wanted to tell him about their experiences in Sunday school and church.

Never underestimate the power of a child's praise.

—JGL

Prints of Peace

> "Don't be concerned about the outward
> beauty that depends on fancy hairstyles,
> expensive jewelry, or beautiful clothes."
> I Peter 3:3

While in the grocery checkout line, I glanced down to discover that my smart outfit of earlier hours was a canvas of color! There was a peanut butter smear here, a milk mustache print there, a bit of finger paint there!

For a moment, I was embarrassed that I'd forgotten to check my appearance before leaving the house. But then I thought, *Well, at least people know I am not neglecting my children!*

And I had to laugh. I was messy because I spent time with my children, being close to them. They had rubbed off on me! Literally.

In the same way, I bear the fingerprints of God when I spend time with Him every day. The company I keep will show. Inner peace will produce outer beauty that no clothing or cosmetics company can come close to promising!

Are you wearing the prints of peace?

—Sheila Soule

AUGUST

DIFFERENT STROKES
FOR DIFFERENT FOLKS . . .
AND THAT'S OKAY!

"Thank you for making me so wonderfully complex!
Your workmanship is marvelous—and how well I know it."

PSALM 139:13–14

*B*elow the beautifully adorned wreath on the door of the palatial home, the mat read, "Welcome."

"Welcome couldn't have been further from the truth," shared Melody. "Mother led the charge as a powerful CEO at work—and at home. The mat should have read, 'Welcome to boot camp,'" Melody insisted.

Melody, on the other hand, preferred a quiet, laid-back home environment where she could spend time relaxing and enjoying her art projects. From the time she could hold a crayon, Melody's dream was to create pictures displaying beautiful flowers, trees, or sunsets in a multitude of colors. She always requested paints and brushes for her birthdays, but seldom received such "frivolous" gifts.

"How can that help you succeed in this world?" her mother would ask, not expecting an answer.

Growing up, Melody never wanted to go home after school, choosing instead to hang out at her friend Lynette's house. Lynette's mom greeted the girls with snacks, eager to hear about their day, and helped with homework.

Melody's mom, Rhonda, on the other hand, greeted her with a list of things to accomplish. Melody ached for a home where she felt safe, loved, and appreciated. She often cried herself to sleep at night, feeling inadequate, awash in low self-esteem. As the years progressed, Melody found creative ways to avoid her mom. The relationship fell apart by the time Melody went to college. "I didn't understand her and she didn't understand me. So we left it that way, rarely speaking," she confessed.

How can we give birth, feed, and raise children in the same house, yet be so different from each other? So many moms, so many kids, so many differences! But God uniquely designed each child for each mom. You and your child were purposely created for each other, regardless if birth or paperwork brought you together.

God is the Creator—and He is also the Provider. And He didn't hesitate to provide us with the tools to understand each other. The Bible is full of wisdom and guidance. Countless books offer immeasurable advice. Classes, friends, counselors, and Web sites help. So how can we communicate with love, compassion, and understanding amid so many misunderstandings?

After all, when a child feels understood, a child feels loved. But moms don't always demonstrate love in a way that our child recognizes.

Feeding them, clothing them, and making sure they have shelter are good choices. But giving them opportunities to thrive and feel loved and accepted for who they are will propel them into successful journeys in this life. That will also bring them through the front door again (and not just to raid the refrigerator).

We get one opportunity at this motherhood job, which came without directions. So what kind of relationships are you building in your home? Besides their favorite song, food, or friend, do you know your child's personality style; his or her dreams; and how to handle conflict, to discipline, and to motivate accordingly? There are four primary personality styles and numerous potential blends of the four styles—therefore, there are numerous potential conflicts.

When Melody's mom, Rhonda, learned that different people have different personality styles, she immediately called her daughter and invited her to lunch. Melody, hesitant to hear her mother's newest complaints, dreaded walking into the restaurant. She said, "There sat my mother, poised and perfectly manicured. Her briefcase was open on the table and she conducted business on her cell phone, as usual. The beautiful gift sitting on the table didn't even spark my interest."

"Hello, Mother," Melody said, scoping out the nearest exit. But Melody found an unexpected conversation. Her mom started talking about their personality styles and why they were so different. Rhonda admitted that she finally understood that her highly driven personality was too overbearing for her reserved, cautious daughter. She said, "I need to slow down, take time to enjoy you, and stop pressuring you to be outgoing and goal-oriented like me!" They discussed what these differences meant over lunch.

Then Rhonda suggested Melody open the gift. Melody beamed at an impressive array of paints and brushes. "Wow. They're perfect, what I've always wanted... and so are you, Mom."

Melody threw her arms around her mother's neck as their hearts and tears joined together for the first time.

The healing began—once they understood. Melody shared, "I can accept myself without feeling like I have to accomplish great things. After years of not speaking, we were able to cry, laugh, and cry again with joy when we realized that it's okay to be different from one another." Melody regained confidence and security. Rhonda said, "I've learned to appreciate my daughter for who she is, because a successful relationship with my daughter is my most important accomplishment."

A child at any age can feel discouraged, worthless, or a failure when he or she feels unable to measure up. We moms can lay a firm foundation for our children's self-esteem and positive self-image. We can identify personality traits as God's workmanship, rather than focus on the differences as perceived deficiencies. We must be brave enough to ask our children what they need from us and be willing to fulfill those desires.

When a mom stands behind her children and understands them for who they are and how God created them, even the impossible seems possible. Maybe we can't change the past, but we can change what we do today, and enjoy tomorrow! Take steps today to understand and appreciate your child and choose to communicate successfully. Go forward in life and put love into action. Lay out the "Welcome" mat and unlock the door to dynamic relationships in your home today!

—SUSAN CROOK

Little Examples

"Good people are guided by their honesty; treacherous
people are destroyed by their dishonesty."
PROVERBS 11:3

"Two soft drinks and two waters, please," we requested at the pizza counter, and then went to fill our glasses at the pop machine. But after my son drank a root beer, my husband, Mark, traded his water for my son's glass and filled the glass with Coke for himself.

Before we left, Mark went to the counter, explained we'd had soft drinks for three people after all, and started to pay.

The manager said, "Don't worry" and wouldn't have even noticed if we hadn't told him. But my husband showed our kids that being honest is right even if it's not a big deal.

Anytime we do something simple like that—returning extra change or something a clerk accidentally puts in our bag, pointing out when we're undercharged at the store—it all adds up. When our kids see us being honest in the little things, it affects their lives.

If we want our kids to be honest in big things,
we have to display integrity in little things.

—JGL

Trusting Our Kids

"How thankful I am to Christ Jesus
our Lord for considering me trustworthy
and appointing me to serve him."
1 TIMOTHY 1:12

When I took my daughter to register for college, I was apprehensive and sad. Waiting in the car for her to join me, I watched a motorcycle screech up and a young woman dismount. Jerking off her baby blue helmet and releasing golden curls across her shoulders, she shouted to someone across the street, loosing an astonishing stream of obscenities.

My daughter arrived and found me remembering news stories about good kids going bad at college.

"If you think I am going to send you to college to learn to cuss like a sailor, drink like a fish, and dress like a pig, you are sadly mistaken," I stormed.

She looked at me in astonishment. "Mother, you know you can trust me."

And I did. I also knew that, long ago, I had committed her to God's care.

"Sorry about that," I murmured, giving her a sheepish smile.

When we've raised our kids well, we need to trust them.

—ANNE McKAY GARRIS

A Shot in the Arm!

"No matter what happens, always be thankful, for this is
God's will for you who belong to Christ Jesus."
1 THESSALONIANS 5:18

Our oldest son was five years old when we returned to the states
after being overseas. He had to have booster immunizations
before he started school. I prayed the entire way to the doctor's
office, hoping he wouldn't notice where we were headed. Then
the familiar words popped out, "Mommy, where are we going?"

"You need some shots before you can start school. They will
keep you from getting sick—isn't that a good idea?" I explained
it would hurt for a little bit but would keep him well later.

When the nurse came in with three injections, Jeremy shut
his eyes tightly and grimaced with each shot, but didn't shed a
tear. I was stunned at his bravery and said, "Jeremy, what did
you think about while your eyes were closed?"

He smiled and said, "I thanked Jesus that I can play and
not get sick."

*Thanking God in painful circumstances is difficult,
but "well" worth it!*

—CONNIE POMBO

Being Instead of Doing

"God replied, 'I am the One who always is.
Just tell them, "I am has sent me to you."'"
EXODUS 3:14

God told Moses to demand that Pharaoh, in the Lord's name, "Set my people free."

Moses knew the Egyptian leaders would want God's credentials before they'd release their labor force, so he asked God what credentials to use. God's answer? Simply, "I AM."

God could have elaborated on his many roles: Creator, Designer of the Universe, Omnipotent Lord, etc. Instead of focusing on the impressive things he *did*, he focused on who he *was*.

We humans are so "do" conscious. We judge people's worth by what they do in life, their positions. As a result, we all try to do too much to prove that we are important.

We moms can take another tactic, a better tactic. While we're proud of kids for what they do, they also need to know that we—and God—just love them for who they are. Their actions are important, but the person behind the actions is more important!

*Kids need to know they're loved not for
what they do, but just because they are.*

—JGL

First Things First

> "You have been Christians a long time now, and you ought to be teaching others. Instead, you need someone to teach you again the basic things a beginner must learn about the Scriptures..."
>
> Hebrews 5:12

It had been a wild day and I was exhausted. I decided I needed a pick-me-up, so I switched on my jukebox with its spinning disco ball and laughed as the kids jumped around to the music.

"Mommy, dance with me," my son pleaded.

The only thing I remember from junior high PE dancing is the two-step, so I started to teach that to my son. But that was too tame for him. He tried to be fancy, but failed. "Honey, I don't know anything about dancing, but I think you have to learn a basic two-step before you can do anything else," I said.

How many times in life are we like my son? We don't put in time on the basics before we expect to do the fancy stuff. Starting at the basics is vital whether we're talking hobbies, learning a new skill, spiritual growth, or even parenting.

Don't expect to have the impact of a Mother Teresa if you're not willing to start by prayer and unnoticed work.

—JGL

Missing the Point

"If I could speak in any language in heaven or on
earth but didn't love others, I would only be making
meaningless noise like a loud gong or a clanging cymbal."

1 CORINTHIANS 13:1

On Red Square in Moscow lies the magnificent eight-domed
St. Basil's cathedral. Legend claims that on its completion, Tsar
Ivan the Terrible asked Postnik, the architect, if he could ever
build anything more beautiful. "Why, yes, Tsar, I think I could,"
responded Postnik, hoping for a new commission.

Ivan the Terrible had Postnik's eyes gouged out.

Ivan missed the whole point.

I, too, can miss the point. How many times have I snapped
at my family on Sunday morning in our hurry to get to church?
Or been more concerned about what I wore to church than the
condition of my heart?

Ivan was a clanging cymbal. And I don't have to gouge
out someone's eyes to be a resounding gong. Worshipping God
starts with love, for Him and for others.

If we don't have love, we are nothing.

—SUZANNE WOODS FISHER

Eyes in the Back of My Head

"The Lord knows people's thoughts. ..."
—PSALMS 94:11

Muffled giggles emanated from the backseat of our car. "What's going on?" I demanded as I felt my long hair being moved.

"She's looking for the eyes in the back of your head," quipped one of our sons as all three children broke out in uproarious laughter.

Many times my children have tried to figure out how I know just what they're doing even when I don't see them. They don't realize that an "oomph" from the backseat always tells me one of my three has just elbowed one of the others in one of their backseat territorial squabbles. Or a creak on the kitchen floor in the middle of the night means I won't find any orange juice in the refrigerator the next morning.

Moms can tell from little clues that their children are doing something they shouldn't. This gives us the appearance of having super powers such as eyes in the back of our head. Scripture tells us that God knows what we are thinking—now there is true power!

Am I aware that my Lord knows all—
even what I am thinking?

—SHERRON SLAVENS

Am I My Sibling's Keeper?

"The Lord asked Cain, 'Where is your brother?
Where is Abel?'
'I don't know!' Cain retorted. 'Am I supposed
to keep track of him wherever he goes?'"
GENESIS 4:9

"Here Elizabeth, let me help you," Gardner said as he gently took his sister's hand and assisted her down the steps.

My eyes watered at the sweetness of it. And with thankfulness, because Gardner didn't know I was watching—he was taking the initiative to take care of her.

I'd always assumed that older siblings automatically consider what little ones can't do and help care for them. So I was disturbed at how many times Gardner *wasn't* kind or thoughtful toward his sister.

Finally, I started teaching Gardner to take care of his sister. "She's just a little bitty thing. She can't do all the stuff we can. She needs our protection, and our help," I explained. To me it was a given, but I saw his eyes awaken—he'd apparently never thought of it that way. Now, although they still had their moments, I saw more and more evidence that he'd taken my words to heart.

*Teaching our children to take care of each
other is one of the keys to a closer family.*

—JGL

Mom and the Miserable, No-Good, Rotten Day

"Then Jesus said, 'Let's get away from the crowds for a while and rest.' There were so many people coming and going that Jesus and his apostles didn't even have time to eat."
MARK 6:31

I was having one of those days that even the legendary Alexander, who had the terrible, horrible, no-good, very bad day, would shudder at. I felt miserable and grouchy. I knew I was being unreasonable with my husband. And boy, was I impatient with my kids!

In fact, my behavior started reminding me of my toddler's—when she needs a nap. I was acting the same grumpy, fretful way. So I put the little ones in the care of my husband, and I went off for an afternoon nap. When I woke up, I felt much better—and we all had a great evening together.

We think our lives are too full to have time for a nap. But Jesus had way more people clinging to him even more constantly than we do. And he still thought it was important to leave their needs behind and get a rest at times.

Sometimes moms need to let the family take care of itself and get the refreshment of a power nap, too!

—JGL

Mentoring Dreams

"Do not withhold good from those who deserve it
when it's in your power to help them."
PROVERBS 3:27

When two friends and I went out to lunch one day, we ended up talking about our kids. And I ended up seeing an example of mentoring right before my eyes.

"My son dreams of being an English professor," one mom shared. "You should hear him talk about old books and the histories behind them."

"Would he like to meet some professors?" asked the other mom, a recent graduate with a degree in English literature. "I can contact mine and talk with him as well."

Some moms are career women. Others have left the career path to work at home or study. It doesn't matter what path we've traveled, or how young or old we may be. The lessons or contacts we glean from life are divine gifts that each of us can share.

So think beyond the box of your home. You can help someone realize an awesome dream.

Assess your skills and expertise.
What can you offer as a mentor?

—CYNTHIA AGRICOLA HINKLE

Growing Through Faith and Dry Panties

"The Lord is close to all who call on him,
yes, to all who call on him sincerely."
PSALM 145:18

"Moooommmyyyyyy! I have to go potty!" I cringe at my daughter's call because it means she has already gone. Another accident. Why does she wait so long to tell me she has to go? Why is she so stubborn?

I suddenly wonder if these are questions God asks about me: Why does she wait so long to ask me for help? Why does she stubbornly try to make it on her own? Why does she only call on me after an accident?

As I clean my daughter's mess and lovingly help her into a clean pair of panties, I realize God does the same for me. I wait until I have an "accident," then I call on Him and He graciously gets me back into the "dry panties" of adult life. Thankfully, I notice that as my faith grows, I call on God more quickly. And just as my daughter grows to have fewer accidents, so do I.

Wonderfully, God is always ready for me
to let Him into my life, accidents and all.

—DIANNE DANIELS

Welcome!

"And anyone who welcomes a little child
like this on my behalf is welcoming me."
MATTHEW 18:5

"Mom, I love Rhonda. She's my favorite lady in the whole world," my son said. He didn't qualify it with "next to you," but I didn't feel threatened.

Rhonda is my good friend. She is also a person who loves children, and mine certainly love her, too!

One reason my kids adore her is that she never ignores them. If she's around them, she doesn't just say "Hi" and not know what to say, like I do with other people's kids. She doesn't just acknowledge them, but she's glad to see them. She welcomes them into her home or into her presence. She takes time to talk with them, to focus on them, to learn their likes and dislikes and remember that later.

Maybe we all can't be as good with kids as Rhonda is, but as we take time to truly welcome them into our lives, their heavenly Father is pleased.

*Perhaps we've reached our highest
when we've bent over to talk to a child.*

—JGL

Mom's Approval Rating

"And may the Lord our God show us
his approval and make our efforts successful.
Yes, make our efforts successful! . . ."
PSALM 90:17

Tonight's evening news reported that our president's approval rating has swooped to a new low. It seems only yesterday it was at an unexpected high. Can you relate?

As a mom, are you relieved your children don't tally your best and worst mom moments and give you daily approval ratings? Imagine having your mothering rating publicized on TV! Wouldn't it be nice if there was a law stating, "If mom doesn't ask how you think she's doing in the area of mothering, don't tell"?

God knew we were going to have ups and downs in our mothering. Some days we spend extra time reading with our children and baking gooey chocolate chip cookies for them. Approval rating...98 percent! Other days we yell at our kids, give them extra chores just because we can, and tell them to get their own supper. Approval rating...5 percent. Ouch.

Seek God's approval for your mothering efforts.

—VICKI TIEDE

Love Flame

"His unchanging plan has always been to adopt us
into his own family by bringing us to himself through
Jesus Christ. And this gave him great pleasure."
EPHESIANS 1:5

"Would you like to keep her?"

"Oh, yes!" I didn't wait for my husband, Russ, or son, Paul, to answer. We'd prayed two years for this beautiful baby.

Miss Penze, the caseworker, had called Friday afternoon. "We have a baby girl for you. You can see her at the adoption agency Monday and decide if you want her," she said.

Most people have nine months, but we had seventy-two hours. We discussed her name at the dinner table. I wanted Kate but neither Russ nor Paul agreed.

"Lori, how about Lori Lea?" I'd seen the name somewhere.

We called our friends and family with the news.

On Monday I looked into Lori Lea's dark brown eyes. Three weeks old. Curly dark brown hair. Perfect.

She fussed a little. I picked her up and instantly a flame of love was lit that has never dimmed or blown out.

Keep her? I might never put her down.

Our Father God experiences extreme love for us,
His adopted children.

—AUDREY HEBBERT

The Miracle Shoes

"For forty years I led you through the wilderness,
yet your clothes and sandals did not wear out."
DEUTERONOMY 29:5

"It's time to get you another pair of shoes, boy!" my husband noted as he mussed our son's hair.

"Another pair of shoes?" I asked. "We just got him shoes a few months ago."

"Well, look," my husband invited, pointing to my son's feet, "those are all worn out."

I sighed. As fast as our kids grow, it seems I'm buying clothes all the time—as well as shoes!

One day as I dragged bags of kids' clothes and shoes into our house, I almost wished I was one of the Israelite parents following Moses. They didn't have to worry about clothes and shoes. Even though they wandered through the wilderness for forty years because of their lack of faith, God still took care of them every step of the way—literally. He not only gave them food and water, but with years of walking, their shoes never wore out! And actually, as the children grew, they must have gotten hand-me-downs from others, so the shoes and clothes went through several lives!

> *If God is practical enough to make clothes
> last way beyond their time, isn't he practical
> enough to provide for our everyday needs?*

—JGL

Tough and Tender

"The Lord is like a father to his children, tender and
compassionate to those who fear him."
PSALM 103:13

I guess different women have their different turn-ons, but one
of the things that makes me adore my husband is watching
him with our kids. Mark helps a lot with our toddler's basic
care—changing her, dressing her, and getting her ready for bed.
It fills me with wonder to watch how gentle and sweet he is with
her. Though like many dads he seems to think his main role in
fathering is to be rowdy with the kids and get them all wound
up, at other times, especially with our little girl, my tough guy
is a bundle of tenderness.

I love witnessing that, and it's the picture I see when I read
Psalm 103:13. God, our mighty, strong, powerful God, is also
soft enough to love us, his little ones.

God's power is big enough to control the world,
and gentle enough to nurture his vulnerable children.

—JGL

What Mom Says

"For the tongue can kill or nourish life."
PROVERBS 18:21

I began the day being a good mom. Before the day was over, I learned how to be a better mom.

It wasn't a big thing that made me angry with my husband, just a lot of little irritations. Dirty socks on the floor...Not one, but three pairs of shoes scattered around the den...And he had left with my car keys again...

On this particular day those annoyances tipped my scales toward anger. I complained to the closest people around me— my children. "Your father..." began my tirade to garner sympathy and make myself feel better.

When I finished venting, my son's somber eyes looked up at me. "Why would you say those things about Daddy?" he asked. Ouch! How foolish I was to think that sounding off would make me feel better. I was immediately reminded of the power of words to nurture or destroy.

The next time I feel like complaining,
I will try to be nourishing instead.

—JERI REDMAN

Weeds and Gardens

"So Peter went over the side of the boat and
walked on the water toward Jesus. But when he
looked around at the high waves, he was terrified
and began to sink. 'Save me, Lord!' he shouted."
MATTHEW 14:29–30

Perspiration trickled down my face, and the sun burned my shoulders as I planted clumps of thyme between the flagstones in our garden.

The little path through the flowers and vegetables seemed so simple and lovely on paper. But like all sweat-equity projects, it has required twice the money and three times the effort that I expected. I wonder now why heavy, flat rocks once seemed so romantic.

"The garden looks really pretty, Mom. Thanks for all your work." The two thin arms wrapped around my neck belonged to the quiet son who rarely expresses thoughts and almost never says compliments.

I paused to savor this gift of words. I saw weeds and more weeds; he saw a garden. I saw yet another unfinished project; he saw a path brimming with beauty and potential.

I'd been staring at the ground for too long. Like Peter, when I looked down I began to sink. It was time to take a break, watch the clouds, and share lemonade and dreams with my son.

*I receive fresh perspective when I look up to see
God's bigger picture.*

—LYNNETTE P. HORNER

When Help Knocks

"You're going to wear yourself out—and the people, too.
This job is too heavy a burden for you to handle all by
yourself."
EXODUS 18:18

"Girl, why don't you let me come over and help you clean your kitchen?" my friend Sally asked. "I know you are so busy. And your house is so beautiful that I'd love to help!"

I answered evasively. Sally was right: I did have a beautiful home. But between working full-time, taking care of my little kids, and other responsibilities, well, housework took the last priority. I was worn out and frustrated, and my home looked unloved.

Moses's father-in-law, Jethro, noticed when Moses was trying to be all things to all people. He told Moses to let other capable people help him. When Moses took his advice, it made a huge difference for him—and for the people he served.

We moms are so used to trying to be and do all things. But maybe it would be better for us—and our families—if we accept, or even ask for, help!

When help knocks on your door,
swallow your pride and let it come in!

—JGL

Taking Our Children to Jesus

"But Jesus said, 'Let the children come to me.
Don't stop them! For the Kingdom of Heaven
belongs to such as these.'"
MATTHEW 19:14

"Jesus loves me," I sang.

To my surprise, two-year-old Elizabeth joined in. I hadn't taught her that song, but she knew it. I wondered how. Then I remembered: she was in the church nursery every weekend and every Wednesday night. The wonderful nursery volunteers were succeeding!

When I married my husband, he had two young daughters. They went to a church they loved, but it didn't have a Sunday school or children's program. My stepdaughters didn't learn a lot of the Bible stories and verses and songs that I grew up with and that impacted my life.

And so I'm especially aware of the great results of our kids' regular involvement in the children's programs at church. Our kids are getting a great faith basis there that supports what we teach them at home. So we take advantage of just about everything our church offers our children!

*Part of the way we take our little ones
to Jesus is to make sure they're in church!*

—JGL

Lacking Nothing

"For forty years you sustained them in the wilderness.
They lacked nothing in all that time. . . ."
NEHEMIAH 9:21

Babies don't come with an instruction manual. After each of my three deliveries, I was sent home from the hospital with this complex, tiny being and was expected to know his needs and how to meet them.

Motherhood is scary. It's okay to say it out loud. You don't have all the answers. You never will. My sons are now adults with their own children. The problems they have now are even bigger than the ones from their childhoods, and I still don't know the answers.

On the other hand, sometimes we are bombarded with too many answers! Everyone has an opinion—just attend a family reunion with a new baby. Answers will come from every angle. But are they the right answers? And how will you know?

With God, you lack nothing! He will give you the answers you seek, if you only ask!

*Write a list of all your parenting questions today,
give it to God, and wait for the answers to come.*

—KATHLEEN ATWELL

The Right Tools

"Work hard so God can approve you. Be a good worker,
one who does not need to be ashamed and who
correctly explains the word of truth."
2 TIMOTHY 2:15

"Dad, do you have any blank business cards?" Alisha asked her dad. Alisha had recently committed her life to Christ and wanted to use the cards to help her memorize scripture.

Later, she came to me, asking if I had a certain Bible translation. I gladly gave her a copy. Then, a week later, she wondered if I had a different translation that she thought would be easier to read.

I happened to have a new, unopened Bible of that translation, with a cute pink cover. I'd bought it for myself but gladly gave it to her.

A couple of weeks later, she asked to keep a study Bible she'd found downstairs. Again, we said, "Sure."

We're happy to give Alisha whatever she needs to learn more about God. Yes, Bibles, Bible dictionaries, commentaries, and other things add up financially when we don't have them around the house. But if we want Alisha to develop her faith, we have to equip her with good tools.

*Providing spiritual tools for our kids is one
of the best investments we can make.*

—JGL

The Teacher

"But when the Father sends the Counselor as my
representative—and by the Counselor I mean the Holy
Spirit—he will teach you everything and will remind
you of everything I myself have told you."
JOHN 14:26

My stomach was in knots. It was my youngest son's first day
of preschool. How would he act when saying good-bye in an
unfamiliar place?

His teacher extended her hand. "Hello, Joel," she said,
calmly. Joel looked like a deer caught in the headlights. I held
my breath and whispered a quick prayer. Slowly, Joel took his
teacher's hand.

"Ben's inside painting," she added. Instantly, Joel relaxed.
He had met Ben on visitation day. My unpredictable four-year-
old sauntered into school without looking back.

I heaved a sigh of relief and thought about the small miracle that had just transpired between my son and his teacher.

Isn't that what God does for us in life? He comforts us and
holds our hand. The Holy Spirit teaches us through his Word
all we need to know for now and for eternity.

Will you take Jesus by the hand and let Him be your teacher?

—SUSAN SKITT

Goodnight, Sleep Tight

"Indeed, he who watches over
Israel never tires and never sleeps."
PSALM 121:4

I wonder how many sleepless nights I caused my mom. When I was an infant, she must have slept with one eye and ear open, ready for my tiniest whimper. As my brother and I grew, she battled our late-night spiders, thunderstorms, and fevers. As teens, my brother and I knew no matter how late the hour, Mom would be waiting up for us. She sometimes scolded, but always told us she stayed up and scolded because she loved us. As grown-ups living far from home, we've probably caused her lost sleep when she knew things weren't just right for us.

Mom's faithful watch gives a human example of the way God watches over us. God never sleeps. He always knows and cares what is happening to us. God keeps such close tabs on us because, as our Creator, he loves us even more than our mothers do.

*Sleep well tonight, knowing that God is
watching over you with love.*

—JANE HEITMAN

271

The One Who Weeps with Us

"Then Jesus wept."
JOHN 11:35

"You'll need to memorize two Bible verses of your choice every week," our Bible professor informed us.

Most of the students trekked straight for John 11:35, which I discovered was the shortest verse in the Bible.

Although that's the shortest verse in the Bible, it's also such a powerful one for moms to remember.

Lazarus, Jesus's friend, had died. By the time Jesus got to the visitation, Lazarus was already buried. He joined the mourners knowing he could raise his friend from the dead. Still, he wept. Perhaps he wept in sympathy and love. Perhaps he wept because life is cruel and death is inevitable for humans. But he cared enough to weep.

Jesus still cares enough to weep. When we mothers deal with difficult parenting situations or experience grief or face whatever makes us want to cry, Jesus understands. He may not always stop the funeral, but he'll always weep with us.

We can take our tear-inducing situation
to our friend Jesus today.

—JGL

The Power of a Praying Mom

"But when you pray, go away by yourself, shut the door
behind you, and pray to your Father secretly. Then your
Father, who knows all secrets, will reward you."
MATTHEW 6:6

Faith was not an overt part of my family. My brother, mother, and I went to church, but Dad was not a Christian, and at home, we seldom discussed spiritual things.

I've wondered how, without strong spiritual nurturing at home, my brother and I have both grown up to be similarly committed to Christ. Neither of us ever rebelled against Christianity. Though we're not perfect, we both seek to have Christ-centered homes.

I think I've found the answer. Though Mom was too shy to talk about her faith, she was a woman of prayer. She was rather secretive, but I often saw her kneeling in her room.

I think my mom prayed us onto the right path. And I believe her lifelong prayers and quiet example of faith resulted in my father coming to Christ shortly before he died—years after her death. Mom may not have talked about her faith, but more important, she lived it, and so its influence still guides us.

May we become such moms of prayer that our children are guided by our spiritual influence whether they see it or not.

—JGL

Praise the Lord and Pass the Philodendron

"This is the day the Lord has made.
We will rejoice and be glad in it."
PSALM 118:24

"These are the best years of your life," my father insisted.

If these are the best, I thought, *I'm in trouble.*

My babies were born thirteen months apart, and postpartum depression and exhaustion clung like smog. Everyone wanted me—my breast-feeding baby, my rambunctious toddler, my devoted husband.

If only I could get both children to nap at the same time!

One afternoon, a period of blissful quietness aroused my suspicion. I peeked into their room.

Jonathan had pulled a planter off the dresser and uprooted the philodendron. Both cribs were littered with potting soil. Telltale rings of dirt circled their mouths.

He'd also opened the Vaseline, and they had papered the walls with Vaseline and Kleenex. I didn't know whether to laugh or cry.

I had a choice to make: I could wish away these precious years, or I could decide not to sweat the small stuff.

I laughed.

Our attitude helps make these years great!

—SHARON SHEPPARD

When Years Seem Like Days

"So Jacob spent the next seven years working
to pay for Rachel. But his love for her was so
strong that it seemed to him but a few days."
GENESIS 29:20

I was one of those "crazy" women who had a baby when older than forty. One interesting thing being an older mom is my friends' reactions. Most of them have children who are teens or older.

"Oh, I miss having a little one around," they've told me for three years now. They like being around my toddler—until the end of the evening draws near. By then, Elizabeth has usually reminded them just how needy toddlers are, and they realize their bodies just can't take it anymore!

Kids take a lot of work no matter what age you are. They're hard years, but in the scope of life, they're such short years, perhaps because our love is so strong and our kids are so dependent upon us.

*Always take time to enjoy your kids; years
of having children at home do pass so quickly!*

—JGL

He Knows

"And the Father who knows all hearts knows
what the Spirit is saying, for the Spirit pleads
for us believers in harmony with God's own will."
ROMANS 8:27

I paced the hospital ward and listened to Tim's labored breathing. He had been unconscious for ten days with meningitis. There was nothing we could do but hope and pray. His birthday was four days away and I prayed, "Lord, please let him be awake on his birthday."

It was frustrating to know that as much as I loved him, only God could help him. I held his little arms, saying, "God is watching over you and we will get through this."

As I turned to sit, I heard a muffled, "Mum," and my little Tim was awake, wondering why a tube had been inserted into his nose.

"Nurse!" I screamed through the hallway. I ran back to his room, and he stretched his arms to me. It was incredible! The doctor checked him and he was quite stable. We had his birthday party right there in his room.

*Give your troubles to God, for He knows
your heart and He can be trusted.*

—CHRISTINE NASERIAN NJERI

Life Is a Beach

"The Lord himself watches over you!
The Lord stands beside you as your protective shade."
PSALM 121:5

"Mom. Mom!" my child demanded, not realizing I was at the beach. I finally heard him, sighed, and returned my mind to my Missouri home.

When the going gets rough—the kids are fighting nonstop, our toddler makes messes, or whatever—I mentally go to the beach.

Nearly every summer, my husband's family gathers for a week on the beach. I love feeling warm sand, watching sand crabs scurry, and listening to ocean waves.

The first year, I wondered why the family lugged so much gear—especially a huge, clunky umbrella—from the house to the beach. But I quickly learned how hot the sand becomes to walk on, and how quickly the summer sun roasts skin. I ran for that protective shade. At other times, the umbrella shielded us from stinging sand the wind spat at us. The umbrella protected us from the harsh realities of life on the beach.

Do you ever feel like motherhood is a dance on broiling sand? Or that you're being burned or stung by the child-induced elements? Let God be your shade, your protection from the harsh realities of the elements of life.

Protective coverings are meant to be taken advantage of.

—JGL

Friends for Kindergarten and Beyond

"So now we can rejoice in our wonderful new relationship
with God—all because of what our Lord Jesus Christ
has done for us in making us friends of God."
ROMANS 5:11

"I'm worried that I won't make new friends," my daughter confessed as we talked about her entering kindergarten. I was worried about making friends, too. Her milestone meant my role
would be reduced in the moms' group I had been a part of for
the past five years. I couldn't continue to lead the group when
I had to leave early for school pickup. The moms in this group
had become my closest friends. What would happen when I
didn't see them regularly anymore? Would they move on without me? Would I find new friends among the kindergarten
moms to fill the gap?

As my daughter and I talked about our fears, I realized that
no matter what friendships come in the future, she and I will
have each other, and we will both have a friend in Jesus. His
promises last through every milestone and every season of life.

*How wonderful it is to have a friend,
not just for life, but for eternity.*

—DIANNE DANIELS

SEPTEMBER

FINDING YOUR INNER "PERFECT MOM"

"That's why I take pleasure in my weaknesses. . . .
For when I am weak, then I am strong."

2 CORINTHIANS 12:10

*Y*ou are a better mom than I was," my mother stated with obvious regret in her voice.

"Not better, just different," I replied.

What a strange, uncomfortable conversation! What began as a nice mother/daughter brunch was turning into an emotionally charged trip down memory lane.

Since my father's death, my mom and I have struggled to figure out our relationship without my dad running interference. We weren't doing very well. My mother was a teacher and a busy pastor's wife during my childhood, and we hadn't formed much of a bond.

In contrast, I have made a conscious effort to be a devoted full-time mom to my two daughters. I try to put them first and always be available to meet any need that they might have. My girls eagerly tell me about school, their friends, their thoughts and feelings. I treasure my relationship with them.

Driving home from the disturbing encounter with my mom, I was in a very contemplative mood. I began by sharing my frustrations with God. "Mom wasn't nurturing and she wasn't there for me emotionally," I whimpered. "Surely, my way of mothering is superior."

As I looked into my rearview mirror to change lanes, I realized that I was not unlike Snow White's evil queen stepmother. "Mirror, mirror in my car. I must be the best mom by far."

What a joke. I laughed, remembering all the times I have felt insecure in my quest to be the "perfect mom."

Many times during my past seventeen years of motherhood I haven't lived up to my goal of being a perfect mom. For one thing, the definition keeps changing. Some days I think I know what kind of mom I should be, and I think I might be able to actually be her. On other days, I feel like even if I knew what makes a perfect mom, I wouldn't be able to attain that perfection. What makes a woman a perfect mom, anyway?

Years ago, desperate for answers, I joined a mom's support group at my church. It didn't help. As I surveyed the moms around the table, I realized that every last one of them excelled in some area of mothering in which I failed. Janelle was teaching her toddlers to speak fluent French. Colette made all of her own baby food from scratch and served her toddler only organic health foods. Susan hand-stitched her children's clothing and concocted creative Halloween costumes for them. Michelle owned her own business and worked outside the home part time, kept an immaculate house, and homeschooled her kids. Needless to say, I did not prolong the blessings and encouragement of that group for very long.

Next, I tried to make friends with women whom I considered poor mothers to make myself feel better. That was mildly satisfying for only a short time because that group of women only brought up more questions.

"If your kids are brats, act up, or do dumb stuff, is that mom's fault?"

"If your child is the proverbial angel, do you get to take some credit for that?"

"Do you try to read lots of parenting books or trust your own instincts?"

"How badly are my offspring going to be scarred for life if I mess up one day? Do I care as long as they live to an age when they can pay for their own counseling?"

During those days of agonizing self-doubt, I managed to find time to pray and read my Bible. God rewarded those efforts and led me to a woman who has been my mentor for eight years now.

Juanita is eighty-five years old. She has five children, nine grandchildren, and eleven great-grandchildren. She was a missionary. She had her own challenges as a mother, from needing to send her children away to boarding school to watching some of her offspring make choices that she disagrees with. When she talks, I listen. When she says God's grace is sufficient, I believe her. Juanita believes that if we are obedient to God, doing what He wants, we are the mothers God wants us to be.

God's grace covers me when I goof up and can't find my inner "perfect mom." Like the time my naked toddler got out the front door while I was on the phone, and was returned by a stranger. Like the time I was ranting about a woman who had wronged me, and my teenager counseled, "Mom, you've got to let it go."

Or the times I didn't take care of myself physically and missed my third grader's field trip and my high school daughter's choir concert because I was bedridden. And for the other times that I've fallen short of perfect, I will boast about my weaknesses because it was and is the time God shows me His power.

By the time I reached my driveway on the day of brunch with my mom, God had reminded me of all the things my mom has done for me in the last few years. Because she worked full-time, she is able to help my girls financially, giving them money for camps, mission trips, and vacations. She comes to every school and church event. Grandma is the ever-ready babysitter.

Sitting in my car, I praise God for perfectly making all moms, in his perfect way, in his perfect time.

—EVANGELINE BEALS GARDNER

Wrestling an Octopus

"We can rejoice, too, when we run into problems
and trials, for we know that they are good for us—
they help us learn to endure. And endurance develops
strength of character in us, and character strengthens
our confident expectation of salvation."

ROMANS 5:3, 4

"I can't do this," I told my husband. I was trying to get my newborn's arm into a tiny sleeve. Jared's arms flailed while his little legs pumped up and down. It was like trying to put a straight jacket on an octopus.

"I'm a total failure," I sobbed. "I can't even dress my own son." As a first-time mom, I was an emotional puddle of hormones and tears.

My husband softly chuckled. "Here, let me help," he offered.

Dressing my baby soon became second nature. I could do it in my sleep. Many times during the first year, I did!

When I think back on those days, I laugh. It's a lot like that in our spiritual walk. God helps us through life's struggles. As we grow and mature in Christ, He teaches us perseverance. One day we'll look back on life's trials and say, "It was worth it all."

In heaven, our perspective on life will change.

—SUSAN SKITT

Silent Wisdom

"But do people know where to find wisdom?
Where can they find understanding? . . .
God surely knows where it can be found."
JOB 28:12, 23

Our son called two weeks before we were to visit him, asking, "Mom, could you possibly come early? I don't know what to do, Sue wants a divorce."

All my motherly instincts kicked in when I saw the pain in my son's eyes. Protect him. Fix it. I hugged and hugged my son, but I knew I couldn't make it all better.

How could I help? What could I say to his wife, who was acting as though nothing was wrong?

Frustrated, I went to the library to think. While sitting there surrounded by shelves of books on every subject, I realized all these books are volumes of silent wisdom until they are opened. This was my answer. The Bible is my source of wisdom, but until it's opened and read, it remains a volume of silent wisdom.

I returned to my son's home knowing I had much advice to give, but until asked, I would remain silent.

As the days unfolded, my son opened many volumes for advice—both practical and spiritual, but the one he opened most contained comfort, love, and acceptance.

*Trusting God for wisdom will
bring direction in every situation.*

—MARGARET WILSON

A Shoulder to Cry On

"Joseph prepared his chariot and traveled to Goshen to
meet his father. As soon as Joseph arrived, he embraced
his father and wept on his shoulder for a long time."
GENESIS 46:29

Joseph was a grown man. His brothers had sold him into slavery when he was just a kid. And now he was a grown man and had been through all kinds of experiences. He hadn't seen or had contact with his father for years—hadn't even known if his dad was alive. But Joseph instantly made good use of his father's shoulders. It didn't matter that they hadn't seen each other in decades—Dad was still Dad, and his son still needed his comfort.

Parents' shoulders are made to cry on. Though different kids express stress and sorrow different ways, they still need us—whether they're little bitty kids or teens or grown-ups themselves.

Usually the older kids get, the more they hesitate to use our shoulders to cry on. So a wise mom watches, keeps in touch, and is ready to offer to be a crying post at any moment.

When you're feeling blue or overwhelmed, there's nothing like taking it to a parent—even a heavenly Parent!

—JGL

The Perfect Blend

"Destruction is certain for those who argue with
their Creator. Does a clay pot ever argue with its
maker? Does the clay dispute with the one who
shapes it, saying, 'Stop, you are doing it wrong!' Does
the pot exclaim, 'How clumsy can you be!'"

ISAIAH 45:9

When we walked into the birthday party at Sally's house, the
kids went off to be with the other kids, and I joined the adults.
As my toddler flitted through the room, the woman next to
me, Cathy, commented, "She's so petite. When I saw her, I told
Sally, 'She's so fragile.' Sally said, 'Don't you believe it!'"

"That's for sure," I agreed. "She's so rough sometimes that
she makes her eight-year-old brother cry."

"Actually, that's a good thing," Cathy said. "When girls
are cute and tiny, they need toughness and strength to protect
themselves."

So many times I'd bemoaned the fact that this sweet-
looking child was such a natural bulldozer and tomboy.

But Cathy's words showed me that maybe God gave this
marshmallow baby a core of steel for a reason. Maybe it's a good
thing that God didn't make her to my specifications.

*God has formed our children with just the right blend of
personalities, traits, and abilities.*

—JGL

Saved Through Childbearing

"But women will be saved through childbearing and by continuing to live in faith, love, holiness, and modesty."
1 TIMOTHY 2:15

When my twins were six months old, I was ready to check out! I not only faced sleep deprivation but also a marriage in trouble, plus the special needs of a hearing-impaired seven-year-old and a high-energy nine-year-old.

I surveyed my options: run away from home, jump in front of a truck, or just go crazy. But God was working! I desperately called upon Jesus to take control of my life and found to my amazement that I was no longer alone and drowning in my circumstances. His presence sustained me. I learned to pray about everything. I found wonderful practical help in the scriptures and in friendships with other Christian moms. I began to relax and so did my household.

Children are a gift from the Lord, but sometimes the demands of the gift overwhelm our inadequate supply of resources. Maybe that's part of God's plan to bring us to Himself? Today, if it all feels like too much, remember it's good to fall on your knees and say, "Help me!" He's willing to save us at every stage, from bearing our children through raising them!

He's your help for today and for all your days to come.

—CATHERINE VERLENDEN ELDRIDGE

Letting Our Children Live Their Lives

"O Lord, you alone are my hope. I've trusted you,
O Lord, from childhood."
PSALM 71:5

My son called from college to try, once again, to persuade us to give him permission to join a fraternity. He was positive that he would be able to influence it for good.

My husband and I weren't so sure. We prayed about it, sought counsel, wrung our hands, prayed more, and finally gave him our blessing. And kept praying.

Two years later, I am in awe of the growing maturity I've seen in my son's life—and so much of it has been a direct result of his being in a fraternity! He participated in an all-Greek Bible study, was asked to lead it the next year, and was elected vice president of the Inter-Fraternity Council, running on a platform of taking responsibility for your actions.

What if we had said no? What if we had let media-inspired fears hold our son back from discovering for himself the ancient words of King David in Psalm 71:5?

*Even parents need reminders that our confidence
rests in God alone.*

—SUZANNE WOODS FISHER

Touchy People!

"Everyone was trying to touch him, because healing power went out from him, and they were all cured."
LUKE 6:19

"Mo—omm! She touched me!"

"Keep your hands to yourself" has to be one of those phrases we parrot the most. Kids are so, well, *touchy* about being touched by their siblings.

The Bible illustrates the power of touch. Jesus could just speak to perform miracles. But at times he also touched, which probably brought emotional healing to people—like the leper who was used to people trying *not* to touch him. Long before scientists researched it, Jesus knew the importance of touch to emotional health.

Our kids may not like siblings touching them, but they don't want us parents to keep our hands to ourselves! I'm learning my kids perk up a bit if I touch them when I walk by—a scratch on the back, a quick tousle of hair, a pat on a cheek, a hug or a kiss, a squeezed hand, even just a touch on a shoulder. All these things keep my kids happier and healthier.

Even the smallest touch brings multiple dividends
in our children's lives.

—JGL

Governing a Great Family

"Give me wisdom and knowledge to rule them properly,
for who is able to govern this great nation of yours?"
2 CHRONICLES 1:10

Solomon had taken over the job as king of Israel from his father, David. And so far he was doing a good job. He was doing so well, in fact, that God expressed his pleasure by offering to give Solomon anything he wanted.

God was talking like the proverbial genie here! If God asked me what I wanted, I'm sure I could have a list ready in a jiffy, starting with a house at the beach!

But Solomon had other goals in mind. His first thought was for the responsibilities and ministry God had given him. He simply asked for more wisdom and knowledge to rule his people properly.

Wow! I wonder what would happen if, every day, we parents prayed, "Give me wisdom and knowledge to rule them properly, for who is able to govern this great family of yours?"

I think I'll try it!

*If we can add wisdom and knowledge to love,
our parenting will be unbeatable!*

—JGL

Two Sparrows

"Not even a sparrow, worth only half a penny, can
fall to the ground without your Father knowing it. . . .
So don't be afraid; you are more valuable to him
than a whole flock of sparrows."
MATTHEW 10:29, 31

My desk overlooks our beautiful backyard garden. Each morning I spend some pleasant time there with my coffee and Bible. It's also a favorite time of day for the bird population as they visit several feeders and splash in the birdbath.

One morning a tiny bird landed on a feeder and enjoyed breakfast. I thought of Matthew 10:29, 31. I began praying (and worrying a bit) for my daughter who was struggling. I petitioned for God's care to keep her from falling.

As I prayed, a bird landed on the opposite side of the feeder and pecked at sunflower seeds. The second bird was a gentle reminder from the Lord—I have a second daughter. Since she seemed to be gliding through life, I assumed she didn't need as much prayer. God reminded me both daughters are of infinite value to Him. Both need His care and equal attention in my prayers.

God loves all of our children.

—SANDRA McGARRITY

The Mercy Rule

"But the Lord still waits for you to come to
him so he can show you his love and compassion.
For the Lord is a faithful God. Blessed are those
who wait for him to help them."
ISAIAH 30:18

It's that time of year! Every Monday night our family tries to
locate football fields in small towns across the state so we can
watch our son play on his school's junior varsity football team.

At one game, our team played great! In fact, they did so
well that at the beginning of the fourth quarter, the refs called
the Mercy Rule. The Mercy Rule is when a team has scored 45
points ahead of the opponent, so the ref calls the game over.
The rule was created so the losing team can save face in light
of defeat.

As I thought about this concept, I was prompted to ask
about my own "mercy rule" in life. How easily do I forgive others when I have been wounded? Is there a limit to how much I
can forgive?

Don't wait for a Monday-night football game to apply this
God-rule in life!

*Be willing and waiting to apply mercy and forgiveness
to someone today!*

—JAMIE SPEAK WOOTEN

Planting in Faith

"Still other seed fell on fertile soil. This seed
grew and produced a crop one hundred
times as much as had been planted. . . ."
LUKE 8:8

"Well, I'm not sure where I learned that," Alisha said after she'd
given her logical views on a societal issue.

I smiled. I knew where she had gotten that. About six
months earlier we'd had a discussion on the topic, and I'd shown
her some research. She had not seemed very receptive at the
time. But now, her words revealed that she'd taken the matter
to heart, thought about it, and made my teaching her own.

When we're parents, we sow a lot of seeds in our children's
lives. Sometimes the seed seems to land on rocky soil, and we
think it's producing no results. We think we're talking to deaf
ears! But at other times, even a seed we thought was futile will
blossom and show us that we do, indeed, have an effect. So
keep sowing that seed—you might be surprised at how firmly it
gets rooted in your children's lives!

*When we sow seeds in our children's lives, we never know
just how vibrantly it may grow!*

—JGL

What's Your Treasure?

"Wherever your treasure is, there your
heart and thoughts will also be."
MATTHEW 6:21

"Shh. Go play; I have to finish this."

"Okay, okay, I'll take care of it in a little while."

"What? Did you say something?"

Those are phrases that I one day realized are often bandied about our house. My husband and I would both tell you that our children are our treasures—our most important assets.

But one day as I caught myself saying words like that over and over again, I started realizing just how much our kids get pushed aside. Mark and I are both self-employed and are very deadline driven. Anything that can be put off often is, and that includes our children.

That's not a problem if it's only for a day or two. But when days stretch into weeks, well, that's a habit that needs to be changed. Then we need to ask ourselves, "Okay, where's our heart?" It's where we're investing our time. We need to be sure that we're not investing so much time in our work that our kids are suffering.

Treasures are meant to be enjoyed and cherished.

—JGL

Strengthened to Shine

"The Sovereign Lord is my strength! He will
make me as surefooted as a deer and bring
me safely over the mountains."
HABAKKUK 3:19

My five-year-old daughter handed me a school announcement
about a parent art show. "Mommy, do this!"

"Katie, what would I submit?" What was she thinking? I'm
not an artist!

"Show them your paintings." She pointed to the creations
hanging on our bulletin board.

"I wish we could submit some of yours, Katie. You're a wonderful artist!"

"So are you, Mommy!"

Katie was as proud of me as I was of her. I'd be embarrassed
displaying my "just-for-fun" artwork. But I wanted my children
to enjoy bold self-expression. What would my actions say if I
refused to participate? God was urging me to be brave.

I entered three paintings. After the show, four moms
approached me. "I never knew you were an artist!" exclaimed
one as the others nodded.

Wow! An artist! I hadn't known either until I faced my
fears of what others might think.

Facing our fears blesses both kids and moms.

—TANYA T. WARRINGTON

"OK, Mom, I Get the Point"

"Work brings profit, but mere talk leads to poverty!"
PROVERBS 14:23

"Mom," my daughter Cherlynn said one morning, "now that I'm in junior high, I don't think I should have to do chores after school anymore."

Teaching God's principles is never more difficult than when children reach adolescence and talk often falls on deaf ears.

"Okay," I replied, "let's try it. Maybe you are too old for chores."

That night, after spending the afternoon with friends, my daughter sat down to her favorite dinner and I handed her a menu listing the price of each item.

"What's this?" she asked.

"Well, since you're no longer helping with chores, it's time for you to start paying for your meals. Oh, and here's a list of things I do for you and what it will cost you to have me continue doing them."

Cherlynn paid to eat her meal, learned a valuable lesson on God's work ethic, and never complained about chores again.

Sometimes applying God's principles is
better than talking about them.

—DORI CLARK

Extreme Measures

"But they couldn't reach him. So they went up to the roof,
took off some tiles, and lowered the sick man down into
the crowd, still on his mat, right in front of Jesus."
LUKE 5:19

Talk about good friends! At some point between the paralyzed
man in Luke 5 and his friends, they decided they would go to
Jesus for help.

Since the man couldn't walk, the friends carried him. But
they didn't arrive early enough to even get into the packed
house where Jesus taught!

Most of us would give up at that point, but not these
friends. They were willing to go to extreme measures to get
their friend to Jesus. They climbed on the roof and made a
big hole in the ceiling. Then they lowered their friend to Jesus.
Jesus commended their faith and healed the man.

Sometimes we parents have to take extreme measures to
get our kids in Jesus's presence. It might call for extreme prayer,
or more time with the child. Sometimes we have to rearrange
our plans. But whatever measures we take, it's worth it.

Never give up on trying to connect your kids with Christ.

—JGL

Apple Pie Provision

"Take delight in the Lord, and he will
give you your heart's desires."
PSALM 37:4

"Can you believe our daughter requested apple pie for her six-teenth birthday?" I lamented to my neighbor, Pauline. "I decorate awesome cakes and she wants pie. My pie crust tastes awful."

"Make oil-and-flour pie crust."

"Tried it. It didn't work."

"Buy a pie."

"Those are horrible things. Besides, we don't have the money."

"We better pray," Pauline suggested.

We did pray.

Later, the phone rang. "Kathy, my husband and I met you at church on Sunday." I remembered the new couple from our home state. "We'd like to bring you something. Will you be home?"

Shortly, the couple arrived and handed me a beautiful, hot apple pie.

"A friend brought us apples. We thought we'd share them with your family."

God knew our daughter's request before Pauline and I prayed. He provided our family's need and our daughter's desire, a birthday pie.

God uses humans to hand-deliver answers to our prayers.

—KATHERINE J. CRAWFORD

Unshakable Love

"And I am convinced that nothing can ever separate
us from his love. Death can't, and life can't. The
angels can't, and the demons can't. Our fears for
today, our worries about tomorrow, and even the
powers of hell can't keep God's love away."
ROMANS 8:38

"You're mean!" my son hurled. "You don't love me and you never
have!"

I didn't rush to comfort him. I knew he didn't feel well physically and was upset about discipline he'd received. His words
didn't shake me. I knew I loved him more than he could ever
understand, and knew we'd talk about it later when he felt better.

A while later, as I approached the kitchen, I saw my son
scurry into the adjacent dining room—avoiding me because
he was still upset.

As I thought about it, God reminded me of times I've had
my own little temper tantrums, accusing Him of not loving me.
Then later I've avoided God, ashamed of my words, but uncertain that He would want me.

"See, my love for you doesn't depend on what you do," God's
spirit whispered to my heart. "It's as unshakable as your love is
for your son."

Whenever you doubt God, remember He loves you
unconditionally—just as you love your own children!

—JGL

Try, Try Again

"And I am sure that God, who began the good work within you, will continue his work until it is finally finished on that day when Christ Jesus comes back again."
PHILIPPIANS 1:6

On the first day of her freshman year in high school, my fourteen-year-old daughter was cut from the volleyball team. She was devastated because being on the team meant so much more than playing volleyball. It meant she belonged.

Near the end of the school year, she ran on the ballot to be the next year's sophomore class treasurer. And lost. That evening, I told her how proud I was of her just for trying. Just for taking the risk of running for a class office. She won, in my eyes, because she had tried. It took two more tries until she finally won the coveted class-treasurer spot.

Regardless of the outcome of her efforts, I'm convinced that she had always been a winner. She had developed resiliency and perseverance. Those characteristics will take her farther than anything won in a first-time victory.

There is nothing that God can't use, even failure,
to shape us and mold us according to His purposes.

—SUZANNE WOODS FISHER

Being Nothing

> "The truth is, a kernel of wheat must be planted in
> the soil. Unless it dies it will be alone—a single
> seed. But its death will produce many new kernels—
> a plentiful harvest of new lives."
>
> JOHN 12:24

One day I asked my two-year-old son what he wanted to be when he grew up. "Would you like to be a fireman?" I asked.

"Noooo," was his soft response.

"How about a policeman, a doctor, or a teacher," I tried. He again shook his little head, no.

"Well, what would you like to be?" I asked.

He thought for a moment, and said, "Mom, when I grow up, I want to be just like you—nothing."

I laughed but his words hit home. My days blur into nights and I seem to have nothing to show for the effort. But as I reflect on it, being "Mom" is the most important thing I have ever done! And now, as the eyes of that little guy now tower far above me, I am convinced those intense days were worth every minute.

Anything you lay aside as you fulfill the role of "Mother" is not wasted, but invested in the future. Keep up the good work. You will reap an amazing harvest!

Whatever our job is, it's not "nothing"!

—SANDRA THIESSEN

Doing What Doesn't Come Naturally

"Do for others as you would like them to do for you."
LUKE 6:31

"Ladies first," my son chirped as he opened the door for me. When we walked to the car, his dad started putting the baby in her car seat. But Gardner just stood there by my open car door. "You'd better get in the car, honey," I directed, wondering why he was just standing there. As I climbed into the front seat, the door shut behind me and I realized, "Oh, he was waiting to shut my door for me!"

I shouldn't have been surprised. Gardner was doing what I'd been training him to do. At eight years old, Gardner has become quite the gentleman, and I'm proud of him. But courtesy isn't something boys—or girls, for that matter—notice on their own. They have to be taught.

Fortunately, courtesy usually brings its own rewards. Gardner likes the surprised smiles and pleased expressions he receives when people notice his manners. Making others feel special makes him feel special, too.

Children often don't know how to act properly—
until we teach them!

—JGL

Enjoy the Seasons

"Teach us to make the most of our time,
so that we may grow in wisdom."
PSALM 90:12

Every year, I so look forward to spring and summer. I have so many plans for when the kids are home from school! But then work or something else interrupts and the end of summer arrives before I know it. In fall and winter, I always mourn for those warm days I lost. Seasons pass so quickly!

I'm learning seasons pass quickly in our lives, too. One day we're debating the questions of having careers versus having children—which to give priority to. Then the seasons include things like juggling kids and careers, or being with kids all day and longing for more adult companionship and more opportunities to pursue our personal dreams.

I hear from other women, though, that in only a matter of a few years, the kids are gone and we have another season when we're needed less and can pursue our passions more. Perhaps a bittersweet season, too!

May God give us the grace and wisdom
to make the most of each season.

—JGL

Facing the Fears

"Then will your face brighten in innocence.
You will be strong and free from fear."
JOB 11:15

Paige described headache, aching muscles, and upset stomach. This "tween" who had always delighted in learning was too ill to go to school. Despite shedding big tears each morning, she became better as noon got closer and was well by evening. The next day the cycle would repeat.

A pediatric checkup revealed nothing physically wrong. Dr. Rogers sat down, looked Paige in the eye, and gently said, "Paige, under no circumstances are you to miss school. Middle school is far different from elementary school. I want you to complete every assignment, eat healthily, and get plenty of sleep."

She looked younger than twelve as she nodded understanding. We did as Dr. Rogers said, and middle-school phobia lasted less than two weeks. I wonder how long Paige would have remained ill had she not faced this fear.

When fears are met head-on,
we gain maturity and confidence.

—ZETA COMBS DAVIDSON

The Gourd Patch

"Dear brothers and sisters, you must be patient as
you wait for the Lord's return. Consider the farmers
who eagerly look for the rains in the fall and in the
spring. They patiently wait for the precious harvest
to ripen. You, too, must be patient. And take
courage, for the coming of the Lord is near."

JAMES 5:7–8

"Here, Mom. Check it out!" My son tossed me a tiny bag of
seeds. "They're from my teacher's garden. In the fall, we'll have
gourds."

I looked them over. "Hard to imagine big gourds coming
from these little seeds. This is a vining plant. We'll need a big
patch of ground."

"Maybe the vacant lot behind us," we both said.

We planted those seeds. Over the next few days, it rained
nonstop. I feared many would wash way. I gave up on them
until I noticed seedlings popping up.

As summer heated, I reminded my son to water and weed
the gourd patch. The plants took off and by fall we had beautiful gourds.

I often wondered if the gourds would survive. Too much
rain, sun, or weeds might kill them. But by holding out patiently,
we were rewarded with a bountiful harvest.

Those who are patient reap a precious harvest.

—KARIN LINDSTROM

The "You're Special!" Plate

"Love each other with genuine affection,
and take delight in honoring each other."
ROMANS 12:10

With kids who are prone to breaking dishes, I have several incomplete sets in my cupboard. But one plate doesn't have any matching pieces. It's a beautiful designer plate I picked up for less than $1 at a thrift store. But it has a lot of worth in our family because it's our "You're Special" plate.

We use this plate at the dinner table periodically. When one of us has a birthday, he or she gets the plate at dinner. Or when one of the kids does something special such as participating in a school project, bringing home a good report card, or making a good play in a soccer game (or simply participating in a soccer game!). Or even when we just want to tell someone "You're Special" for no reason at all! It's just one of the little things we do to honor and celebrate each other.

*Start a fun new tradition in your
family with a "You're Special" plate.*

—JGL

A Way Through the Wilderness

"For I am about to do a brand-new thing. See, I
have already begun! Do you not see it? I will make
a pathway through the wilderness for my people to
come home. I will create rivers for them in the desert!"

ISAIAH 43:19

I've always been a suburbs gal. However, I love forests. As a
kid, I played in the woods. As an adult, I love visiting national
parks and driving side roads into forest nooks.

But whenever I'm in a forest, I don't explore the under-
growth—I stick to the paths because the trees and roots and
grass and thickets are just too dense to be able to get through.

That's the kind of scene I picture when I read Isaiah 43:19. I
see a forest filled with dense, weedy emotions, attitudes, actions,
and sins that separate us from being able to get to God. Then
I envision God swooping through the forest with a sickle, a
bulldozer, or whatever other equipment is necessary to break
through the thicket and clear a path for us. Just as we'd do anything to help our kids reach us, he'll do anything to help us
reach him!

*When you feel something is separating you
from God, ask Him to clear your path.*

—JGL

Proper Nourishment

"Who is a faithful, sensible servant, to whom the
master can give the responsibility of managing
his household and feeding his family?"
MATTHEW 24:45

When my children came in from school, they were usually eager
for a snack. A cookie or granola bar and a glass of milk were
just what they needed before grappling with their homework
or setting off for some after-school activity. If I had instead
served roast beef, potatoes, a vegetable, salad, and cheesecake,
it would have been too much for the moment. It would have
overwhelmed them.

In the same way, I learned to give them spiritual food in
the right portions. As opportunities arose to teach them spiritual truth, they didn't need to hear everything I had learned
through years of experience. Nor did they need a summary of
everything I had gleaned from the Bible. Though tempting to
heap up piles of truth and ladle out rich wisdom, just a morsel
or two was all they really needed at a time—and was more easily digested.

*Truth in the proper portions will whet our children's spiritual
appetite, but too much at a time may turn them away.*

—PHYLLIS FARRINGER

Random Acts of Spiritual Blessing

"For I long to visit you so I can share a spiritual blessing
with you that will help you grow strong in the Lord."
ROMANS 1:11

A few years ago, random acts of kindness were all the rage. People focused on just doing nice things for others. I thought of that when I read this verse—this seemed like random acts of spiritual blessing!

I also thought of my kids. *How can I practice random acts of spiritual blessing on my kids?* I wondered. As I started thinking about it, ideas came to mind. For my older stepdaughters, I could send e-cards with scripture messages and words of encouragement and blessing. For my elementary-school-age son, perhaps exploring rocks with him and talking about God's role in nature and science would be a fun blessing. My toddler would love it if I sat with her on my lap and read Bible-story books to her. I realized sharing scripture and the blessing of God's love could lace many family experiences if I just get in the habit.

*How can you share spiritual blessings
with your children this week?*

—JGL

Clay Memory

"So each generation can set its hope
anew on God, remembering his glorious
miracles and obeying his commands."
PSALM 78:7

As soon as I peeked into the kiln I knew I had a problem. My favorite pot, the one that had been slightly crooked after I threw it on the wheel, was crooked again. Nuts! I had worked so hard to straighten it.

I lifted it from the kiln and looked at it more closely, shaking my head in dismay. Clay memory had struck again. Clay memory is the tendency for pots that have been out of shape and subsequently corrected, to return to their original form. It can be disastrous for potters.

But the same principle at work in humans, who are also made of clay, can reap wonderful results for moms. At times, children trained to follow God walk away from Him for a time. But spiritual "clay memory" brings them back. If mothers continue to pray, those same loved ones eventually return to the values they were raised with.

*Be comforted and trust God to work
with your child's memory.*

—JEANNIE ST. JOHN TAYLOR

Follow the Leader?

"And a little child will lead them all."
ISAIAH 11:6

"Please Mommy!" Elizabeth was relentless. She wanted to play outside so badly. But she couldn't go outside alone and I had too much work to do to take her outside. I tried to get her involved in other things that would keep her occupied, but no luck.

What a dilemma! I know being outside getting physical activity in the fresh air is so much better than Elizabeth watching even the best videos. But my work needed top priority.

Finally, I took my notebook computer outside with me. I sat in the shade and put on an old baseball cap to cut down on the glare so I could see the screen, and tried to work.

Surprisingly, it worked well. Elizabeth ran around the yard while I typed away. The breeze felt lovely on my face and the sun toasted my toes. I felt invigorated from being outside. *I need to listen to Elizabeth more often,* I thought.

Sometimes our kids have the best ideas!

—JGL

Keep Trying

"I command you—be strong and courageous!
Do not be afraid or discouraged. For the
Lord your God is with you wherever you go."

JOSHUA 1:9

"Gardner, what's wrong?" Elizabeth asked her big brother.

I turned around. Gardner's head was down and his shoulders shook. He finally explained he couldn't defeat a bad guy on his Nintendo game.

"Honey, remember the last time you were upset because you couldn't defeat someone?" I said. "You kept trying and eventually figured it out."

"Yeah, but I've tried thirty times now," he sobbed.

"When Thomas Edison was trying to make the lightbulb, he tried hundreds of times," I said.

"I know." Gardner gulped.

"He said at least he figured out hundreds of ways not to do it. You just have to keep trying and it will work out eventually."

I thought of Gardner's teen sister. It seemed that no matter what I did, I couldn't get close to her. I was about to just give up when my own words struck me. Gardner and I both decided to keep trying.

If we don't keep trying, we'll certainly never succeed.

—JGL

OCTOBER

WHERE'S ALBERT SCHWEITZER WHEN YOU NEED HIM?

"We were as gentle among you as a mother feeding and caring for her own children. We loved you so much that we gave you not only God's Good News but our own lives, too."

1 THESSALONIANS 2:7–8

hen it comes to sickness and disease among our children, I have a deal with my husband. I handle fevers, sniffles, and anything that oozes from any naturally occurring body cavity; this includes, but is not limited to, the nose, the mouth, the ears, and the "unmentionable" areas. He handles all trauma cases: broken bones; puncture wounds; concussions; and anything that requires stitches, staples, or casts.

This division of labor works out nicely for us for several reasons. One, Rick gags at the first whiff of what nurses euphemistically call "loose bowel movements," and he gets nauseous at the sight/smell/sound of—well—*nausea*. This makes him pretty much unavailable when the kids are leaking from either end of their bodies. Two, I tend to panic whenever one of my children comes home with a bodily injury. I try to remain calm for the child's sake, but that's difficult for me when he is standing in front of me with a pair of scissors protruding from his thigh (yes, that really happened).

We learned early on that it's better for us to specialize. Our first son, Josh, was born with severe jaundice; his skin had the festive autumn glow of a ripe pumpkin. They finally let us bring him home when he was eight days old, but we had to make periodic visits to the clinic for blood tests. With newborns, blood is drawn from the soles of the feet instead of from their teeny-tiny fingers. If a needle prick doesn't do the trick, the nurse "milks" the foot by gently squeezing it. This can sometimes take several minutes. It did with Josh, and he screamed the whole time. I don't mean he cried or sobbed or whimpered. He *screamed.*

And I was devastated. I knew that this procedure was necessary. I knew that Josh wasn't in pain; he was just mad that the nurse was grasping his foot so firmly. I knew all this with the calm, logical part of my brain (yes, I can be logical, but only when it's absolutely necessary). The calm, logical part of my brain wasn't in charge at that moment, however; the hormone-driven new-mom part of my brain was in the driver's seat. I had to leave the room. Rick, on the other hand, held Josh firmly on his lap and observed everything with an engineer's detachment.

Rick definitely is the family champ when it comes to blood and bones, and I am profoundly grateful. There has to be *someone* calm enough to drive to the emergency room. (When Jason stabbed his leg with the scissors, Rick actually ate a bowl of cereal before the two of them headed to the hospital. "We may be there a while," he explained very matter-of-factly. "I don't want to get hungry." Feel free to imagine my reaction.)

But when it comes to anything icky, Rick is one big wimp. If one of our children crawls into bed with us just in time to puke all over my grandmother's quilt, Rick bolts for the bathroom. If a feverish baby fills his diaper with certain "deposits," Rick adjourns to another part of the

317

house. He's not trying to shirk his fatherly duty; he simply cannot handle the aromatic fluids produced by sick children.

I've learned to deal with Gross Childhood Output, or GCO as I call it. Since my husband is useless in this area, it's not like I have a choice. Mouth breathing helps. So does a clothespin on the nose—it hurts like crazy and looks goofy, but desperate times require desperate measures. It also helps if I remind myself that, not long ago, these fluids were actually solid food. It's the same stuff I served for dinner, just liquefied and chemically altered. Okay, this doesn't really help that much. I just wanted to *prove* that I can be logical when the situation calls for it.

I do have one weapon that helps me when I'm emptying the bedside bucket or washing saturated sheets for the seventh time that day. I like to think of Jesus washing the disciples' feet. Jesus and His disciples walked everywhere they went. They traveled along dirt paths and desert trails. They wore sandals. By the end of the day, their feet must have been filthy.

When Jesus tied a towel around His waist and knelt before the first disciple, He didn't complain about the dirt under the nails and the sand between the toes. He didn't turn up His nose in disgust. Instead, He tenderly lifted the man's foot, removed the worn-out sandal, and dipped the foot in the cool water. He lapped water over the top of the foot and gently rubbed the toes clean. He removed the foot and rubbed it dry with the towel. Then He lifted the next foot.

Yes, Jesus did this to teach the disciples a valuable lesson about servanthood, but He also did it because He loved them. Imagine how refreshing it was to have clean feet after a long, exhausting day of travel. Imagine also how refreshing it was to their spirits to know that their Teacher cared enough to take care of this most basic need.

I like to think that when I care for my ailing children, or when Rick drives one of them to the ER *again*, we are showing them the same kind of love Jesus showed His disciples. We care enough about them to bind their wounds, soothe their hurts, and clean up their messes. That says more to them than thousands of "I love yous."

Parenting can be a dirty business. And I'm the one who gets to do it.

—RHONDA WHEELER STOCK

Child's-Eye View

"I will that you, Lord, with all my heart; I will
tell of all the marvelous things you have done. I
will be filled with joy because of you. I will sing
praises to your name, O Most High."
PSALM 9:1–2

I'm sweeping the patio, yet one more time. This week the winds
have been wild. The leaves get tracked into my house. When
I'm not changing diapers, washing faces, and settling argu-
ments, I'm cleaning up leaves so the kids won't eat them and
the house won't get trashed. I'm feeling disgruntled.

I hear Savannah giggling. She has a leaf in her hand. Her
eyes are wide and intent in the amazement of her new discov-
ery. She throws it in the air, watches it float, and retrieves it.

As I watch her I find her enthusiasm and joy contagious.
I feel, once again, the joy every child of God should have in
His creation. The leaves are no longer a burden, but things of
wonder and beauty. The tedium of daily duties melts. I sit on
the ground, sharing with this precious child the love and joy of
His amazing creation.

*With a child's-eye view of God's wonders,
we can learn anew how to give thanks.*

—DONNA LEE LOOMIS

Pretty Feet

"And how will anyone go and tell them without being sent? That is what the Scriptures mean when they say, 'How beautiful are the feet of those who bring good news!'"
ROMANS 10:15

I hardly had time for a shower, let alone a pedicure, before my son's flag football game. My feet were very telling of a mom who had run around barefoot on hardwood floors all day and gardened outdoors. I slid on my flip-flops and headed off to the game. No one will notice my feet today, I thought.

"I like your flip-flops," another mom said. "Thanks," I replied as she continued to stare. I glanced down and, in horror, beheld worn, pasty-looking feet with chipped nail polish. Utterly embarrassed, I curled my feet under the bench for the rest of the game.

I'm comforted to know that God's idea of "beautiful feet" is different from mine. The meaning of this verse isn't limited to evangelists. As moms, we have the unique position of bringing the good news of Jesus to our children, which gives new meaning to our daily routines.

Your feet are beautiful no matter when you had your last pedicure.

—LARYSSA TOOMER

God's Tattoo

"See, I have written your name on my hand. Ever before
me is a picture of Jerusalem's walls in ruins."
ISAIAH 49:16

My oldest stepdaughter adored the teen singing sensation Hanson when she was a young teen. She scribbled their name all over the place—her folders, her jeans, her father's desk mat, and especially her hands—they had "Hanson" or "I love Taylor Hanson" scribbled on them. She had posters of the three boys on her bedroom wall and locker at school.

Kids like to keep the names of their crushes before them.

When the Israelites accused God of no longer loving them because they were going through tough times, He told them He loved them so much that He had their name written on His hands and had a picture of their troubles before Him.

It's the same with us. No matter what problems we go through, God is mindful of them. He has our image before Him, and He has our names on His palm to tell the world we're His.

God has your name on His palm because
He likes to think about you so much!

—JGL

The Umbrella of Protection

"Children, obey your parents because you belong to the Lord, for this is the right thing to do."

EPHESIANS 6:1

"I feel God wants me at camp this week," Alisha announced one Sunday night. For weeks, I'd told her we wanted her to go to the camp. She balked at obeying her parents—until she got the direct word from God. I decided it was time to teach her the "umbrella principle" afresh.

So one night, I gave umbrellas to the kids. They looked bewildered, although the younger ones were delighted.

I told them to put the umbrellas over their heads. "What is an umbrella for?" I asked.

"To keep the rain off of us," they said.

"Right," I added, "it protects you. Pretend Daddy and Mommy are the umbrella God has put up to shield you. As long as you stay under the umbrella by obeying what we tell you, you'll be okay. But if you don't follow orders, you're stepping away from the umbrella and just might not have the same protection."

That drove the message home!

Just as we're umbrellas shielding our kids,
God is the umbrella covering all of us.

—JGL

Who's Driving Your Car?

"Do not be afraid of the terrors of the night,
nor fear the dangers of the day."
PSALM 91:5

"Be home by midnight," I told my son and his friend as the screen door slammed behind them. The friend looked like an alien from some distant galaxy, with his multicolored hair, hardware dangling from his face, and tattooed arms. I watched them climb into the alien's UFO of sorts and drive away.

Before long I questioned my intelligence in letting my son leave. I began worrying. Does he have money to call home? Will that other kid drive safely?

I no longer worried about whether he needed a diaper change or where I put his pacifier. But while times change and bring different worries, God's message remains the same: Pray and be thankful, and peace will be yours.

When my son walked through the door in one piece, I knew then that God does not want us to worry and fight Him for control of life's steering wheel. So, sit back, relax, and try to enjoy the ride.

When God's driving, we can enjoy the ride.

—CARA STOCK

Challenged to Grow

"But grow in the special favor and knowledge of our Lord
and Savior Jesus Christ. To him be all glory and honor,
both now and forevermore. Amen."

2 PETER 3:18

Gary Richmond, a former zookeeper, tells of watching a giraffe giving birth. He was astounded that the giraffe gave birth standing up—a ten-foot drop for the newborn.

Also amazing was the mother's treatment of the baby. As soon as the little one landed on the ground, the mom kicked it forcefully until it was on its feet. Then she knocked the baby down and kicked it until it got up again.

Gary wondered why the mother seemed to be so cruel. Someone explained: in the wild, giraffes roamed in herds for safety. A mother and baby away from the herd were vulnerable. The mother needed to get the baby up and strong enough so they could catch up with the herd and be safe.

Though none of us would kick newborns, we give our children age-appropriate challenges in all areas of their lives and they learn to stretch and grow.

Just as God challenges us to growth,
we can encourage our children's growth.

—JGL

Comforting Arms

"I will comfort you there as a child is
comforted by its mother."
ISAIAH 66:13

Like every other mother I know, I remember the birth of all four
of my children. I recall the ensuing years when my children
suffered skinned knees, fractured bones, and broken hearts.
They always depended on me to comfort them and reassure
them that they would heal and be okay. They knew that their
mother's love was one thing they could count on!

I raised very independent children; they have learned
through the years to be self-sufficient. Yet at times they still
come to me for comfort when worried or in emotional pain.
They know no matter how old or experienced they are, I will
always be there to love and comfort them in their troubles, just
as God gives us the comfort we seek from Him in our emotional, physical, or spiritual distress.

*God's loving arms are always available when I need comfort
from the worries and cares of this world.*

—BETTY KING

Under Siege

"I am not afraid of ten thousand enemies
who surround me on every side."
PSALM 3:6

My time and energy are under attack on every flank. I leave the office on Friday with more unfinished tasks than I had on Monday morning. Driving home, I am battered by the reminder to schedule an oil change and to have the tires rotated. I retreat to my fortress. Sigh. I find solace from the world at the dinner table with my family. Then dirty dishes ambush me. Around the corner, the overflowing hamper prepares an assault. The laundry room conceals stacks of clean clothes, yet another onslaught. The adversaries of my agenda lurk everywhere.

I plan my counterattack. I launch a cleaning campaign. Our refrigerator art gallery catches my eye. I pause. How I cherish the people who make all this mess. I am so blessed to be a part of their lives. I thank God to be the mom.

Be sure to make time to be thankful for your family.

SUSAN PARIS

If You Say So . . .

"'Master,' Simon replied, 'we worked hard all
last night and didn't catch a thing.
But if you say so, we'll try again.'"
LUKE 5:5

Peter was still a fisherman called Simon when Jesus borrowed his boat to stand on while he spoke to a shore filled with people. After he finished speaking, Jesus told Peter to go out a little farther and his nets would be full of fish.

Now that directive didn't make sense. The men had fished all night and gotten nothing. How could this guy who wasn't even a fisherman give them advice?

But Peter decided to trust Jesus and try again. They took in so much fish that the boat nearly sunk.

Sometimes it seems as if God asks us to do illogical things, or things that we think won't work. Maybe something like, "Try a devotional time with my kids? Yeah, right . . . they never listened before!"

"Kiss my kids before they go to bed every night? They're seventeen and fifteen—they won't want that!"

"Take a day off work to spend with my kids when they're home from school?"

But when God directs us, he also has reasons for doing so.

Is God asking you to do something that doesn't seem to make
sense? Go for it—and get your nets ready for the blessing!

—JGL

Love Means . . .

"But I confess my sins. I am deeply
sorry for what I have done."
PSALM 38:18

"Love means never having to say you're sorry."

That was the popular statement when I was growing up. I remember I had a figurine of a boy and girl that spun to the *Love Story* theme and had those words on the front of it. It was such a romantic notion—that people who loved each other never had to apologize.

Then I got married. There's nothing like marriage and kids to blow all your romantic notions! I find love means *always* having to say you're sorry!

When a bunch of people live in one house, it's so easy for feelings to get hurt, for misunderstandings to abound, and for people to catch you acting like a bad example. A child whose feelings you hurt doesn't understand that love means not having to say you're sorry. In fact, resentment builds if we don't admit our mistakes and apologize.

*Love truly means quickly admitting and
apologizing for our errors.*

—JGL

When Mom Can't, God Can!

"Keep me safe, O God, for I have come to you for refuge."
PSALM 16:1

It was a great day for a bike ride. I was behind my daughter, Carol, staying safely in the right-hand lane. Suddenly, a fiercely barking dog ran into the street and startled her. As she pedaled faster and faster, watching him over her right shoulder, the bike veered to the left, and she didn't realize she was heading straight into traffic.

I could only watch in horror as I saw her crossing into the second lane of traffic. She couldn't hear my warning, and I couldn't catch up to her. Thankfully the drivers slowed down until the dog gave up and she could get back to the right side of the road.

Sometimes danger attacks our children and we can only watch. But just as God was with Carol on that bike ride, he is with them during other dangerous times, too, when we cannot be.

When mom can't be there, God is!

—MERILYN MILLIKAN

When the Loving Gets Tough

> "Love never gives up, never loses faith, is always hopeful,
> and endures through every circumstance."
> 1 Corinthians 13:7

"Someone else can take care of your dad," a friend said when my father grew ill. "You have a family to care for."

But Dad had no one else, and I wanted to be there for him. So, for the next five months, I was Dad's primary caregiver, taking him to doctors and sitting with him in the ERs and hospitals and skilled nursing facilities. I paid his bills and took responsibility for him.

But I wasn't alone. Every step of the way, my kids helped me. They also spent hours with Grandpa and took care of him. They never complained, although our whole family revolved around his needs.

Initially, I'd thought about shielding my kids from this painful stage of age and dying. But they learned valuable lessons about honoring parents, teamwork, family, sacrificing your own interests for someone you love, and persevering when life gets tough.

Sacrificial love in tough situations is the
best kind of love for our children to learn.

—JGL

Life's Shooting Stars

> "Look up into the heavens. Who created all the
> stars? He brings them out one after another,
> calling each by its name. And he counts them to
> see that none are lost or have strayed away."
> ISAIAH 40:26

We bought the old dressers at a garage sale. Three-year-old Sean and six-year-old Ryan were excited about transforming the dressers with a coat of paint. After we sanded, primed, and painted, we were ready for the fun part. The boys would stamp stars all over the dressers.

I showed them how to avoid smudges and drips, and then let them go at it. All was going well when Sean dragged a stamp.

I said, "Oh, you smudged that one."

"No, I didn't," he replied. "That's a shooting star."

I looked again and saw a shooting star falling through the night sky. I also saw that while I had aimed for perfection and conformity, he shot for creativity and individualism.

That star reminds me that we cannot be perfect because only God is perfect. In His perfect love, He sees us as individuals and loves us, smudges and all.

God loves each one of us just as He created us: uniquely.

—MARY GALLAGHER

The Rewards

"Wise words bring many benefits,
and hard work brings rewards."
PROVERBS 12:14

Playing his Nintendo DS was Gardner's favorite pastime, and for weeks he'd longed for a certain new game. He carefully saved his allowance and offered to do extra chores to earn more money. Each day he checked his savings several times in case the amount had miraculously grown.

One night when he was talking about his money and the game he wanted to get, I teased him with, "My birthday's coming up. Are you going to get me a nice present?"

"I'm not going to wait until your birthday. I want to go buy you a present tomorrow because I love you so much and you're such a good mom," he said decisively. He paused, and I could almost see the calculator adding amounts in his brain. He got a worried look. Then he smiled and said, "Mom, you're more important than a game."

*Thankfully, sometimes parenting has
the nicest heart-stirring rewards.*

—JGL

When Guys Bond

"So God created people in his own image; God patterned them after himself; male and female he created them."
GENESIS 1:27

"So, what's a highlight of being a parent?" the small-group leader asked.

My husband answered, "Last night I taught my son to make vulgar noises on his arm."

I rolled my eyes. Gardner is at that age when he and his dad like to make rude noises and, well, act like guys.

My initial response is to teach my son to just stop it. But I realized this is a male form of bonding. As I watched my guys try to outdo each other in making rude noises, I realized it was becoming almost a nightly ritual—and they seemed to better enjoy each other's company all day long. At times I say, "Enough!" And I don't tolerate it at inappropriate times. But who am I to keep dad and son from communicating—even if I don't understand the language?

Boys will be boys—and maybe a
smart mom remembers that!

—JGL

The Cutting Edge of Opera

"Now there are different kinds of spiritual gifts, but it is
the same Holy Spirit who is the source of them all."
1 CORINTHIANS 12:4

Twenty years ago when we took our son for a kindergarten evaluation, the teacher suggested we keep him home another year because he couldn't cut well with scissors. We were devastated! Our bright five-year-old was anxious to start school with his friends. After several days, we decided he was ready and we enrolled him in school.

As young parents, we wasted days agonizing over whether he would keep up with his peers. Through the years, we discovered that all children move at their own pace, developing skills they need when they need them. God gives every child different gifts.

Today, Chad is a confident opera singer with a master's degree in performance. He has traveled the globe pursuing his passion.

Chad wasn't destined to be a famous artist who creates masterpieces, but he has never been denied an opera role because he couldn't cut well with scissors.

*Instead of worrying over what our children
can't do, we can help them find what they can do.*

—JENNIE HILLIGUS

The King of Compassion

"When the Lord saw her, his heart overflowed
with compassion. 'Don't cry!' he said."

LUKE 7:13

"Hey man." A stranger approached my husband as he pumped gas. "I need to buy oil for my car so I can go see my sick dad, but I forgot my wallet."

I looked around and saw no empty car—only a bar across the street.

My husband didn't look for collaboration as he opened his wallet. God's given Mark a gift of compassion, and many hard-luck stories—whether financial appeals, or excuses from our kids—get the benefit of his doubt. His heart just overflows with compassion. Kinda like Jesus, I guess.

Compassion was also a main element of Jesus's life. Day after day, He was bombarded by people who had needs. Jesus truly felt their pain, and used His abilities to help them.

Jesus still has more compassion than we can ever fathom. He has compassion for moms as they do the best job possible to raise their kids. When we need sympathy or help, Jesus is happy to be there for us.

When we have needs, we can turn to
the one whose compassion is unending.

—JGL

Too Tired To Pray

"Share each other's troubles and problems,
and in this way obey the law of Christ."
GALATIANS 6:2

My youngest son was born with a condition called esophageal reflux. As a result, he spent the first three months of life eating, throwing up, crying, and sleeping in fifteen-minute increments. An additional diagnosis was added as a result—failure to thrive.

Complicating matters, my other son was not quite two. Some days were more than I could bear. Most days I was too tired to think. My nerves were shot; I lived on diet sodas and crackers.

But I was blessed with several wonderful neighborhood "grandmas." Whenever it seemed I was at my very end, I'd walk next door and hand them the baby. They'd hold and rock him, allowing my sanity to return. Once my son had surgery and things settled down, I found out something else they'd been doing. Praying! Even though my boys are now sixteen and eighteen, I still praise God for those women's prayers.

*Do you know of another mom who needs the
life-giving, and life-saving, power of prayer?*

—LAURA BROADWATER

Just Trust?

"For the word of the Lord holds true,
and everything he does is worthy of our trust."
PSALM 33:4

Two-year-old Nathan jumped onto a pile of sofa cushions and smacked his head on a wooden footstool. He ran to his mom, who dried his tears and hugged him.

Later, he jumped off the stairs, into Mommy's arms. He didn't doubt that she would catch him, even though he had gotten hurt under her watchful eye earlier. Nor did he doubt that she would catch him even though he had not been a good listener that day—he'd fought with his brother over a toy and refused to sleep during his naptime.

His trust in his mother's care was not affected by his performance or even his hurts.

It is a simple formula that children employ. We adults are the ones who tend to complicate matters. We fret about whether our prayers are being heard, whether we will get an answer, and doubt that we deserve either.

*May we all have the faith of a child and boldly approach
God, in full confidence that we are loved with an
everlasting love and that He is worthy of our trust.*

—SHEILA SOULE

I Didn't Really Mean It!

"But if instead of showing love among yourselves
you are always biting and devouring one another,
watch out! Beware of destroying one another."
GALATIANS 5:15

"Sometimes I think you don't like me at all!" I looked into the grief-stricken face of my friend Kevin. "You always say such, well, mean things!"

Kevin was my good friend and I loved him dearly. Admittedly, I teased him a lot, but it was only teasing. Surely he *knew* I ribbed him so much only because I thought he was wonderful.

Obviously, he did *not* know that.

I learned a lesson from Kevin that has stayed with me: why say uncomplimentary things even in teasing? Even though it usually is meant affectionately, sometimes there's a barb behind teasing. And it's too likely to be misunderstood—especially by our kids, who tend to take it to heart.

Over time, I've broken the habit of teasing and really bite my tongue when temptation strikes. Instead, I try to show affection by using words that are lavish praise and *can't* be misunderstood.

*"Say what you mean and mean what
you say" is a good axiom for all of us!*

—JGL

Do As I Do . . .

"And you should follow my example,
just as I follow Christ's."
1 CORINTHIANS 11:1

I don't remember learning to read, but when I was a kid, my head was always in a book. At night, instead of sleeping, I was often curled under the covers with a flashlight and a book.

My parents never told me to read. But I think they still set me on this lifelong love because I saw them read. They read the newspaper every day. Dad was a blue-collar laborer, but at home, he often sat and read different volumes of the encyclopedia for pleasure. And Mom was always reading a church magazine or novel.

Besides being an example, my parents also provided the means for me to pursue this habit—I wore out several library cards.

I learned from my parents that a way to instill good habits in my kids is to model the behavior, and to make the tools accessible.

*Whether they realize they're doing it or not,
kids follow our examples.*

—JGL

How to Be a "Perfect" Mom

"For by that one offering he perfected forever
all those whom he is making holy."
HEBREWS 10:14

"It's all up to me now." Driving away from the hospital with my precious bundle snuggled in the carrier in the backseat, I had my first case of the yips. Anxiety, guilt, self-doubt all rolled into one. Axe murderer or Nobel Prize winner, the child was my responsibility. What was I thinking? I don't need that kind of pressure!

The pressure didn't lessen as my children grew into sweet, wonderful kids. What if I messed them up, did something wrong, scarred them for life? Yikes!

Then I understood God was the one who gave me the job of parenting, and He's the one who perfected me for it.

God knows my makeup and the makeup of my children, and He determined that we are a perfect match. Of all the mothers in the world, there is only one perfect mom for Lauren, Alan, and their little sibling on the way, and that's . . . me!

I don't have to "be" the perfect mom—
God perfected me for the job.

—PAULA WISEMAN

Decisions, Decisions!

> "One day soon afterward Jesus went to a mountain to pray, and he prayed to God all night. At daybreak he called together all of his disciples and chose twelve of them to be apostles."
>
> LUKE 6:12–13

Decisions. Like all moms, I make them all day. Within a week, we make hundreds of decisions without any prolonged thinking.

But once in a while a decision comes along that *does* require more consideration. I'm so used to making decisions that sometimes, I take all the burdens for tough decisions on myself.

Recently, I've learned to go to a couple of other sources. I've learned my husband is more than willing to share the burden—if I just tell him about it instead of trying to handle it on my own.

And especially on kid matters, I also seek the advice of friends who are further along in the parenting process.

I'm also learning many times I miss the first step in tough decisions—asking God what I should do. Jesus was God's son, but even He prayed about decisions. In fact He spent the whole night in prayer before He appointed His disciples.

*If even Jesus needed input on decisions,
how much more do we!*

—JGL

A Lesson from the Laundry Room

"You slaves must obey your earthly masters in everything you do. Try to please them all the time, not just when they are watching you. Obey them willingly because of your reverent fear of the Lord. Work hard and cheerfully at whatever you do, as though you were working for the Lord rather than for people."

COLOSSIANS 3:22–23

The laundry room was silent, and the door was shut.
I did not want to face what lay behind that closed door. My two-year-old daughter had probably dumped out an entire bag of pet food, or was busily soaking socks in the dog's water bowl again.

With dread, I creaked open the laundry room door.

"Hi, mommy!" Katie's blue eyes glowed proudly. In shocked amazement, I saw that she was hard at work placing the entire clean contents of my dryer inside an empty laundry basket.

Every day, we face the choice my daughter did: with no one but the Lord for our audience, we can choose to make a mess or choose to use our time to bless others, no matter how small or unnoticed the task.

Our reward? Blessing the heart of the One who matters most, and storing up praise that will last forever.

How can you use your time to bless others
when only God is watching?

—KATHERINE CRADDOCK

My Daughter, Myself

"How can you think of saying, 'Let me help you get
rid of that speck in your eye,' when you can't see past
the log in your own eye? Hypocrite! First get rid of the
log from your own eye; then perhaps you will see well
enough to deal with the speck in your friend's eye."
MATTHEW 7:4–5

My oldest daughter was driving me nuts with her whining. She
was only four, but I was concerned about her attitude. I poured
out my prayers in a notebook: Where is this coming from, Lord?
How can I guide her and train her when she's so negative and
stubborn?

The voice that responded was quiet, succinct, and clear:
"Repent."

I knew I was hearing the Lord, and he wasn't referring to
my daughter. He was addressing me! I had a negative attitude
toward motherhood, and some days I would have resigned
gladly if someone just showed me where I could turn in my
paperwork.

I sighed. "Lord, forgive me for my complaining, for my
impatience. Help me to love my children as you do," I prayed.

A week later, I was amazed at how quickly Lindsey's behavior improved after I confessed my sins!

*Lord, help me to take a good look
in my spiritual mirror each day!*

—LYNNETTE P. HORNER

Faith of a Child

"The Lord is my strength, my shield from every danger. I trust in him with all my heart. He helps me, and my heart is filled with joy. I burst out in songs of thanksgiving."

PSALM 28:7

"Thurman, watch out!" my mother shrieked.

"I can't do anything," my father calmly replied. "We're floating."

So that's why those houses are built on stilts, I thought, looking out the window. I couldn't see any pavement—just floodwater climbing up the doors of cars. Then I put my head against the window and went back to sleep.

On another vacation, we were driving to the top of Pike's Peak—in the days before the narrow roads were lined by guardrails or closed in bad weather. As we drove higher, the gentle summer snow became a blizzard. We couldn't see other cars on the road—couldn't see the road or its edge. I remember my mother shrieking, "Turn around!" and my father saying, "Where?"

We have pictures to prove the danger, but I slept through most of it.

Sleeping sickness? No, I implicitly trusted my father. I knew he could get us out of any situation.

When it comes to trusting our heavenly Father, maybe we should regain the faith of a child.

—JGL

Little Shadows

"Every time I think of you, I give thanks to my God."
PHILIPPIANS 1:3

No matter how often I clean my office, it's soon a mess again. It's not because I'm a total slob. Like my kids always claim, "I didn't do it!"

My toddler did. Two baby dolls nap on top of files in an open file drawer. With them safely in bed, she has spread coins on the papers I refer to as I type. Even more goodies abound on the floor.

I try to keep her out of my office so it has a shot at being clean and I have a chance to concentrate, but otherwise, I've learned to ignore it and to let her play by me.

What can I say? She likes to be with me. Maybe if she hangs out with me now—even if it messes up my office—she'll want to hang out with me as she grows older. What mom could ask for more?

Even when it's inconvenient, we can thank
God that our children want to be with us!

—JGL

God's Top Ten List

"See how very much our heavenly Father loves us, for he allows us to be called his children, and we really are! . . ."

1 JOHN 3:1

For Mother's Day my son gave me a Top Ten list of why he loves me. It includes things like "She tickles me" and "She finds time to play with me."

I thought it would be cute to write a Top Ten list telling all the reasons why I love him. I soon noticed the flaw in this idea. I do not love my son because of anything he does for me; I love him because he is my child.

God doesn't make a Top Ten list for His children either. We may be tempted to think He does. We may imagine it contains things like "She attends church every week" or "She gives to the poor," but we can't earn His love or cause Him to love us more than He already did when He gave His life for us. He does not love us if or when, He simply loves us.

God's love is unconditional.

—MARY GALLAGHER

The Ghost That Comforts

"And I will pray to the Father, and he will give
you another Counselor, who will never leave you."
JOHN 14:16

As my sons went through a tub of Beanie Babies to play with, my older son badgered my younger son, trying to convince his younger brother to pick the ghost Beanie. My older son demanded, "You have to play with the ghost! What are you so afraid of?"

My youngest wailed, "I'm telling Mommy! I don't want to play with that. I'm too scared to play with the ghost!"

Without hesitation, my oldest son explained, "There's nothing to be scared of. Don't you know that it's the Holy Ghost?"

My younger son's countenance changed immediately. "Oh! Hi, Holy Ghost," my youngest exclaimed as he hugged the ghost Beanie to his heart.

While humorous, the exchange between my sons reminded me of how much easier we could take life's challenges if we remember that God sent His Holy Spirit to comfort us in the midst of our doubts and fears.

*When we are fearful, we can be comforted
by God's Holy Spirit.*

—MaRita Teague

Calling in Backup Help

"If two of you agree down here on earth concerning
anything you ask, my Father in heaven will do it for
you. For where two or three gather together because
they are mine, I am there among them."
MATTHEW 18:19–20

For the whole year, I tried to make it to the moms' prayer meeting. I wanted to get to know the other Christian moms in my son's school, and to pray with them about our kids' needs. But with my work schedule—and our family schedule—it just wasn't feasible.

Thankfully, I discovered an alternative: e-mail prayer. When I face tough stuff with my kids and long for someone else to pray about it, I have special friends I can send e-mails to. The last time, they even prayed round-robin—each person typing a prayer and clicking "reply to all" so everyone would get the prayer and add theirs to it, like the "two or three gathered together" that the Bible mentions.

It's better to find support and encouragement and prayer backing in person. But when that's not possible, think creatively. Try an e-mail prayer loop or other means with your mom friends!

Never hesitate to get prayer backup!

—JGL

The Real Treat

"If we say we have no sin, we are only fooling
ourselves and refusing to accept the truth."
1 JOHN 1:8

"Aaah!" I shrieked as the lion entered the room. I guess my histrionics were pretty effective.

"Mommy, it's only me!" my son quickly reassured.

Didn't you just love it when you dressed up for Halloween or a fall party and your parents pretended they didn't know you? Kids love playing make-believe!

We parents sometimes play make-believe, too. We may make believe we're perfect and never do anything wrong. The problem is that our kids see through our pretense as clearly as we see them in their seasonal costumes.

The main thing is not to pretend we're perfect when we're not. We can honestly let them know, "Mommy doesn't act like she should sometimes, either. Let's pray for each other, and I'll work on it."

As they see us honestly acknowledge and work through our imperfections, they learn how to do that in their own lives.

*We can't trick our kids about who we
really are, but we can treat them to a good
example even through our human failings.*

—JGL

November

Thanksgiving Shadows

"Teach us to make the most of our time,
so that we may grow in wisdom."
Psalm 90:12

I will always remember a Thanksgiving Day many years ago. My husband, Bob, and our two children drove to my parents' home in St. Louis. By afternoon on this feast day, the aroma of roasting turkey and cornbread dressing floated through the house. My twin sister, Alberta, and I chatted as we helped in the kitchen. Our husbands and kids relaxed in the living room.

Our children, Karen, seven, and John, five, sauntered into the kitchen. "Where's the turkey?" John called out. I pointed to the oven where it hid in a baking bag. "We'll eat soon," I said, giving him a hug.

Full of restless energy, John found his cousins, Mark and Diana, in the next room. He began to chase them through the house.

"Hold it!" Bob yelled. They slowed to a trot. Then thirteen-year-old Mark got away from John and sprawled into a living-room chair. A satisfied grin spread across his face.

I studied Mark, a big-boned, soft-spoken teenager. I adored him. Sunlight danced across the top of his head on the synthetic fibers of the light blond wig he had worn for several years.

We must savor every minute today, I thought. I looked away so Mark couldn't see my misty eyes. At family gatherings we didn't mention Mark's dreaded disease—leukemia. Since his diagnosis at age six and a half, many prayers and chemotherapy had brought long remissions. Our family prayed for Mark's healing and saw God's faithfulness in many ways. But recently, medical reports showed worrisome changes.

What does a mother do in such a situation? I wondered. Alberta, a strong Christian, trusted the Lord with all her heart, a mother's heart—filled to the brim with love. She and her husband, Ron, gave Mark wonderful experiences and nurtured him in the Christian faith. Mark grew in closeness to Christ and relied on the Bible as his guide.

Pushing my thoughts aside, I headed to the dining-room table, where rust and yellow mums from the yard formed a triumphant centerpiece. Every year Mother covered the table with her favorite linen cloth, sterling silverware, and fine china.

"Time to serve the food!" my mother called out. Alberta and I carried in cauliflower with cream sauce, giblet gravy, and steaming dressing. Ron and Bob lifted the plump turkey to a large platter. Diana watched every move. Then my beaming father took his place at the head of the table to carve the turkey.

Little John, in a dress shirt with a red clip-on tie, sat next to Mark. He always wanted to be near Mark.

"I want lots of turkey!" Mark said with an eager smile. He nudged John, "How about you?"

When the family was seated, all ten of us joined hands around the table. Heads bowed. A hush. Then my mother began her spontaneous prayer. "Thank You, Lord, that we are all gathered here together." Her voice broke. "We praise You, O God...."

Tears burned my eyes. Mother continued to thank God for specific things. Then she said, "Bless each one here at his deepest need." My father tightened his big hand around mine.

An indescribable sweetness swept over us as. It was like we had come into a great cathedral. God's presence is so gentle and real.

God strengthened us for the days ahead. Mark valiantly fought his illness, but he got weaker. Still he kept his sense of humor. He remained sensitive to others' needs. One day Mark saw his mother immersed in her Bible. Her face must have revealed her heavy heart. "Don't worry, Mom," he said lovingly. "That's what God's for."

Mark lived fully his rich relationships with God, his family, and his friends. Five months after that Thanksgiving, he went to heaven just as Easter was dawning across our world. *It's much too soon!* I cried in my grief. We all missed Mark terribly.

When the chilly winds of November sweep over me each year, I often think of our last Thanksgiving with Mark and God's nearness. We still miss Mark. Yet I have a deep, unexplainable assurance of God's steadfast love and mysterious ways. He comforts us and brings us to a place where we want to thank him for endless blessings even amid our personal losses.

—CHARLOTTE ADELSPERGER

Can You Hear Me now?

"The eyes of the Lord watch over those who do
right, and his ears are open to their prayers."
1 Peter 3:12.

I had just finished Gary Chapman's book, The *Five Love Languages of Teenagers*. And took plenty of notes. So, while my son ate his breakfast, I enlightened him with love-language lingo. (Every twelve-year-old's dream conversation, of course!)

As I rambled, Josh stopped mid-slurp of Captain Crunch to ask a poignant question:

"Mom."

"Yeah, honey?" *My ears tuned with expectancy.*

"Which land animal is the loudest—a howler monkey, a hyena, or an African elephant?" he asked, his eyes pasted to the back of his cereal box.

It's tough to connect with your son when his mind is . . . well, on another continent. We parents understand that, although it may not be easy—especially over Captain Crunch. Staying in touch with our children is worth all the effort we can muster.

God feels the same about us. In our frenzied mommy worlds of lunches, laundry, and to-do lists, connecting with God remains simple: through prayer. God longs to enter our preoccupied state and listen to our hearts—*His ears tuned with expectancy.*

God's ears are tuned to us with expectancy.

—Elizabeth Duewel

Someone's Watching

"Thereafter Hagar referred to the Lord, who had
spoken to her as, 'the God who sees me'..."
GENESIS 16:13

You won't receive a standing ovation when you change the
twentieth diaper of the day. No one will congratulate you when
you read *Green Eggs and Ham* a hundred times without skip-
ping a word.

No one will see your victory dance when you remember to
remove the clothes from the dryer the same day you put them
in. And on nights when you don't know who has shed more
tears, the baby or you, it's awfully hard to feel like the Proverbs
31 woman. You may wonder if your work really matters.

But if God saw an expectant mother alone in the desert,
surely He's watching over you.

He has seen all the ouchies you've kissed, the sleep you've
missed. He's counted the tears you've cried and the hours spent
rocking a fussy babe.

As you nurture your children, you are truly doing what
pleases Him, and you are not alone.

Remember that He is "the God who sees."

—CINDY HVAL

Follow Your Mom-stincts

"So, my dear brothers and sisters, be strong and steady,
always enthusiastic about the Lord's work, for you know
that nothing you do for the Lord is ever useless."
1 CORINTHIANS 15:58

"The kind of music you listen to does affect your thoughts and
the way you act," I told my teen stepdaughters. They rolled their
eyes and looked at me as if I were crazy.

But now, scientists have now done a study that backs what
many Christians have said for years: hearing sexual lyrics in
songs can encourage teens to have sex at earlier ages. The study,
released in the August 2006 issue of *Pediatrics*, found that
kids who listened to pop music with sexual lyrics drastically
increased sexual involvement within two years, compared with
teens who didn't listen to pop music with sexual lyrics.

The encouragement we can find in studies like this is the
reminder that we can follow our instincts. Whether or not a
study has yet been done on whatever we feel may be spiritually,
emotionally, or physically harmful for our kids, we should, for
the most part, trust our instincts.

*As you guide your kids, keep following
the insights God gives you.*

—JGL

Like Pulling Teeth!

"Don't think only about your own affairs, but be
interested in others, too, and what they are doing."
PHILIPPIANS 2:4

"How was your day at school?"

"Okay."

"What interesting things happened today?"

"Nothing."

Those are pretty much the answers I get from our teen,
whether it's school or coming home from a party or whatever.
Sometimes it's like pulling teeth trying to get in a conversation
with your kids.

I've learned a couple of things over the years that help. One
thing I've learned is that even my talkative kids aren't ready to
talk the minute they get home from school or an event. But if
I'm working in a common area in our house, after ten or fifteen
minutes, they'll wander to where I am and start chatting.

I also find that my children are likely to get chattier if we
get involved in a project together (even if it's cutting potatoes
for dinner). And our teen gets chatty if we go out for a long
drive or shopping together.

*When your kids don't seem to want to communicate, keep
trying and letting them know you're interested in their lives,
and they'll open up in their timing!*

—JGL

Hidden Dangers

"Fear of the Lord gives life, security,
and protection from harm."
PROVERBS 19:23

Ten-month-old Zachary crawled into the bathroom chasing
the cat. Darjeeling jumped into the tub to keep from having
her tail pulled. Zachary pulled up on the edge of the tub and
babbled at her.

"Dat!" he scolded her, reaching for her tail. She jumped out
and he turned to pet her, losing his balance. I stepped forward
as he fell backward. I caught him with his head scarcely an inch
off the hard tile floor. Much of my day is spent protecting my
son from dangers he doesn't know exist.

Later, I closed the basement door so Zachary couldn't fall
down the stairs, and remembered when God closed the door
on a relationship in my life, probably saving me from a broken
marriage. At the time, I didn't understand. All these years later,
I realized, God protects His children, too.

*So many times God protects us when we
don't even know we're in danger.*

—CORA ALLEN

NOVEMBER 6

Putting Words in Our Mouths

"So we have continued praying for you ever since we first
heard about you. We ask God to give you a complete
understanding of what he wants to do in your lives, and
we ask him to make you wise with spiritual wisdom."

COLOSSIANS 1:9

I don't see my oldest stepdaughter, Nicole, very often anymore.
She got married three years ago, and has moved 200 miles away.
Between her and her husband's work schedules and ours, we
seldom connect in person.

We talk to her on the phone, but without the frequent contact, I'm not quite sure how to pray for Nicole.

Then I found Colossians 1:9 and decided it's a good verse
to pray for all of my kids, but especially Nicole and my teen
stepdaughter, Alisha. Both are trying to plot their futures and
grow in their faith.

When we don't know what to pray for our kids, we can
ask the Lord to show us Bible verses that we can pray for our
kids, placing their names in the verses. Then, we can share the
verses with our kids. It's just another way to let them know we
care!

*When we don't know what to pray, we can
borrow our words from God's Word.*

—JGL

Got Friends?

"Two people can accomplish more than twice as much as one; they get a better return for their labor. If one person falls, the other can reach out and help. But people who are alone when they fall are in real trouble."

ECCLESIASTES 4:9–10

I started to leave, but my friend shut the door in front of me. We had just had a bittersweet conversation about my unmarried daughter who was becoming a mother. Now I was on my way to meet her for her first doctor's appointment. My friend looked into my already tearstained eyes and said, "Just remember, you will never have this moment again. Make the most of it and walk in love—Grandma!"

That's what a mom's friends are for! Challenging us through our hurts, lending an emotional hand, and seeing clearly when tears blur our focus. Or they're there for times of crisis, like my other friend, who brought me some new clothes as I prepared to fly out of town unexpectedly after news of my dad's heart attack. Seeing the emergency, she knew I'd need a few things!

Friends—they're just always there!

—KAREN MOREROD

NOVEMBER 8

No Surprises for God

"You saw me before I was born. Every day of my
life was recorded in your book. Every moment
was laid out before a single day had passed."
PSALM 139:16

Today after dinner my husband gave me the big news. We've
taken thousands out of savings to pay basic bills for several
months, our health insurance is rising to $1,500 a month, and
we can't even afford to drive 600 miles to see Granny as we'd
planned.

Anyone want a serving of depression for dessert?

You've been there. At times like these we face choices—
not just financially and in our attitudes, but in our faith.

After my husband gave me the glorious news, we prayed
together. Then I saw Psalm 139:16 on my computer screen.

If God is truly God, and knows all things, as He says in His
Word, then He knows about this financial mess. He also knows
how He'll see us through it—after all, He's brought us through
tough times before.

So I'm choosing to skip the depression dessert and hop
straight to the after-dinner cup of faith. Join me?

Since God knows our future, we can look to Him.

—JGL

Just Because You're His

"Can a mother forget her nursing child? Never!
Can she feel no love for a child she has borne? But
even if that were possible, I would not forget you!"
ISAIAH 49:15

My son David was four months old. He had on the cutest clothes—a yellow-and-white shorts outfit with a cute bunny on it. As my husband and I stood before the church during the dedication service, I thought of how much I loved this child. He had done nothing for me—no crayon drawings, no macaroni artwork. In fact, during my pregnancy, he had caused me morning sickness, hours of labor, and pain. After his birth he had given me sleepless nights and dirty diapers and required constant attention.

Yet my overpowering love for my son was almost palpable. I would have gladly laid down my life for him. I glimpsed what unconditional love is in its simplest and purest form—the love of a parent for a child. And I realized how God loves us, even when we do nothing for Him but cause Him pain and grief. We are His children.

*God's love for us has no requirements
and no strings attached.*

—CONNIE DUNN

Rubble Trouble

"A person without self-control is as
defenseless as a city with broken-down walls."
PROVERBS 25:28

"Rubble, rubble, toil and trouble," I muttered. Frazzled over rebuilding our hearth, I altered Shakespeare's line to lighten my mood. So many delays! When you factored in work, family, and curious pets, completion seemed impossible. When my daughter's flailing tantrum increased the mess, anger flared in me and I stifled a yell. Be the grown-up, I told myself.

I knelt and regrouped the scattered bricks. Surprisingly, my youngster helped. "It's good to share how we feel," I said, "but we also need to respect each other."

On the other side of our makeshift wall, her eyes filled. "Words are like bricks," I added, silently grateful for this unfolding insight. "They either come between us and make us stumble, or they keep us safe."

After we dismantled our barrier—both physical and emotional—that newly opened space was perfect for hugging.

In Christ, we can temper our tempers.

—LAURIE KLEIN

Love Snuggles

"Most important of all, continue to show deep love for
each other, for love covers a multitude of sins."
1 PETER 4:8

"I can't do it!" Simon cried out. He was having the hardest time
learning to read.

"C'mon, sweetie, try to sound out this letter," his mom,
Christy, encouraged.

But Simon puckered up his face angrily. Despite her coaxing, Christy could get nothing more out of him.

The next day Christy sat on Simon's bed. "Lord, what can
I do to help Simon learn to read?" Christy prayed. She picked
up a picture Bible sitting by the bed and thumbed through it.
A picture caught her eye of Jesus holding children on his lap.
"Maybe that will help," she thought.

That night when it was time to work on reading, Christy
plopped on Simon's bed and pulled him onto her lap. They
hugged and chatted for a while. Then she picked up Simon's
book.

Simon was still less than totally willing to learn, but he
seemed more willing to try, safe in his mother's arms.

Sometimes a little love snuggle goes a long way.

—JGL

The Miracle of "Always Enough"

"So she did as Elijah said, and she and Elijah and her
son continued to eat from her supply of flour and oil
for many days. For no matter how much they used,
there was always enough left in the containers, just
as the Lord had promised through Elijah."

1 KINGS 17:15–16

Elijah was on the run from people who were trying to kill him.
At first God had ravens bring him his meals (v. 6). But then God
directed him to go visit a widow in Zarephath to be taken care
of. When Elijah arrived there and asked for food, the woman
told him she had enough food to make one more meal and then,
without provisions, she and her son would die.

Elijah told her to go ahead and give him some food, and
the Lord would not let her supplies run out until the famine
was over. And that's what happened.

Moms give so much. Do you ever feel like you're just running out of what you need to keep going and giving? As we
follow God's nudge to keep giving, even when our resources are
low, somehow we keep going, and moment by moment, we find
what we need.

Do you feel low on resources?
Keep giving and see how God provides.

—JGL

Built on a Rock

"Listen to me, all who hope for deliverance—all who seek the Lord! Consider the quarry from which you were mined, the rock from which you were cut!"

ISAIAH 51:1

The front door closed softly; I heard the car starting and was suddenly afraid. My husband and my mother left and I was flying solo with a baby for the first time.

Back and forth, gently swaying, I slowly rocked the tiny child in my arms. The oak rocking chair from my grandmother's house comforted me with its cozy creaking.

My little boy snuggled in the pale blue baby afghan knit by my other grandma. He slept peacefully, as if he already knew her loving hands.

I watched in awe at how easily my own mother bathed and handled her new grandson. She laughed and talked with him, loving each moment.

Now it was my turn as the mom, but I wasn't building on bare ground. I could be thankful for a rock-solid foundation of family, friends, and faith. I was still scared, but I wasn't alone.

You never really appreciate your mother—
until you become one.

—SUE LOWELL GALLION

On the Other Hand

"In the same way, wisdom is sweet to your
soul. If you find it, you will have a bright
future, and your hopes will not be cut short."
PROVERBS 24:14

"I can always count on one of my kids loving me!" exclaimed my aunt.

She was right! As a mother of five children, she could relate to my household of six children. In one conversation, I had confessed that on any given day, one or two, or even three, of our teens were getting into trouble and vowing that they hated us "parentals."

During that phone call, my aunt had chuckled and agreed that it was also the truth in her big family. She warned me that even in adulthood someone in her brood always seemed to be in a crisis of some kind.

During this phone call, my encourager turned my thought around for me. In one sentence she turned my groan into rejoicing. With multiple kids, one of them likes you on any given day. What a special blessing of being a mom.

*Hang on to those blessings to make it through
the trials of parenting.*

—TANYA T. WARRINGTON

The Tools God Uses

"Then Jesus was filled with the joy of the Holy Spirit and
said, 'O Father, Lord of heaven and earth, thank you
for hiding the truth from those who think themselves
so wise and clever, and for revealing it to the childlike.
Yes, Father, it pleased you to do it this way.'"

LUKE 10:21

"Mom, do you know how crystals are formed on rocks?" my son
Gardner asks me. Or he might ask about rainbows or fog.

"No, what makes this happen?" I respond. And Gardner
proceeds to tell me.

I'm amazed that this child I gave birth to understands sci-
entific concepts that I still haven't grasped yet! If an emperor
were displaying make-believe clothes around here, I think
Gardner would be the first to say, "He's naked!"

The realization of how our kids see so clearly is enough to
make you laugh. Maybe that's why Jesus was filled with joy in
Luke 10:21.

Sometimes kids, and those with childlike simplicity, understand the basics—especially of faith—more than those of us
who are older and supposedly wiser. I'm learning I can't underestimate my kids—that God can teach me His truths through
my children, if only I'll listen.

*Wise people are willing to learn through any
tools God uses to teach with—even children.*

—JGL

Using Teachable Moments

"My teaching will fall on you like rain; my speech
will settle like dew. My words will fall like rain on
tender grass, like gentle showers on young plants.
DEUTERONOMY 32:2

"Mom, do you know about the earth?" my son asked.

"Why don't you tell me?" I invited.

My little scientist proceeded to tell me how the earth spins, how gravity works, and where the earth is lined up in the planets.

Then it was my turn. I told him that if our planet were just a bit slower or faster or closer to or farther away from the sun, the planet couldn't sustain life.

"God made everything balanced," I explained, taking advantage of a "teachable moment."

"Teachable moments" are simply times when life gives us an example to teach a good lesson in a natural way. At times teachable moments just happen, but I've also learned to be intentional. For instance, if I take my kids to a park that has a huge stone, I might ask the kids how God is like a rock. If we see ants at work, I use them to illustrate teamwork.

*Let's put some thought into building more
teachable moments into our days.*

—JGL

The Perfect Touch

"Your own soul is nourished when you are kind,
but you destroy yourself when you are cruel."
PROVERBS 11:17

My toddler was screaming, flailing his arms and legs in every direction. His face was blue with the effort of producing a five-alarm scream heard all over the Publix Supermarket in Miami. Crawling behind the checkout counter to escape my son's tantrum seemed like the best possible solution. But a kind woman in her fifties gently laid her hand on my shoulder and whispered in a sweet voice, "It's okay, honey, we've all been there."

Immediately, I burst into tears—relieved to know someone understood!

That toddler is now twenty-five years old and teaches high school. Gone are the two a.m. feedings, the animal-cookie crumbs glued to the car seat, and those terrible temper tantrums! What remains are the memories of those mentoring moms who touched my life with their presence when I needed it the most. They let me know I wasn't alone in this awesome task of mothering and prayed me through the difficult times.

*Take some time today to thank a mentoring
mom who has touched your life!*

—CONNIE POMBO

Look to the Future!

"But Lot's wife looked back as she was following along
behind him, and she became a pillar of salt."
GENESIS 19:26

Have you ever made any parenting mistakes?

I did. When I married my husband, I became a full-time
stepmom, though I'd never been a parent before. I tried to do a
good job, and my motivations were good. I set out to love the
girls and treat them as my own. I did as good a job as I could
in a tough situation, but looking back, I wish I'd been a little
different in some areas.

So much of parenting is a matter of live and learn. But
sometimes I look back at stepparenting mistakes I made and
get discouraged. I feel immobilized, as if I should just quit parenting the stepdaughter who's still in her teens. At those times
I have to pray and turn my sights to the days ahead instead of
the days behind.

*Every parent makes mistakes, but as we let go of the past,
we can enjoy the present.*

—JGL

Taking Our Cross with JOY!

"He was willing to die a shameful death on the cross because of the joy he knew would be his afterward...."

HEBREWS 12:2

Do you ever mull over all the hours you've clocked in, the unappreciated commitments you've fulfilled, or the noble ambitions you've sacrificed? Ever just stuck another meal on the table, calculated the career income you've missed, and secretly wondered if your God-given abilities are being squandered?

The focus usually doesn't make a very happy mommy.

As Jesus headed to Calvary, can you imagine Him feeling sorry for Himself and thinking, *Oh, poor me . . . my Father better take note of all I'm suffering right now, because this is horrible!*

God knew there would be a cross. He knew the sacrifice that would be required of His only begotten son, and He chose to willingly fulfill it. Because of God's incredible love for us, Jesus took up His cross with *joy*; as mothers, we definitely need more of that kind of love.

Let's not be martyr-moms; let's take up motherhood with joy!

—ANN DUNAGAN

Pictures of Harmony

"So then, let us aim for harmony...
and try to build each other up."
ROMANS 14:19

"Mom, can I have this photo album?" my son asked.

We have a lot of unfiled photos, so I told him to have at it.

He worked hard, and finally, he was done. "Mom, wanna see my photo book?" he asked.

We sat on the couch and turned pages together. Some of his selections were surprising—like the one of when he was young and had his "blankey" superhero cape or the school picture of a child I didn't think he even liked. I asked him why he chose some of the photos, and his answers gave me insights into how his mind worked. Through his pictures, I learned some of his favorite activities, birthday cakes, and Christmas presents—as well as special family moments he remembered. It was a fun bonding time as it reminded us of the importance of family and memories and as we talked about how God had put us together as a family and provided for us.

*Recalling memories is a great way to build
harmony and unity in our families.*

—JGL

The Body You've Always Wanted

"You should be known for the beauty that comes from within, the unfading beauty of a gentle and quiet spirit, which is so precious to God."

1 PETER 3:4

As a busy mother, sometimes the only running you do is from errand to errand, and the only weights you lift are groceries and your four-year-old, into her car seat. It can seem impossible to have the time or energy to take care of yourself. However, we're bombarded by magazine and television images of perfect, thin, gorgeous women, and it's hard not to feel a little bit insecure.

The next time you look into the mirror, feast your eyes on this: that body of yours brought a life into the world; those arms can wrap themselves around your whole family; and that back is strong enough to bear everything from broken toys to broken hearts. And what you can't see is even more amazing: a heart full of unlimited, unconditional love—the love you give your family, and the best reminder on earth of the kind of love God feels for you.

You are strong and beautiful.

—TRACY DONEGAN

Thank You!

"I remember the days of old. I ponder all your great works.
I think about what you have done."
PSALM 143:5

"How's the parade?" I asked as I walked through the family room.

"It's okay," Alisha replied, curled up on the well-worn emerald couch with a cup of hot tea, watching some girl wearing a princess gown waving at her from the TV.

I padded to the kitchen in my smiley-face slippers and put the turkey in the oven. The aroma began to fill the house almost as soon as I sat down to watch the parade with Alisha. During the lengthy commercial breaks, I started making the pumpkin pie and worked on other preparations for the big meal.

Our whole family loves Thanksgiving and its traditions—on this day we didn't even have any extended family coming over, but we still fixed the whole spread.

Most of all, we enjoy having a day that focuses on thanking God. Over the turkey and dressing, we talk about how the Pilgrims specifically came here to find religious freedom.

*Amid the crazy bustle of the day, don't forget
to teach your kids whom they need to thank!*

—JGL

Traditions of Faith

"And in the future, your children will ask you,
'What does all this mean?' Then you will tell them,
'With the power of his mighty hand, the Lord
brought us out of Egypt, the place of our slavery."
—Exodus 13:14

"Hey, babe, put the candy corn by each plate, will you?" I asked
our teen.

"Sure," Alisha replied.

We have a tradition for our Thanksgiving dinner—we
place kernels of corn or candy corn by each plate. For each
kernel a person has, he or she has to tell something he or she is
thankful for. Extended family members dining with us seem to
enjoy sharing our tradition, too.

The Bible is full of examples of people following traditions. If we look at biblical culture, we see lots of traditions like
annual feasts focusing on praising God for various things. One
of the most popular Old Testament traditions was building rock
monuments. When God did something special in people's lives,
they would build a small pile of stones, often at that location.
Then, every time they passed that pile, they would remember
what God had done, which boosted their faith in Him.

*Spiritual traditions can be a wonderful
way to teach our children truths about God.*

—JGL

Actions and Feelings

"There must be a spiritual renewal
of your thoughts and attitudes."
EPHESIANS 4:23

"These kids are making me crazy," I told my husband. "Do you think we could sell them?"

Sure, I was joking . . . mostly!

We were just going through one of those tough family times—a toddler destroying the house, an elementary schooler with learning problems, a teen facing challenges. It wasn't anything major, but it was getting me down. I caught myself thinking negative thoughts about my family.

"Lord, this is not good," I prayed one day. "Please help."

A phrase floated through my mind: "If you think enthusiastic, then you'll be enthusiastic."

When I was in leadership training years ago, that was our mantra. We were taught to act like a leader even if we didn't feel like one at the moment, and the feelings would come. And it actually worked.

"You need to reshape your attitude," God seemed to whisper. "If you act enthusiastic and positive about your family, the feelings will come."

Surprisingly—or maybe not—it worked.

Often when we act like we should, the feelings will follow.

—JGL

In the Gap

> "I looked for someone who might rebuild the wall of righteousness that guards the land. I searched for someone to stand in the gap in the wall so I wouldn't have to destroy the land, but I found no one."
>
> Ezekiel 22:30

As I drove to church that morning, I told God I was giving up on my son. After my friends and I had prayed for my son, he'd given up on drugs. But now he'd joined a cult that didn't believe in Jesus.

As I sat in the church service, a woman told about how God had worked in her son's life. Her story was similar to mine. Her son had gotten involved in drugs and turned away from the Christian faith in which she had raised him, but she, and her prayer partners, had faithfully stood in the spiritual gap in his life by praying for him. And God had delivered him and brought him back to faith in Jesus.

Earlier that morning I had told God I was giving up on my son because my prayers were not being answered. I believe that woman's testimony was His answer to me. I bowed my head and prayed for courage to wait on God's timing and to continue to pray for my son and love him.

Our prayers for our kids never go unrewarded,
even if we don't see immediate answers.

—Angela Joseph

Let It Snow!

"'Come now, let us argue this out,' says the Lord. 'No matter how deep the stain of your sins, I can remove it. I can make you as clean as freshly fallen snow. Even if you are stained as red as crimson, I can make you as white as wool.'"

ISAIAH 1:18

"Mom! Mom! It's snowing!" my son cried as he burst into the house. Snowfall is always a welcomed event around our house— by my son, anyway.

Gardner dashed out to the deck and gathered fresh-fallen snow to pour Kool-Aid over and make his own snow cones.

As I watched him out the kitchen window, I thought of Isaiah 1:18. What a promise of hope! Though we may do wrong, God loves us enough to make us pure, clean, and crisp again.

Have I told my son that enough? I wondered. *He knows about asking God to forgive him when he does wrong. But have I empha-sized enough the wonderful promise that God makes us as white as snow?*

Gardner ran inside for a hot cocoa break. As I stirred marshmallows into the mixture, I decided to take advantage of the moment and started in. "Did you know the Bible talks about snow?"

God loves us, and our children, enough to make us pure!

—JGL

Walking with Spiritual Wisdom

"Asking God, the glorious Father of our Lord Jesus Christ,
to give you spiritual wisdom and understanding, so that
you might grow in your knowledge of God."
EPHESIANS 1:17

When our son James shipped off to Fort Riley, Kansas, we prayed, "Lord, put strong believers in his path. Help our son see Jesus. Keep him safe and please give him vocal-for-Jesus acquaintances to guide him through these lonely days."

After a night of little sleep and lots of prayers for our boy, our phone rang.

"Mom, Dad, it's James." As if we didn't recognize his voice.

"You won't believe what happened today. A sergeant fell in step with me when our platoon ran across the parade ground. We talked. I guess I sounded lonely." James took a deep breath. "You two been praying? That sergeant asked me to attend church with him on Sunday."

Before long James reported other stories of "coincidental" happenings. We were assured that God knew where our young private lived and He cared enough to place believers in his pathway more than once.

Ask God to give you spiritual wisdom so the
Lord can use you to draw people to Him.

—KATHERINE J. CRAWFORD

Unending Forgiveness

"Then Peter came to him and asked, 'Lord, how often should I forgive someone who sins against me? Seven times?' 'No!' Jesus replied, 'seventy times seven!'"
MATTHEW 18:21–22

My stepdaughter had hurt me time and time again. In fact, at that stage in her life she was pretty pleased with herself if she could visibly cause me grief.

One morning as I drove to work, I sensed the Lord telling me, "Forgive her."

"Again?" I responded. "How many times am I going to have to forgive her, God?"

Boy, I really set myself up for that one. Instantly, words from Matthew 18 flashed through my mind, including the "seventy times seven."

I realized that morning that Nicole was my "seventy times seven" person. The way our personalities clashed, I was sure she'd hurt me—intentionally or not—490 or more times. Or, as some theologians tell us Jesus meant here, endlessly.

And I'd need to keep forgiving her—just as I hoped she'd forgive me—until she grew up, our communication grew better, or one of us changed.

Keep forgiving those seventy times seven people in your life!

—JGL

Imitators!

"Follow God's example in everything you do,
because you are his dear children."
EPHESIANS 5:1

Ijjjjjaaabbortoxbado. The alien words filled my computer screen.

"Oh no!" I cried.

I waded through a couple of error screens, some other opened files that now also had other alien words inserted into them, and found one of my most important files in the desktop trash.

I explored the extent of the damage and relaxed a bit. I tend to stress when I walk into my office and occasionally find that little fingers have danced across my keyboard. My computer is important to me. I carry it with me almost as often as other people carry PalmPilots or purses. But I forget to back up my iBook so I panic when alien hands strike.

From experience, I know that little Elizabeth giggled with glee as she did it—thinking she was being just like Mommy. I remind myself that imitating parents is part of a healthy growth pattern in kids' lives—as long as we are good examples.

While we're doing imitable actions, let's also let our kids see spiritual qualities in our lives that they can imitate.

—JGL

The Sales Season

"Tell them to use their money to do good. They
should be rich in good works and should give
generously to those in need, always being ready to
share with others whatever God has given them."
1 TIMOTHY 6:18

"So, you wanna get up early to go shopping in the morning?" I
asked our teen, Alisha.

"No!" she exclaimed. I'm afraid none of us are early birds
in our family. Our friend, Rhonda, hits the store the day after
Thanksgiving to catch the six a.m. bargains, but though I love
savings, I'm more likely to take advantage of the stores' late-
night hours.

Alisha's shopping habits are turning out to be similar to
mine, I've discovered.

Shopping with Alisha has also taught me that whether we
shop in the morning or at night, the Christmas season is a
great time to teach our kids how to be wise with money. A
shopping excursion with each of our kids can be like a field trip
to teach them about sales, what it means to buy now and pay
later, and figuring how many Christmas gifts are necessary or
what's practical to spend on presents.

Kids learn their spending habits from us.

—JGL

DECEMBER

FORGET ABOUT CHRISTMAS

"The light shines through the darkness,
and the darkness can never extinguish it."
JOHN 1:5

"I'd like to forget all about Christmas," my mother remarked one gray December afternoon many years ago. I had been patting glass wax on the Merry Christmas stencils I had taped to our front-door window. The sponge fell from my hand as my mouth dropped open. "Mother," I said in disbelief.

"It's just so much work and . . ." She turned away, her shoulders slumping.

I didn't know what to say or do. What on earth was wrong with her? How could she say such a thing? From my twelve-year-old perspective, Christmas was the very best time of the year. I loved every part of it. The baking, decorating, snooping for gifts hidden in the cedar chest, walking through gently falling snow to the Christmas Eve candlelight service at our little church in Forest Glen. . . .

"Oh, please let it snow again this Christmas," I whispered as I carefully removed the stencil around a star that had dried to a bright white.

Almost fifty years later I still find myself wishing for snow (after I get all my shopping done), but so much else has changed. Even if glass wax still was manufactured, I wouldn't have the time or patience to stencil my windows. Now I slap on bright vinyl cut-outs. They're quick, easy, and not messy. When I'm feeling especially nostalgic, I spray snow in the corners of the panes. White Christmases are a rarity, as are carefree days.

I think I'm beginning to understand how my mother may have felt. It is so easy to get caught up in the pressures and worn to a frazzle. I vow to take Christmas in stride this year—to start earlier, to spend less, to focus on what really matters. Yet a far more formidable foe threatens to steal my joy as I think about Christmases past and how things used to be.

The years have flown so quickly. My children no longer charge down the stairs to empty their stockings. The nest is empty—and Christmas just isn't the same. I no longer spend hours in toy stores searching for Tommy Turtle, Legos, or baby dolls that cry "mama." Hunting gifts for my adult children isn't as fun—or as easy. It takes more energy and dollars. Now that I'm sixty-one, neither seem to go as far. But God is teaching me a wonderful truth. I have a choice! I can live in the past and feel sad. I can live in the future and feel fearful. Or, as He intended, I can live in the present and rejoice for all He has given me—right now, today.

The blessing of learning to relate to my children in new ways as I let go and allow them to make their own choices. . . . It's not always easy. Sometimes my protective, motherly instincts yearn to take over. I want to pull them onto my lap, hold them close—and tell them what to do! But mothering them isn't smothering them. They need to be free to live their own lives.

The blessing of my husband's arms around me. . . . I think of how our love has grown deeper through all we

387

have weathered together. Another choice! Daily choosing not to take our marriage for granted. Choosing instead to keep working at it so that it keeps getting better and better.

The blessing of knowing "Jesus Christ is the same yesterday, today and forever" (Hebrews 13:8). When I find myself longing to go back to the way things used to be or getting anxious about the future, I can choose to accept His gift of peace. *Immanuel*, "God is with us"—with me—right now, this very moment. And He promises never to leave or forsake me.

Yes, my mother wanted to forget all about Christmas that year. None of us knew it at the time, but she was struggling with manic depression. Years later she struggled with an illness similar to Alzheimer's. Tough decisions needed to be made when my stepfather died and she could no longer live in the home that had been hers for almost thirty years. Yet I'll always remember the Christmas we moved her into our home. Her hands shook as she unwrapped ornaments for the artificial tree we had put up in her bedroom.

"This is mine," she said as if fearful that this, too, would be taken away from her. But then, unexpectedly, she smiled as she hung the star on the tree. Even though her mind was clouded with confusion, I knew God's presence and the light of His love had penetrated—if only for an instant. Indeed, when things seem the darkest, His light shines the brightest.

Forget about Christmas? Never! Because Christmas is so much more than the baking and decorating and gift buying. It is the celebration of "good news of great joy for everyone!" (Luke 2:10). And it is a joy that is so much deeper, so much richer, than the carefree joy of childhood.

> "The Savior—yes, the Messiah, the Lord—
> has been born . . ." (Luke 2:11).

—MARLENE BAGNULL

Light It Up!

"Your word is a lamp for my feet and a light for my path."
PSALM 119:105

For six winter days we were without electricity, thanks to an ice storm. We huddled in front of our gas fireplace and underneath piles of blankets, trying to stay warm. I missed the light almost as much as the warmth. On that first day, we headed to the local Wal-Mart, which was warmer than our house and lit by their independent generators. The shelves were nearly bare, but in the hunting supplies, I found little flashlights with colorful elastic bands so we could wear them around our heads, like miners' lights.

The little flashlights were actually designed for children, and the kids took right to them. They had fun realizing that every time they looked at me, their dad, and each other, the lights lit up what they were looking at. They looked down at the floor and danced in the pattern of the light as they wiggled their heads.

As I watched the kids walk in the lights they cast, it reminded me of why we make the effort to teach them scripture. God's word in their hearts is like those flashlights. It illuminates every step they take and shines God's light on all they do.

Light up your life, and your children's lives, with God's word.

—JGL

The Unanswered Questions

"The Lord is close to the brokenhearted; he rescues
those who are crushed in spirit."
PSALM 34:18

"Jonathan didn't make it," my brother-in-law explained over the
telephone in a grief-soaked voice. "They couldn't get his heart
started again after the surgery."

Oh, Lord, why? my mind and heart cried.

I was still reeling from the shock of the toddler's death
when cries erupted in the living room. Four-year-old Mark
thrust a score pad in my face.

"Mommy. They said I lost the game. They're cheating!"

I glanced over the calculations of his older siblings. "Mar-
kie, they're right. You did lose the game." He stared at the paper
in disbelief. I knelt down to console him. "Sweetheart, when
you're older, you'll know how to add the numbers yourself. For
now, will you believe me?"

I heard an echo of my words from God's heart: "You don't
understand now. In this death, will you believe me?"

Oh, Father, we hurt, but we choose to trust in you, I decided.

Some answers must wait until heaven.

—SANDY EWING

Gift-Wrapped by God

"There was nothing beautiful or majestic about
his appearance, nothing to attract us to him."
Isaiah 53:2

My journey to motherhood did not go as scripted. No maternity dresses, baby showers, or prenatal visits heralded the arrival of our little boy—a malnourished six-year-old who didn't speak English. My childhood dreams of blond-haired, blue-eyed babies were replaced by this black-haired, dark-eyed kindergartener named Angelo.

Angelo reminds me that God's gifts are often wrapped in unexpected packages. The Bible is filled with stories about the surprising people God chose to fulfill His plans. Jesus was the ultimate surprise. The Jewish people expected a king, but the Savior was born to poor parents. People wanted Jesus to show power; He focused on humility.

At seven, Angelo's interests are developing, and we already see a zany sense of humor and a gift for languages. I don't know what God has in mind for Angelo, but the joy, laughter, and love he has brought into our lives would be missing if we had rejected this "uniquely wrapped" gift from God.

*May we never reject any of God's gifts
because the "packaging" is not what we expect.*

—Kimberly Baldwin Radford

Mundane Chores, Open Hearts

"Then make me truly happy by agreeing
wholeheartedly with each other, loving one another,
and working together with one heart and purpose."
PHILIPPIANS 2:2

"What do you like about John?" Mom asked.

I almost dropped the glass I was drying. Mom and I didn't usually get on such a personal conversational level to talk about my boyfriends.

Blame it on the dishwashing! Mom's kitchen wasn't big enough for a dishwasher. So every night, my job was to help Mom wash and dry dishes. And as we looked at the dishes and not at each other, each of us lost a little of our shyness. I wasn't accustomed to talking about my dreams, but sometimes Mom drew them out over the dish suds.

These days I have a dishwasher—and wouldn't trade it for the world! However, I try to find other mundane ways of spending time with my kids. I've found that when we work together on brainless projects like making brownies, my kids will figuratively let down their hair and we can connect soul to soul.

Making time for mindless chores together can open the heart.

—JGL

Caught You!

"Think of ways to encourage one another
to outbursts of love and good deeds."
HEBREWS 10:24

"I caught you!"

"I didn't do it!" is usually the automatic response I hear from my kids.

"Yes, you did; I saw you!" I reply

"What?" they say, honestly bewildered, trying to think of what bad thing I could have caught them doing in the past few minutes.

"I caught you helping your sister get a drink."

"I caught you doing more cleaning than your chores required."

"I caught you throwing your trash away."

I finish the words with a "Thank you" or "I'm proud of you" or "Way to go." And my kids glow with pleasure.

Sometimes we parents are so focused on catching bad behaviors to correct that we forget to even notice all the things our kids are doing *right*. How much nicer it is to receive praise than a scolding. And how much more motivating to continue the behavior!

*Make a special effort to catch your
kids doing good things this week.*

—JGL

Gentle Reminders

"The heavens tell of the glory of God. The
skies display his marvelous craftsmanship.
Day after day they continue to speak; night
after night they make him known."
PSALM 19:1–2

Pretzel wreath Christmas ornament. Popsicle stick basket.
Hand-crafted Derby cars. Thumb-print pottery dish. Our son's
childhood creations fill our home! Brent brought home school
and church handicrafts and gifts throughout his childhood.
Time has taken its toll on the pretzel Christmas wreath ornament. Each year I find myself gluing a broken part before hanging it gently on the family tree!

Do these objects coordinate with my home décor? Not
really. Would they sell on eBay? No. Are they of worth? Priceless! These mementos are tangible evidence of Brent's love for
me, and they remind me of the wonderful relationship I share
with my son. Relationships give life meaning.

Much like Brent's childhood artifacts, God also places
cherished reminders of his love for us throughout his creation!
Seashells. Snowflakes. Pond ripples. Sun beams. Rainbows. We
must develop eyes to see these reminders as we live our daily
lives.

Relationships with God and one
another make life worth living!

—SUSAN MOORE

Winning the Battle, Losing Myself

"Live in harmony and peace. Then the God
of love and peace will be with you."
2 CORINTHIANS 13:11

"Not this way! That way!" yelled three-year-old Kyle as I passed our exit. I was hoping the drive would lull him to sleep—we both needed him to nap today. My ignoring his outbursts usually hushed him, but this time he continued his tirade.

"Be QUIET!" I matched him decibel for decibel, not exactly the peaceful mom I strive to be.

Perhaps it was a moment of inspiration or desperation, but I decided to pull over until he calmed down. Taking him into the front seat, I held him close, his head on my shoulder. "We'll stay here until you can relax," I told him. He settled quietly into me and I felt my own breathing slow and my jaw unclench.

Snuggling a toddler while they pitch a fit isn't recommended by most parenting books, but I realized it's not worth winning the battle if, in the end, I lose myself.

A war is not won that doesn't result in peace.

—MARY PIELENZ HAMPTON

Just Like Mom?

"[Uzziah] did what was pleasing in the Lord's sight,
just as his father, Amaziah, had done."
2 KINGS 15:3

"He did what was evil in the Lord's sight, just as his father had done" or "He did what was pleasing in the Lord's sight, just as his father had done."

All through the books of Kings when the scriptures describe the kings who ruled, we find the words, "just as his father had done." It's amazing how many times these rulers followed their fathers' leadership example in life. If the father did evil, most of the time, the son did, too—and sometimes the son even did more evil than the father. On the other hand, if the father pleased the Lord, chances were that the son did, too.

As I read this, it makes me wonder, *What kind of spiritual example am I giving my children to follow?* If our lives were written out as these scriptures are, would we be listed as "pleasing in the Lord's sight"?

The Bible gives us plenty of tips on how we can be pleasing in the Lord's sight and a good example to our children—now all we have to do is follow them!

—JGL

Having Fun

"So rejoice in the Lord and be glad, all you who obey
him! Shout for joy, all you whose hearts are pure!"
PSALM 32:11

On opening night of the Christmas play, I gathered the cast of
children and began my last-minute directions: talk loudly, don't
rush your lines, hold for the laughs, don't turn your back to the
audience, smile during the songs.

A little voice interrupted, "Is it okay if we have fun, too?"

How often, in my headlong rush to "Get things done," I
forget to have fun. God provides us with the capacity to experience joy, and he even gives us much to be joyful about. I find
joy in my family, in my work, in my beautiful home. But I often
get so caught up in my daily activities I forget to be joyful. I
need to be reminded. Just as my children's faces glow with
excitement and joy, I'd like to show as joyful a face to the world
as the children do.

It is okay to have fun.

—JEAN CAMPION

Blessed to Be a Blessing

"I was naked, and you gave me clothing..."
MATTHEW 25:36

Amid twisted hangers, bulging drawers, and way too many clothes, the kids and I began our major closet-cleaning attack. It took days, but as we conquered our last pile, we felt victorious—with sacks for the Dumpster and sacks to give away. Best of all, we finished just before I left on a short-term missions trip to Uganda.

Soon I was surrounded by orphans adorned in only rags and ripped-up shirts, and often with bare bottoms. I thought of these precious children and my family's ridiculous "conquered" closets. Then I felt the Lord whisper, "I'm the One naked on these streets!" Immediately, I went and bought armloads of children's clothing, but the situation turned pathetic. Mothers came from everywhere, holding up naked babies and begging for help. The need was beyond me.

Back home, our family raised funds to clothe that whole village, and this year, we even started an orphanage. The world's need is huge, but it's not beyond God!

*Let's show our kids that we're blessed
so we can turn and be a blessing!*

—ANN DUNAGAN

For Our Own Good

"This is my happy way of life;
obeying your commandments."
PSALM 119:56

"God has two reasons for any of the commands he gives in the Bible," Josh McDowell explained. "He gives us rules and guidelines either to protect us, or to provide for us."

When I was a teenager, I heard Josh McDowell say this at a youth rally and it changed my life. I realized that although I might not understand all the proclamations in the Bible, I could trust that they're designed to help me live a better life.

I've shared this statement about God's rules with my kids, but it's also been my guiding principle in making rules as a parent. I tell my kids, "I make rules for two reasons: to protect you, or to help provide a good life for you."

When I make rules, I weigh them against this—it helps me make sure I'm making rules for a real reason. And it also helps me explain those rules to my kids.

*God's rules are made to enhance our lives,
not frustrate them!*

—JGL

It's Not about the Bubbles

"Though good advice lies deep within a person's heart,
the wise will draw it out."
PROVERBS 20:5

"I won't take that Christmas gift to my teacher!" my six-year-old son announced as we headed out the door.

"Why not?" I said, my teeth clenched.

"I don't want to."

I grabbed my purse, but then I stopped. I had been praying Proverbs 20:5 that week, but changed the verse to, "The purposes of a child's heart are deep water, but a mother of understanding draws them out."

I took a deep breath and sat by him. I started to ask him questions and discovered the issue was that I had wrapped the gift in a red-and-green burlap sack. He was mortified by such a "weird" gift.

I quickly rewrapped it and avoided a bad day for both of us.

So often I've reacted to my children only by what I saw on the surface, not realizing those were just the bubbles made by the commotion beneath.

*When you see the bubbles rising,
take time to see what's causing them!*

—TAMARA VERMEER

Peace at Home on Earth

"God blesses those who work for peace,
for they will be called the children of God."
MATTHEW 5:9

"But he started it!"

That has to be one of the top ten phrases that make a mother crazy.

My mother had an effective answer for that phrase when my brother or I blurted it out. She'd say, "It doesn't matter who started it; *you* end it."

I guess that's what a home full of peace is all about—all of us taking responsibility to end the strife.

That's not easy to do—especially when three or more people live together every day and know each other's weaknesses and idiosyncrasies. At times the togetherness is bound to grate a bit.

When I read Matthew 5:9, I noticed the little verb *work*. That's one of those little verbs that packs a huge punch! Peace doesn't come naturally—anytime we want it, we have to *work* for it. It's not impossible to achieve, but it does take effort, even in our homes.

Peace on earth begins at home.

—JGL

His Understanding Is Unlimited

"Have you never heard or understood? Don't you know
that the Lord is the everlasting God, the Creator of all
the earth? He never grows faint or weary. No one can
measure the depths of his understanding."

ISAIAH 40:28

"Lord, I'm trying so hard, but I'm failing so often," I cried. "I'm
so weary."

We'd been through challenging times: three moves in four
years, several job changes, I'd gone from being single to a full-
time stepmother, my first baby was born with a heart problem
and ended up in the ER every year, my husband and father
both encountered fairly severe health problems, and our whole
family seemed to wallow in quagmires of stress.

And now I felt so discouraged and overwhelmed in my spiritual walk. I felt I needed to be *doing* more before God would be
pleased with me.

Surprisingly though, he just seemed to whisper, "Don't
worry; I understand."

What a comfort to know that he fathoms everything we're
going through. When our hearts and our spirits feel one way,
but reality is pressuring us another way, he understands. And
because our heavenly father understands, he gives grace.

*When we fall short of who we want to be, God knows our
hearts and our circumstances, and offers us understanding.*

—JGL

Trust God's Timing

"But I am trusting you, O Lord, saying,
'You are my God.' My future is in your hands. . . ."
PSALM 31:14–15

With two children celebrating birthdays during the Christmas season, I spread out the expense by purchasing their gifts throughout the year, which I then hide in closets. By the time I need the gifts, they've either become buried on the shelves or I've forgotten where I hid them.

As a mother of three young children, it often seems my God-given gifts also get hidden in a closet. Days filled with changing diapers, preparing meals, and folding laundry leave little time for personal ambitions! So I store my talents and dreams away for another day.

If you're in a similar situation, know that God has not forgotten about your gifts. In His perfectly orchestrated plan, He's using your current season to shape you into a greater likeness of Jesus. When He does finally take your gifts off the shelf, you will be better prepared spiritually to use them for His glory.

*Don't worry about the gifts on the shelf; they'll come to light
in the right time.*

—RENEE GRAY-WILBURN

Faith for the Impossible

"Mary responded, 'I am the Lord's servant, and I am willing to accept whatever he wants. May everything you have said come true.' And then the angel left."
LUKE 1:38

Young, unmarried, and pregnant in a culture where women were once stoned for getting into that kind of condition. What a world of condemnation Mary entered when she said yes to God!

She had to know she'd face her neighbors' scorn, land her family in scandal, and possibly lose the man of her dreams.

It takes a lot of faith in God, and love for Him, to agree to be part of such a seemingly crazy, impossible plot. Not only was Mary willing, but then she also praised God, thanking Him for the honor. Maybe that was her secret to saying yes—knowing that with God, nothing is impossible. Most of us won't face the same kinds of challenges Mary faced. But still, as women and moms, God calls on us to tackle tough tasks sometimes—sacrificing for our kids, loving and giving when our resources are low, trusting God with our children's futures, and so much more.

May we have the same faith as Mary when
God asks us to do what seems impossible!

—JGL

Never Enough

"A relaxed attitude lengthens life; jealousy rots it away."
PROVERBS 14:30

"More, more, more...never satisfied," I muttered in the direction of my young daughter, who was begging for the newest American Girl doll.

"Puhleeeeze, Mom? Look, she even comes with a neat bag and all this extra stuff," she pleaded, complete with pouty eyes and protruding lower lip.

More, newer, better...she always wanted the latest doll, the newest outfit, the coolest accessory.

But then I realized I am not really different.

I also like the "in" colors, the brightest jewelry, and the most current accessories. I find that my daughter isn't the only one who isn't always satisfied.

But God isn't surprised with us; after all, as far back as the Israelites, He's heard the moaning and groaning, griping and complaining of dissatisfied individuals.

Instead of focusing on what we don't have, we need to relax and seek the intangible peace of God, which never goes out of style.

Fashions and styles come and go,
but God's love and peace are eternal.

—KATHY PRIDE

Actions of Love

"Dear children, let us stop just saying we love
each other; let us really show it by our actions."
1 John 3:18

Bread dough writhed in the old metal bowl as my mother turned the handle on the dough hook. I watched apple peel curl around my fingers as I prepared apples for the pies she'd make. Saturdays were baking days.

Mondays were wash days, and outside, the still-warm clothes were hung in the sunshine. Tuesdays, Mom ironed. She let me iron towels, hankies, and pillowcases, but she did Dad's shirts. Mother's love was seen in these weekly rituals, and when her hands weren't busy crocheting tablecloths or doilies, she was making us new clothes.

Times have changed but mothers haven't. They still fill kitchens with delightful smells and prepare Christmas surprises and provide clothes. Mothers still care more than anyone else about your special hopes and dreams, no matter what your age. Everything they do says "I love you."

Show your children you love them—and tell them, too.

—V. Louise Cunningham

Preparing the Way

"You yourselves know how plainly I told you
that I am not the Messiah. I am here to
prepare the way for him—that is all."
JOHN 3:28

John sounded pretty exasperated. People kept wondering if he felt shunned or frustrated because this new man, Jesus, was getting all the attention and baptizing people just like John was.

John finally said, basically, "Look, can't you see? I don't care if he gets more attention than me—he *is* more important to me! In fact, my job is to point people to *him*! I'm only here to prepare the way for him!"

The last words of this verse, "I am here to prepare the way for him," stuck in my mind. I began to think of this in terms of our parenting role. Could it be that our primary job in our parenting role is to prepare the way for God in our children's lives? To prepare them to hear His voice and follow His guidance? To prepare them for a lifetime of serving Him?

*In all the tasks of parenting, let's make sure
that we're not too busy to remember our
responsibility to prepare our children for God.*

—JGL

Moms Make It Special!

"Her children stand and bless her.
Her husband praises her."
PROVERBS 31:28

"I'd forgotten how much fun Christmas could be!" my husband told me. He explained that he and his two young daughters weren't used to getting cool gifts for Christmas. He never knew what to get his girls. But during my months as the stepmom, I'd listened to the kids and made mental notes. At Christmastime, I got gifts that fit their desires and needs—a far cry from my husband's habit of grabbing anything at the store on Christmas Eve!

He also liked the way I brought more meaning into the season, with decorations and music and traditions and scripture.

I was pleased at this praise. It does take hard work to give gifts that will tell each family member how special he or she is, and to make the holiday meaningful. But even though it's a hectic time of the year, and even when your family forgets to say anything, it's worth that extra effort you make, Mom!

God blesses our efforts to make
Christmas joyous for our families.

—JGL

Rejoice!

"Oh, what joy for those whose rebellion is forgiven,
whose sin is put out of sight!"
Psalm 32:1

"I have had it with all of you! I have tried to be nice since your parents have been away on vacation this week. What do you do? Fight one another, flood all the bathrooms, spill food everywhere in the house, trash your rooms, and act like zoo animals at the church Easter play! You have left me no other option but to put you all on punishment for the next two days. Go into your rooms and start cleaning them! I will call you when dinner is ready!"

They started giggling. "Jozlynn, what's so funny?"

"Aunt Faith, Mommy always told us Jesus died so we can be forgiven for all the bad stuff we do. So, we can be happy Jesus has a short memory! We hope you do, too."

"I forgive all of you!" We all laughed. I am glad He does not remember our sins. That is a reason to rejoice.

God forgives His children so we can rejoice and forgive ours.

—Faith Waters

Where Is Baby Jesus?

"Thank God for his son—a gift too wonderful for words."
2 CORINTHIANS 9:15

"Where is Baby Jesus?" my four-year-old asked as he gazed upon the heaping pile of Christmas presents. They had engulfed the Christmas tree and snaked across the living-room floor. That Christmas Sean had become so interested in Nativity scenes that he started to collect them. He toted his personal manger scene everywhere, reminding us all what Christmas was truly about.

Sean anxiously looked around and tugged on my sleeve again. "Mommy, where is baby Jesus?"

I pointed to the mound of boxes and bags. "He's behind there."

We pulled the gifts away to see the manger scene that had succumbed to the great wall of gifts. It was a gentle reminder that too often Jesus is pushed aside to make room for dazzling lights that catch our eyes and shiny wrapped gifts that offer us temporary satisfaction. The first Christmas gift—the greatest gift of all—can easily be forgotten as we grasp for sparkling packages the world offers us.

Accept the greatest gift of all: God's love for you.

—MARY GALLAGHER

Happy Birthday, Jesus

"The Savior—yes, the Messiah, the Lord—has been born
tonight in Bethlehem, the city of David!"

LUKE 2:11

"If it's Jesus's birthday, aren't we going to sing 'Happy Birthday'
to him?" my young son asked.

"Sure," I replied. "Let's sing."

My son had a great point. So, the next year, I let my kids
make and decorate a birthday cake.

Okay, cake, candles, birthday song. Anything else? I wondered.

Of course. A gift. What do you give the God who has
everything? Like the animated video *Little Drummer Boy* and
I were teaching my children, we can give ourselves to Jesus at
Christmas. I pondered how to make the idea concrete for my
kids. Some people give themselves to Jesus by serving dinner
at a mission. Some people give gifts in Jesus's name to needy
kids through Samaritan's Purse or the Prison Fellowship Angel
Tree.

This year, my kids and I are going to brainstorm and figure
out a way to give a gift to Jesus—a gift that comes from our
hearts and lives.

On Jesus's birthday, don't forget the one
who's the focus of the celebration!

—JGL

The Surprise

"Not that I was ever in need, for I have learned to get along happily whether I have much or little."
PHILIPPIANS 4:11

Christmas was coming and it looked as though it was going to be a bit skimpy. We bought a few small gifts. Then the children and I baked, sewed, and drew pictures to give. Things were about ready when my mother, who was very creative with a small amount of money, arrived on Christmas Eve carrying a large box.

The children were up early the next morning, waiting with anticipation. It was time to open presents. To my great surprise, when we got to their grandma's gift, nothing was in that big, beautiful box.

The children looked in it again, and Grandma smiled. "Invisible rabbits," she said. She stroked one of the pretend rabbits. "Oh, oh, there it goes," she exclaimed as she ran after it. Immediately the children were caught up in the excitement. It was all they needed.

I doubt they remember anything else they received—or didn't receive—that year.

Our needs and others' needs are not
always what we think they are.

—HILAH C. WAGNER

Giving with Love

"For God so loved the world that he gave
his only Son, so that everyone who believes
in him will not perish but have eternal life."
JOHN 3:16

"You can give without loving, but you can't love without giving,"
my mentor used to tell us.

Moms generally know the truth of that more than anyone.
Moms are the ones who tend to notice and meet even the little
needs. Recent studies show that moms are so busy meeting
needs that they even cut down their sleep time to try to have
more time in their days. As a result, they aren't as healthy as
they should be. Sometimes moms literally give until they hurt.

God understands that feeling. We celebrate the joy and
the awe of Christmas because God loved us enough to give
until it hurt. When He gave humans our lives on earth, we
messed up that gift, so He gave us the only thing He had that
could give us spiritual, eternal lives—His son.

*Today, as you spend the day giving of yourself
and making sure everyone in your family is
happy, remember the gift of love God gave you.*

—JGL

Instant Obedience

"That night Joseph left for Egypt with the child and
Mary, his mother."
MATTHEW 2:14

Imagine the scene: the Wise Men have left and Joseph and
Mary probably talked about their visit for hours—what it meant,
the fun of being visited by dignitaries, the lavish gifts they'd
brought. Perhaps they even had a hard time sleeping because
of the excitement.

But then in the middle of the night, Joseph was awakened.
God was telling him to pack up immediately and leave.

I probably would have moaned, "Sure. First thing tomorrow."

But not Joseph. Before dawn, they were history in Bethlehem! And Joseph's quick obedience saved Jesus from death.

As moms, we've all had those times when God has nudged
us to do something—maybe it's putting down dinner preparations to go hug a child, or maybe it's trusting a child when he
or she wants to do something, or maybe it's giving a child a
second chance.

Even when it's not a life-and-death matter, God has His
reasons for telling us to do something, regardless if it's inconvenient or seems like an odd request.

May we, like Joseph, learn to practice instant obedience.

—JGL

Good Is God

"Whatever is good and perfect comes to us from God
above, who created all heaven's lights. Unlike them,
He never changes or casts shifting shadows."

JAMES 1:17

I have a grudge against Santa Claus. Every Christmas he gets the credit for the new bicycle, the pop-up play tent, the expensive baby doll. My children are in awe of him: How did he know exactly what they wanted? What an amazing guy!

I wonder if God ever feels like this when I fail to give him credit for his awesome gifts: the pattern the morning sun makes as it filters through the trees, the way a hot shower feels after a workout, the flash of delight on my son's face when he nails one to center field. When I forget that good books, caramel lattes, and belly laughs are all gifts from His hand.

In each of these things, God says, "I love you! I love to see you smile. You can count on me to provide!"

Just as we delight in blessing our children, God delights in blessing us. Let's give credit where credit is due.

All good things come from God.

—BECKY FULCHER

Tickled Pink!

"And a voice from heaven said, 'This is my beloved Son,
and I am fully pleased with him.'"
MATTHEW 3:17

When Jesus wanted John to baptize him, John balked. "Who am I to baptize you?"

But Jesus pointed out that this was the way God wanted it. Then we read some of the coolest words in the Bible: "This is my beloved Son, and I am fully pleased with him."

Mom, did you ever stop to realize that God probably says the same words about you? You go through your days trying to raise your children to love God. You take care of the needs of your household—both at home and perhaps even at a full-time job. You minister to the needs of your whole family, and even find time to help others. Why *wouldn't* God be pleased with you? He's probably tickled pink!

Today, remember you're God's beloved
daughter and He's so pleased with you!

—JGL

Yee-Haw for Kids!

"For everything that is hidden or secret will
eventually be brought to light and made plain to all."
LUKE 8:17

"Yeee-haaaaw!"

I knew I shouldn't have done it. But hey, we were in the
Colorado Rockies, on a hay wagon driven by Stetsoned wran-
glers, going to a mountain cookout complete with a singing
cowboy. Shouting a full-bodied "Yeee-hawww!" as we headed
out just seemed like the thing to do at the time.

Little Elizabeth looked at me, entranced at newly learning
this talent her mommy had.

"Yee-haw!" she cried with excitement, making everyone
laugh.

Now, months later, in the coldness of the holiday season,
little Elizabeth still goes around shouting "Yee-haw!" whenever
it may cross her mind: at Wal-Mart, in the grocery store, at
friends' homes, during church. . . .

I've given up trying to explain the context in which she
learned to "yee-haw." Instead, I threaten my other family members within an inch of their lives if they tell where she picked
up the full-bodied yell—and hope that's the only thing she
repeats!

We have no secrets from the world after we have kids!

—JGL

Faith for the Future

"My future is in your hands . . ."
PSALM 31:5

As I looked around the dining-room table, I realized, "This is a great time in life." Our family was at a good, happy stage. And part of me wished we could stay put in that secure stage forever.

In Luke 9, Peter wanted to stay put. When he saw Jesus talking to Moses and Elijah, he was ready to set up permanent tents! But the glory moments ended and they moved on.

Like Peter, sometimes I resist moving on. A negative voice taunts, "How do you know it will be this good ahead? What if bad things happen to your children?"

So instead of just enjoying this life stage, I'm tempted to worry about the future.

I'm learning we can't cling to the security of the past or even today. We have to keep moving our family into an insecure future. But thankfully, we don't move into the future alone.

We can enter the future confidently, remembering
that God has already been there.

—JGL

Pressing Ahead

"Forgetting the past and looking forward to
what lies ahead, I strain to reach the end of
the race and receive the prize for which God,
through Christ Jesus, is calling us up to heaven."
PHILIPPIANS 3:13–14

The end of the year can be stressful when we look back and think of all the things we planned to do that year—and didn't get done. As I face the New Year, I wonder, Will I finally get myself together enough to be able to accomplish everything I plan and have the kind of year I want?

So many expectations! Perhaps that's why some of us don't make lists of New Year's resolutions—we moms have enough hopes and expectations without a list that we can't live up to!

As I face the New Year, I have to consciously put the old year behind me—its surprises, its disappointments, its failures, and even its successes. If I don't consciously do this, I enter the New Year so focused on the failures of the year before that I am hindered mentally and emotionally.

Today, let's pray Paul's words in Philippians 3:13–14 for ourselves and for our families. May God help us not focus on what's behind, but press ahead to all that He has for us and our families this year, and beyond!

*As you enter this New Year, forget what's behind you—
and press ahead with faith!*

—JGL

About the Editors and Contributors

Charlotte Adelsperger is an author and speaker who has written three books, and pieces for more than a hundred different publications and compilations. Charlotte speaks to various groups on ways to encourage others. She is thankful for her husband, Bob, and for her grown children, Karen Hayse and John Adelsperger. Charlotte lives in the Kansas City area and can be reached at *author04@aol.com*.

Cora Allen is a freelance writer living in Kansas City with her family.

Candy Arrington is a freelance writer whose publishing credits include *Today's Christian*, *Focus on the Family*, *Encounter*, *The Upper Room*, and *Writer's Digest*. She and her husband, Jim, and two teenage children live in Spartanburg, SC.

Kathleen Atwell is a married mom of three sons, grandma to a precious boy, and a lifelong seeker of answers. She lives in Missouri, where she writes, babysits, and scrapbooks.

Marlene Bagnull is the mother of three grown children and the director of the Colorado and Greater Philadelphia Christian Writers Conferences. She is the author of eight books, including *My Turn to Care—Encouragement for Caregivers of Aging Parents.*

Sandi Banks is mom to six children, gramma to ten, and gave birth to her first book, *Anchors of Hope*, in 2002. Other published contributions include stories in *Reader's Digest* and the *Kisses of Sunshine* series.

Jamie Birr is a part-time postal carrier and freelance writer. She lives in Elkhart, Indiana, with her husband, three children, and two very spoiled dogs.

Laura Broadwater has been happily married for twenty-two years, and is the proud mother of two teenage boys. She loves reading, writing, dancing, painting, and teaching.

Annette Budzban is a weekly religion columnist and freelance writer who has been published in several Christian magazines. Her e-mail is *ahrtwrites2u@aol.com*.

Dianne E. Butts (*www.Dianne EButts.com*) has written for more than fifty Christian magazines and a dozen compilation books, including *A Cup of Comfort Devotional for Women*. When she's not writing, she enjoys riding her motorcycle with her husband, Hal, and gardening with her cat, P.C. They live in Colorado.

LeAnn Campbell is a retired Special Education teacher. She began freelance writing in 1990 and has had over 1,200 articles in more than 100 publications. LeAnn and her husband have six adult children, eleven grandchildren, and one great-grandson.

Jean Campion, the mother of three, bills herself as a free-range writer and editor working from her rural home in southwest Colorado. Her first book, a historical novel, was published in summer 2006.

Ginny Caroleo and her husband, Mike, enjoy homeschooling their two teenagers and working in children's ministry at their church in New England.

Sandy Cathcart is a mother of five and grandmother of fourteen. She lives in the mountains of Oregon and often speaks and writes about her learning experiences with her family.

Dori Clark has been married to Duane for forty-five years. She is the mother of three and grandmother of eight. A member of Oregon Christian Writers, Dori has written devotions for *God's Word for Today* and *Word in Season* and has had articles and stories published in *Live*, *Lifewise*, *Discipleship Journal*, and *My Little Friend*.

Shae Cooke, mother and former foster child, shares her uplifting messages of God's hope worldwide. Visit her Web site and her writing ministry at *www.shaecooke.com*. Write or e-mail to P.O. Box 78006, Port Coquitlam, B.C., Canada V3B 7H5 or *shaesyc@telus.net*.

Katherine Craddock is a pastor's wife, freelance writer, and mother of two who makes her home outside Washington, DC, in Chantilly, VA.

Katherine J. Crawford lives in Omaha, Nebraska. She is a wife, mother and grandmother, a freelance writer and a contributing author for *www.pmpawareness.org*. Her Web site and e-mail addresses are *www.katcrawford.com*, and *lionheartedkat@cox.net*.

Susan Crook is a certified human behavior consultant with a master's degree in communication, graduating magna cum laude. Her career experience as the former assistant director of the Kansas City Chiefs Cheerleaders and successful business owner uniquely qualifies Susan as an inspirational national speaker and author who equips and motivates others to build strong, effective relationships. Susan's passion and desire is to serve God by empowering others to live victorious lives! She is the author of *Personality Insights for Moms*. For more information, visit *www.SusanCrook.com*.

V. Louise Cunningham has been involved in writing curriculum for her women's Sunday school class for sixteen years. She has had three books published, as well as fifty skits and hundreds of devotionals. She is also a wife, mother, grandmother, great–grandmother, and hospital volunteer.

When **Dianne Daniels** is not busy enjoying her two young daughters, she writes Christian nonfiction to help and encourage other mothers. She is also committed to ministering to moms through MOPS (Mothers of Preschoolers) International.

Inspiring words come so naturally to **Sally R. Danley** that her boss had her e-mail them daily to coworkers before she retired. Today her work is published across the country.

Zeta Combs Davidson is a freelance writer in Kansas City, Missouri, who loves baseball and the Kansas City Royals.

Tracy Donegan, a freelance and children's book author, is proud mother to Nate and Emily.

Karla Doyle is "just a mom" living outside of Washington, DC, who dares to be happily married. Her best advice to moms is, "Whenever possible, wherever your children are, be there." She has never regretted following that advice.

Elizabeth Duewel is married, with three children—Brittany, Joshua, and Brooklyn. She spends a great deal of her time trying to keep up with her kids and playing in the dirt in her garden.

Ann Dunagan is a homeschooling mother, an international minister, and the author of *Hand Commands* (for children) and *The Mission Minded Child* (for parents and teachers). She and her family live near Hood River, Oregon.

Connie Dunn is a mother of three grown children and three grown stepchildren. She was a single parent for twenty-two years. She currently resides in Kansas City with her husband and two of her children.

Dee East retired from the Delaware Department of Transportation, and has been a widowed mother of three sons since 1970, grandmother of four, caregiver for her ninety-two-year-old mother, and a minister to the needs of widows through The Widow's Might.

Liz Hoyt Eberle has been a mom for many years. She needed God to parent—then and now. Liz lives and writes things of the heart in the Texas hill country and can be reached at *eberle2@hotmail.com*.

Catherine Verlenden Eldridge is a retired computer programmer who loves to teach Bible studies, pray for people, draw, write, and quilt. She rejoices in the gift of her family: her delightful mama, "pushing ninety"; her wonderful husband, Jim; and her six grown kids and ten grandkids.

Contributors

Pamela Enderby is a writer and women's ministry leader. She loves to encourage young moms with notes of inspiration, free child care, and mini-getaways. She's also basking in her new role as grandma.

Sandy Ewing is a mother of five and grandmother of thirteen. She is a freelance writer and speaker and lives in Estes Park, Colorado, with her husband, Tom, and bichon frise, Mei Mei.

Phyllis Farringer lives in Olathe, Kansas, with her husband, Doug. An empty nest mom, she also likes to write and participate in activities at her church.

Suzanne Woods Fisher has been a contributing editor to Christian Parenting Today magazine and has written feature articles for many publications. Her first novel, *Copper Tailings*, will be available in April 2007.

Misty Fontenot is a single mother of two daughters and lives in Texas. She owns a home business and is also beginning a new career as a freelance writer.

Becky Fulcher, mother of two, is published in periodicals and book compilations. Living in Colorado, she enjoys painting, cooking, and teaching the Bible to teenagers and children.

Mary Gallagher is a reading teacher and writer. She lives in southern Ohio with her husband and two sons.

She has been published in *A Cup of Comfort for Christians* and *Writing on the Run Tip of the Week*.

Sue Lowell Gallion is a freelance writer and mom in Leawood, Kansas.

Evangeline Beals Gardner is a full-time stay-at-home mom who is also a freelance writer, sings on the worship team at church, and teaches piano lessons from her home.

Anne McKay Garris is a retired newspaper editor and author of the book *Grandma Was Right, 39½ Slogans to Raise Children By*. She lives with her husband, Berle, in Clearwater Beach, Florida.

Nancy B. Gibbs (*www.nancybgibbs .com*) is a pastor's wife, mother and grandmother. She is a writer, newspaper columnist, and motivational speaker.

Viola Ruelke Gommer (*vgommer@ aol.com*) is a retired nurse educator and health-care executive. She is the wife of a retired United Methodist clergyman, mother of two, and grandmother of six. Many of Vi's writings and photographs have been published by *Mason-Crest*, *Upper Room*, *The Secret Place*, *Barbour*, *The Quiet Hour*, and *Chicken Soup for the Nurse's Soul*. She has been involved with the United Methodist Volunteers in Mission in Russia, Bolivia, Guyana, Dominican Republic, Cuba, Haiti, and Zimbabwe.

Alicia Gossman is a court clerk and mom of three boys who own a dog named Chuck. She enjoys reading, writing, and watching HGTV.

Renee Gray-Wilburn is a full-time mom of three—Conner, Cayla, and Chandler—and a part-time freelance writer. She has written for *Focus on Your Child*, *Clubhouse, Jr.*, and *Quiet Hour* magazines.

Shanna Bartlett Groves has contributed stories to *A Cup of Comfort* books for sisters, nurses, and mothers-to-be. She has written for the *Kansas City Star* and *Kansas City Homes and Gardens* magazine, is a member of the Heart of America Christian Writers Network, and founded the Kansas City Chapter of the National Association of Women Writers.

Pam Halter is a homeschooling mom and children's author. She lives in New Jersey with her husband, Daryl, two daughters, and three cats. Her son and daughter-in-law made her a first-time grandma in October 2006.

Mary Pielenz Hampton is author of *A Tea for all Seasons* and several other illustrated devotional books. She lives with her husband and sons in the Pacific Northwest.

Audrey Hebbert lives in Omaha, Nebraska, where she is a freelance writer and a volunteer Bible teacher and mentor for young Christians. She enjoys her two children and their families, including three grandchildren. Her Web site is *www.audreyhebbert.com*.

Jane Heitman, a freelance writer and library technician in Colorado, is a contributor to *A Cup of Comfort Devotional for Women*. She has been published in many Christian and educational markets.

Karen Heslink is a retired elementary teacher, mother of two daughters, and an aspiring author who has written for *I Love Cats* magazine, *Giggles & Grace*, and *Riders & Reapers*. She lives in Lancaster, Pennsylvania, with her husband and two cats.

Elizabeth Hey is a freelance writer specializing in travel, profiles, and inspirational articles. She and her husband live in Kansas City with their three teenagers.

Jennie Hilligus is a mom of two grown children and has recently acquired a new son-in-law. She and her husband have been married twenty-six years. They enjoy boating and have just become the proud parents of a new Honda Goldwing—though she says she refuses to become a "biker babe"!

Cynthia Agricola Hinkle is author of the Christmas Arch Book Star of Wonder and has contributed to several compilations. She lives in southwest Ohio with her husband, Andrew; son, Peter; and daughter, Jessica.

CONTRIBUTORS

Lynnette P. Horner is a mother of four from Littleton, Colorado, who loves to encourage "close encounters" with God through prayer. She also belts out tunes with the car radio and hopes other drivers don't notice.

Cindy Hval is a freelance writer from Spokane, Washington. She and her husband, Derek, are raising four sons, ages six to sixteen. Her work has appeared in *Northwest Woman* magazine and the *Spokesman Review*.

Sally Jadlow is wife of one, mom to four, and grandma to eleven. She serves as a chaplain to corporations in the Kansas City area and teaches creative writing at a Christian school. Her poetry book, *Sonflower Seeds*, took first place at Oklahoma Writers' Federation, and her novel, *The Late Sooner*, was published in October 2006.

Diana L. James is an author, speaker, writing teacher, and freelance writer.

Imogene Johnson lives in rural Lawrenceville, Virginia, with her husband, O.W., and is retired as a secretary with the Virginia Correctional Education system. She is an adult Bible teacher and a choir member at the Lawrenceville Baptist Church, where God blesses her with examples and inspirations for her writing.

Angela Joseph is an occupational therapist who likes to write fiction materials and non-fiction devotionals in her spare time.

Married for 31 years, **Charlotte Kardokus** has two children and two grandchildren. Besides being a freelance writer, Charlotte is the Public Service Representative for the State of Oregon.

LaRose Karr is a wife, mother, grandmother, church secretary, freelance writer, and speaker. She enjoys speaking and ministering to God's people. Her work appears in various compilation books and devotional guides and she can be reached through e-mail at *larosekarr@bresnan.net*.

Betty King is an author, *Life Style and Devotional* newspaper columnist, and freelance writer. She is an inspirational and motivational speaker who lives with multiple sclerosis. Visit her Web site at *www.bettyking.net* or e-mail her at *baking2@charter.net*.

Laurie Klein is widely published. A founding editor of *Rock & Sling: A Journal of Literature, Art and Faith*, she is completing a spiritual memoir that celebrates the worldwide journey of her praise chorus, "I Love You, Lord."

Mimi Greenwood Knight is a freelance writer and artist living with her husband, four kids, four dogs, four cats, and a disagreeable bird in south Louisiana. Her articles have been included in *Parents* magazine, *Working Mother, American Baby, Sesame Street Parents, Today's Christian Woman, Christian Parenting Today*, and *Campus Life* magazine as well as in several anthologies. Contact Mimi at djknight@airmail.net.

Jane Landreth is a Christian freelance writer. Her first published articles and stories were inspired from activities done with her son. Doing things together was an important part of family life.

Karin Lindstrom lives in Gardner, Kansas, with her husband and son. She's authored numerous devotionals, stories in children's magazines, and a children's book.

Jeanette Gardner Littleton has written 3,000 articles and eight books—several with her husband, Mark—including *Hugs for Coffee Lovers*. Jeanette has been an editor for several publications, including *Moody* magazine, and has edited a bunch of books. She's currently a freelance writer and editor, and enjoys codirecting Heart of America Christian Writers Network (*www.HACWN.org*).

Donna Lee Loomis is a mother of three, grandmother of six and counting, who has been an in-home childcare provider for forty years. She says, "I delight in the ways children open up my adult heart and put me in touch with my Lord and the child in me."

Susan Lyttek, wife of Gary since 1983; homeschooling mother of two boys, Erik and Karl; and coach for Write At Home, an Internet writing class for homeschoolers, snatches moments to write before their school day begins in the shadow of the nation's capital.

Sandra McGarrity lives and writes in Chesapeake, Virginia. Her writing has appeared in books and magazines. She is the author of two novels.

Karen McKee has a degree in English from Regis University and works as a librarian in Grand Junction, Colorado. She and her husband have been married almost forty years.

Merilyn Millikan was a stay-at-home mom for twenty years, then a single mom for twelve years. She worked as a nurse, then a full-time missionary for fifteen years, before retiring.

Pat Mitchell is a freelance writer living in Kansas City, Missouri. As caregiver to her elderly mother, she finds herself privileged to return some of the care she received from her mother while growing up.

Rani Moodley is a clinical psychologist with a doctorate in management studies. She works as a leadership development consultant, counselor, professional speaker, and writer.

Susan Moore has a doctor of education degree and is a university professor of education, wife, mother, and grandmother who lives in Olathe, Kansas.

Karen Morerod is a freelance writer and, most of all, loves being a mother of five!

Christine Naserian Njeri is a Christian inspirational writer.

Susan Paris freelances from Grand Junction, Colorado.

Connie L. Peters writes from Cortez, Colorado. She has two adult children, but not an empty nest. She and her husband care for a developmentally disabled adult who also provides many illustrations of God's love and care.

Connie Pombo is an author, speaker, and founder of Women's Mentoring Ministries in Mt. Joy, Pennsylvania. Her greatest accomplishment, however, is being mom to her two grown sons.

Kathy Pride is a mom, author, speaker, and parent educator. Her first book, *Winning the Drug War at Home*, was released in April 2006 from AMG.

Angela Welch Prusia is a former middle-school teacher who stays home with her children and writes during (most) naptimes.

Kimberly Baldwin Radford and her husband, Colin, work with the poor through their nonprofit organization, HELP Madagascar (Health, Education, & Lifeskills Projects). They live with Angelo, two cats, and two dogs on the island nation's beautiful east coast.

Susan Estribou Ramsden is a wife, mother of one daughter, and grandmother of one granddaughter. She is a retired teacher who finds joy in writing Christian poetry.

Anita Lynn Ramsey lives in Smithville, Missouri, with her husband and four children.

Katy McKenna Raymond writes from her home in Kansas City, where she lives with her husband in their recently emptied nest. Her three children and daughter-in-law live nearby, close enough to pour a frequent cup of comfort into her life. Katy's hard at work finishing her first novel, a romantic comedy about a couple's mid-marriage crisis. You can find Katy's blog at *www.fallible .com.*

Jeri Redman lives in Woodbridge, Virginia. She holds dear the privileges of being wife and mother, and she delights in helping women discover contentment and joy in these roles.

Colleen L. Reece calls herself "an ordinary person with an extraordinary God." She learned to read beneath the rays of a kerosene lamp in a home without running water or electricity. Approximately five million copies of her 140 books have been sold to date.

Rhonda Rhea is a pastor's wife and mother of five. She lives near St. Louis, though she confesses she spends most of her time either circling the county delivering teens or wrestling them for her car keys. She is a radio personality and also appears on TV programs throughout the country. Rhonda is a humor columnist for publications in the United States, Canada, and South Africa, and she has several Christian humor books out, including *Who Put the Cat in the Fridge*, *Turkey Soup for the Soul—Tastes Just Like Chicken*, and *I'm Dreaming of Some White Chocolate*. Her newest book, *High Heels in High Places*, is scheduled for release in 2007.

Micki Roberts is a member of Romance Writers of America and its inspirational chapter, Faith, Hope, and Love. She serves as editor for *Herein Is Love*, the FHL Newsletter. She is also a member of American Christian Fiction Writers. Micki is a contributor to *Penned From the Heart*, Volumes 9–12, and *Divine Stories of the Yahweh Sisterhood*.

Stacy Rothenberger, homeschooling mother of five, enjoys sharing her joys and struggles of mothering through the written and spoken word.

Carolyn Byers Ruch is a mother of four amazing teenagers (yes, all under one roof) and one even-tempered husband. She takes many deep, cleansing breaths from her home in Hatfield, Pennsylvania.

Tara Rye is a speaker/teacher/writer/ and radio personality in Omaha, Nebraska. She and Greg have been married for fourteen years and they are blessed with two delightful children who keep them on their toes.

Her greatest comfort is to have a cup of chai tea with her two dogs lying next to her as she reads her Bible early in the morning before the family wakes up. Feel free to contact her at *www.tararye.com*.

Susan Kneib Schank lives in Parkville, Missouri, with her fabulous husband, James, and precious five-year-old daughter, Ivy Rose. Susan is a member of the Society of Children's Book Writers and Illustrators, Juvenile Writers of Kansas City, and Heart of America Christian Writers Network. She is also a Library Media Specialist in the Kansas City, Missouri, School District. When not writing, working, or spending time with her family, Susan sings with the Kansas City Symphony Chorus and volunteers for Lakeside Nature Center.

Carmen Schroeder is a stay-at-home mother of four children, ages two to eight. She enjoys encouraging women of all ages, through speaking and writing, on how to live a life of wholeness according to God's Word.

Carol Hatheway Scott is the mother of seven children, ranging from fifteen to thirty-six years of age, and the grandmother of thirteen. She and her family have lived as missionaries in Mexico, Guatemala, Grenada, and Brazil.

Lori Z. Scott loves her husband, Jim, and precious children, Michael and Meghan. Check out more of her writing at *www.extremedivamedia*.com. She lives in Indiana.

429 ⌒

CONTRIBUTORS

Kim Sheard's writings have appeared in *A Cup of Comfort Devotional for Women*, *Today's Christian*, and *Brave Hearts* magazine. She lives in Fairfax, Virginia.

Heidi Shelton-Jenck is the mother of four children and works as a freelance writer for educational and Christian projects. Her husband (and best friend) is a Presbyterian minister.

Sharon Sheppard is a wife, mother, and grandmother. A former college English teacher, she currently works as a freelance writer and speaker.

Leslie J. Sherrod lives in Baltimore, Maryland, with her husband and two children. Her first novel, *Like Sheep Gone Astray*, was published in 2006.

Susan Skitt is a stay–at–home mom who's never home! She writes and speaks from Bucks County, Pennsylvania. Contact her at *skskitt@comcast .net*.

Sherron Slavens has seven published devotionals and seven scheduled for future publishing. Married forty-eight years, she is a mother of three and a grandmother of three, a speaker for the Colorado Alzheimer's Association, and a Stephen Minister (a trained lay minister) in her local church.

Sally Smith is a guidance counselor who enjoys speaking, reading, writing, and baseball. She and her husband, Jerry, are raising their children, Steve and Heather, in Carl Junction, Missouri.

Sheila Soule is the homeschooling mama to four wonderful and challenging children. Married to her handsome prince Jeff, they reside in California. Her fondest hope is to see the bottom of her laundry hamper. You can reach her at *Sheila@profaith .com*.

Maribeth Spangenberg is wife to Steve and mother to nine children. She considers it a blessing and a ministry to be able to encourage other mothers.

An escapee from the corporate world, **Susan Stanley** is a full-time wife (to husband Trent) and mom (to son Nathan). She writes during naptimes and at night.

Cara Stock is a married mom of two and grandmother who is learning to give the keys of her life to the Lord. She lives in Missouri with her husband, son, and various four-legged friends.

Rhonda Wheeler Stock has been a freelance writer for sixteen years. Her work has appeared in *Today's Christian Woman*, where she was a regular contributor, and in several other publications. She has also written curriculum for several publishers. She and her husband live in Kansas and are the parents of three boys and a girl. Rhonda teaches junior high special education and enjoys prowling around flea markets, thrift stores, and antique shops.

Jeannie St. John Taylor, a former teacher with a master's degree, works full-time as an author/illustrator crafting books for women and children in her Portland studio. She has published fourteen books, with three more to be released in 2006. Her latest project, *No Ordinary Woman*, is a make-you-cry booklet intended to convince women of their incredible value.

MaRita Teague teaches Sunday school to children, sings in the choir, and teaches college English at Northern Virginia Community College. She lives in Northern Virginia with her husband and two sons.

R. J. Thesman has been writing professionally for more than thirty years, publishing more than 300 articles and stories in various publications. She has self-published several books, which were used to teach English to international students. R. J. operates an editorial service called Do It Write and also works full-time for a Christian ministry. She enjoys gardening, interior design, cooking, and journaling.

Sandra Thiessen lives with her husband of twenty-three years in Centennial, Colorado. Together they enjoy four children, one daughter-in-law, and a little grandson. Sandra enjoys singing and speaking to various groups about the care and goodness of God.

Vicki Tiede is a homeschooling wife and mother. She is the founder of Grace Lessons Ministries, a speaking and writing ministry designed to encourage and equip women to face the inevitable challenges of marriage, motherhood, and walking with Christ.

Laryssa Toomer is an Army wife and mother of three children. She is a Bible teacher, frequent speaker, and writer, and she resides at Fort Bragg, North Carolina.

Ann Varnum hosts the longest-running television talk show in Alabama. She is the author of *Sunny Side Up—An Inside Look at Early Morning TV*, coauthor of two cookbooks with her sister, Martha, and is a freelance writer. She and her husband, Jerome, have three children and five grandchildren.

Tamara Vermeer has a background in journalism and marketing and lives in Colorado with her husband and three children. She is an avid reader with a heart for reaching out to women through Bible studies, writing, and coffee.

Lisa Vitello is wife to Guy and mom to six great kids. She publishes the *New Harvest Homestead* newsletter for women who enjoy living a simple, old-fashioned lifestyle. Visit her Web site at *www.newharvest homestead.com*.

Hilah C. Wagner resides in Salem, Oregon, with her husband, Arnold, also a writer and a cartoonist. She's the mother of three grown daughters who have become her dearest friends. She also has five delightful grandchildren.

431

Contributors

Tanya T. Warrington, a freelance writer, loves being a mom. She wouldn't trade in a single one of her hormonal teens.

Faith Waters is an ordained minister in the African Methodist Episcopal Church. She is also a youth consultant and freelance writer. She resides in Pennsylvania.

Karen H. Whiting (*www.karenhwhiting.com*) has ten published books, including *Secrets of Success for Women: The Home.* She is a mother of five and grandmother of three.

Wife and mother of two, **Karen Whitson** writes from Shawnee, Kansas, where she and her husband both enjoy God's blessings with home-based businesses in writing and accounting.

Jennifer Whyman is a mother of three. She is fighting middle age with lots of eye cream and long walks. She loves a good cup of hot chocolate in the morning!

Margaret Wilson has taught interdenominational Bible studies for thirty years and has written many courses of Bible study. She has also enjoyed speaking at retreats and the counseling that results from her close interaction with women. Margaret and her husband, Jerry, are longtime residents of Southern Oregon, where they raised their son and daughter, who have each blessed them with two grandsons.

Paula Wiseman lives in Robinson, Illinois, with her husband, Jon, and children Lauren, Alan, and Rachel. She has written for children and teens and is currently working on a novel.

Lucy Woodward has been an author since 1971. She has written plays, poems, devotionals, two inspirational books, and a novel.

Jamie Speak Wooten passionately challenges women to truly know God and His Word in their lives. She creatively relates biblical truths to daily living through Speak for Christ Ministries and in her weekly e-Devotional entitled "Hey Girlfriend . . . It's Almost Friday!" Jamie currently serves as a women's ministry director, conference speaker, and visiting teacher at the seminary. She is the proud mother of three priority blessings: James, Jordan, and Jenna.

Elisa Yager is mom to two great kids, and when she's not writing, she works full-time as a Manager of Human Resources at a manufacturing firm located in Allentown, Pennsylvania. Currently Elisa is working on a Civil War novel that takes place in her hometown in Hunterdon County, NJ.

Barbara Youree is author of six children's books with missionary themes and a series of four Christian historical romances. Her work has appeared in several magazines, both secular and religious, including devotionals in *The Upper Room.*

SUBJECT INDEX

433

Subject Index

Scripture Index